THE KIDS ARE IN CHARGE

CRITICAL PERSPECTIVES ON YOUTH

General Editors: Amy L. Best, Lorena Garcia, and Jessica K. Taft

Fast-Food Kids: French Fries, Lunch Lines, and Social Ties
Amy L. Best

White Kids: Growing Up with Privilege in a Racially Divided America
Margaret A. Hagerman

Growing Up Queer: Kids and the Remaking of LGBTQ Identity
Mary Robertson

*The Kids Are in Charge: Activism and Power in Peru's Movement
of Working Children*
Jessica K. Taft

The Kids Are in Charge

Activism and Power in Peru's Movement of Working Children

Jessica K. Taft

NEW YORK UNIVERSITY PRESS

New York

NEW YORK UNIVERSITY PRESS
New York
www.nyupress.org
© 2019 by New York University
All rights reserved

References to Internet websites (URLs) were accurate at the time of writing. Neither the author nor New York University Press is responsible for URLs that may have expired or changed since the manuscript was prepared.

ISBN: 978-1-4798-6299-3 (hardback)
ISBN: 978-1-4798-5450-9 (paperback)
For Library of Congress Cataloging-in-Publication data, please contact the
Library of Congress.

New York University Press books are printed on acid-free paper, and their binding materials are chosen for strength and durability. We strive to use environmentally responsible suppliers and materials to the greatest extent possible in publishing our books.
Manufactured in the United States of America
10 9 8 7 6 5 4 3 2 1
Also available as an ebook

For all the kids raising their voices for justice and dignity
and all the adults who listen and take them seriously

CONTENTS

Introduction

On July 28, 2015, Peru's National Independence Day, over a hundred working children and their allies marched through the streets of Lima, demanding that their national government recognize their rights as workers and as political subjects. Their press release, banners, and flyers called for the government to cease trying to abolish child labor and to instead focus on protecting working children from exploitation and providing them with better social services and schools. Children, they argued, should be allowed to work so long as that work is dignified and is not causing them harm. Further, they asked the authorities to respect their political organization, the Movimiento Nacional de Niños, Niñas y Adolescentes Trabajadores Organizados del Perú (MNNATSOP, the Peruvian National Movement of Organized Working Children and Adolescents), to include them in all policy decisions related to working children, and to "listen and take into account what we propose for our lives and our communities." This march was not just attended and led by children, but was entirely planned by a committee of ten young activists, ages eleven to fifteen, who had been elected to leadership by their peers in the movement. They were supported in this organizing by four *colaboradores* (adult supporters), but the young people themselves were the primary decision makers, wrote all of the materials for the event, and did the outreach and publicity.

The march started out fairly subdued, with just a handful of the young activists chanting. Led by eleven-year-old Andrea and fifteen-year-old Patricia, the NATs (*niños y adolescentes trabajadores*, or working children and adolescents) quickly became more comfortable, getting louder and louder as they yelled, "Alerta! Alerta! Alerta que camina: los NATS organizados de América Latina!" and "Los niños lo dicen y tienen la razón, sí al trabajo digno y no a la explotación."[1] By the time we had reached the main plazas in the center of the city, they were totally enthusiastic protestors: dancing, laughing, and jumping up and down in rhythm with the chants. Despite its small size, the march captured the attention of many bystanders, who expressed surprise at seeing children leading a march, as well as curiosity about the movement's reasons for defending children's right to work. After moving through the center of Lima, past several plazas full of people, the group stopped in a park and several teenage leaders spoke about why they were there. They expressed their firm belief in their rights to political, economic, and social inclusion, and the need for then president Ollanta Humala to follow through on the commitments he had made to children, including to working children. The crowd of both participants and bystanders cheered loudly after each speech, and the young activists wrapped up the event with an escalating call-and-response series of "Que vivan los NATs!" "Que vivan!"

As the event was winding down, one of the *colaboradores* asked my partner and me whether we would help out by walking Andrea back to her home in a nearby neighborhood. A diminutive Afro-Peruvian with an infectious smile, Andrea was overflowing with energy and practically bounced through the streets as she led us back toward her house. Although we knew our way around the area fairly well, we let Andrea guide us, following her directions on which route to take to her house. Along the way, she told us proudly that she "knows this area like the palm of my hand." She pointed out various landmarks, including her favorite place to eat ceviche, greeted a few neighbors as we got closer to her house, and kept up a running commentary about how my partner and I should be careful because we are foreigners and people might try to cheat or steal from us. She warned us not to go down certain streets, to avoid a particular park, and to be alert because her neighborhood is "not safe." In a crowded area around the Plaza de Armas, she paused to make sure we were all still together, ushering my partner forward when he fell behind a bit. I tried to reassure her and explained that we had lived in Lima for many months, and that we both travel a lot through various neighborhoods of Lima on foot and feel comfortable in these spaces. When we got to her house, she smiled, told us this is where she lives, and then offered to walk us back toward the center of the city so we could catch a bus back to our apartment. I gently reminded her that the whole point of our journey with her was that the *colaboradores* wanted us to take her home, not the other way around! She reluctantly agreed to this, but reminded us one last time to be careful and gave me her cell phone number, "in case you get into any trouble."

Both the march itself and our interactions with Andrea that day are reflections of the critical approach to childhood that has been developed over the past forty years by the Peruvian movement of working children. In the march, working children engaged in a public politics of protest, arguing for children's greater inclusion in economic and political life. They demonstrated their ability to organize and engage in collective political action and challenged widespread assumptions about child workers. Against increasingly globalized narratives that imagine the ideal childhood as a time of only play and learning, or as a time without responsibilities, the NATs argued directly for their right to work a limited number of hours in safe, dignified, and protected conditions and explicitly claimed that work and a happy childhood are not necessarily incompatible. They also emphasized their own political and economic capabilities, redefined childhood as a space of meaningful and critical participation, and identified themselves as public subjects and collective actors, directly challenging more widespread discourses that frame children only as objects of socialization and as innocent, passive, and privatized individuals. But Peru's movement of working children is not just interested in children's political and economic inclusion; it also seeks to transform intergenerational relationships, making them more egalitarian and increasing children's power and authority in their everyday interactions with adults. This everyday intergenerational politics was evident in Andrea's confidence and her totally empowered take-charge attitude. Andrea is not just an eleven-year-old activist with political experience who can lead a march and express her own fully developed arguments about children's rights; she is also an eleven-year-old who knows her way around her city, trusts herself to effectively navigate its potential dangers, and is not afraid to tell two adults that she is more knowledgeable and skilled at this than they are. The fact that we were foreigners certainly helped mark us as less competent than Peruvian adults, but Andrea claimed significant power and authority in this intergenerational interaction. Andrea entirely rejected the idea that she needed protection, positioning herself instead as a protector; she saw herself as being in charge of and responsible for us, not the other way around. Like many other NATs involved in the movement of working children, Andrea has learned to value her expertise and to question assumed intergenerational hierarchies that place adults "above" children.

* * *

The Kids Are in Charge explores the specific case of Peru's movement of working children in order to question, destabilize, and disrupt many commonsense ideas about children and childhood. Both this book and the movement itself directly challenge five widespread assumptions: (1) the binary difference assumption, or the assumption that children and adults are essentially different kinds of humans; (2) the natural assumption, or the assumption that childhood is a natural and universal category, with fixed traits and characteristics; (3) the passivity assumption, or the assumption that children are uncritical sponges who absorb the perspectives of adults; (4) the exclusion assumption, or the assumption that children should be prevented from participation in both work and politics; and (5) the power assumption, or the assumption that adults' power over children is just, inevitable, and/or necessary, and should not be diminished. These five assumptions are not universal, and they can look and sound somewhat different in different social and cultural contexts, but they are powerful and increasingly pervasive narratives about childhood that circulate globally through popular media, international human rights institutions, children's organizations, and other transnational programs and interventions that address education, families, communities, and children's lives.[2] This book draws on the knowledge and experience developed in the critical space of Peru's movement of working children to reconsider and question each of these assumptions and to offer an alternative approach to childhood and intergenerational relationships.

THE BINARY DIFFERENCE ASSUMPTION. Ideas about childhood are also always ideas about adulthood: the two categories are positioned in opposition to one another. Many of the dominant ideas about modern Western selfhood—that we are rational, free-willed, independent individuals—rely upon a binary logic in which children are *not* those things.[3] The logic of the binary suggests that children are fundamentally different from adults, and that their needs, desires, and ways of being in the world are essentially distinct from those of older individuals. While I do not dispute that there are differences between a four-year-old and a fifteen-year-old, and between a fifteen-year-old and a thirty-seven-year-old, there are also many differences *among* fifteen-year-olds globally, historically, and in any given social context. Some fifteen-year-olds may have more in common with some four-year-olds, and some may have more in common with some thirty-seven-year-olds. Like all binaries, the adult/child binary obscures the similarities between the two social categories and overemphasizes differences. Following upon the theoretical work done by many other scholars of childhood, I encourage readers to not take the meaning attached to differences of age for granted. Instead, we should make these differences the subject of inquiry; we should ask ourselves why we think that children are different from adults in any given situation, and whether, perhaps, they are not actually as different as the binary assumption suggests.

THE NATURAL ASSUMPTION. Critical sociological, historical, and anthropological approaches to the study of childhood consistently argue that childhood is a social construction, that it is not an inevitable biological category, and that its meanings are not universal, fixed, or natural.[4] What it means to be a child, and children's social roles, responsibilities, and capabilities are flexible and context-dependent.[5] What children are allowed to do, what they learn to do, and therefore what they *can* do all vary across cultures and time periods.[6] Age is not destiny. However, the natural assumption appears frequently in everyday social life, usually with very specific sets of claims: fifteen-year-olds are self-centered, or twelve-year-olds can't really think abstractly, and so on. And while there may be some truth to some of these claims, the sociology of childhood, as an approach, encourages us to be skeptical of the tendency to see children's experiences or children's capabilities at a given age as inevitable. What it means to be a child is context-dependent and malleable. Against the natural assumption, the movement of working children shows how childhood looks different when kids are treated as capable political actors and are given the opportunity to develop, learn, and participate in a collaborative intergenerational social movement.

THE PASSIVITY ASSUMPTION. The first two assumptions undergird a whole set of more specific ideas about childhood, including the assumption that children and adults are very differently situated in relation to the enduring sociological question of agency and social structure. Adults are usually assumed to possess agency, or to have the capacity to critically interpret the world and to act creatively upon that world, while children are frequently assumed to be passive objects of socialization, fully produced and constrained by their social contexts. This is evident in the recurring claim that children are "sponges" who absorb the ideas of adults around them, while adults are independent, autonomous, critical thinkers whose ideas are their own. Drawing from critical social theory and childhood studies, I take the theoretical position that individuals of all ages are products of social environments *and* active subjects who interpret, navigate, and act upon those environments.[7] The passivity assumption is particularly relevant for the movement of working children and this book because many people assume that children who are involved in social movements or who engage in political speech are merely pawns of adult activists. Children who are politicized are frequently described as manipulated, with their political education being depicted as brainwashing and their claims dismissed as mimicry.[8]

These narratives assert that children are incapable of critical political analysis, while adults are positioned as agentic critical thinkers. *The Kids Are in Charge* rejects this depiction of activist children as simply dupes of all-powerful adults, but that does not mean that they are entirely free of adult influence. Instead, like many sociologists, I take the position that everyone's ideas may be both socially produced *and* critically considered. Therefore, rather than challenging the passivity assumption by claiming that children are also autonomous, free-willed, and rational individual agents, I highlight how both children and adults in the movement of working children are shaped by the larger social context of childhood and are actively contesting and questioning some elements of that context.

THE EXCLUSION ASSUMPTION(S). Dominant narratives about child labor presume that work is antithetical to a "good" childhood and that work harms children. Working children are regularly depicted as tragic figures, victims who have "lost their childhood" and who need to be saved from the "scourge" of child labor. This book presents a very different view on children's work, highlighting how children's work is not always exploitative and is not always a negative feature in children's lives, although it is sometimes both of these things. Children's work is not the focus of my analysis, but I introduce readers to children who enjoy their work, who find work to be fulfilling, and who are fighting for their right to work in dignity. They argue that working can be an asset for children, providing them with valuable knowledge and skills. They directly reject the idea that their total exclusion from work would be in their best interests and instead argue for the value of children's inclusion in economic life.

These children also challenge their ongoing exclusion from political decision making and political authority. Children's exclusion from politics relies heavily upon the first three assumptions, as well as an ideal of childhood innocence that suggests that children should not be concerned with social and political problems.[9] This ideal of innocence ignores the fact that many children are living these problems on a daily basis and do not have the option to ignore them.[10] Children experience racism, sexism, homophobia, poverty, violence, war, and other injustices; they live in political and politicized worlds, and therefore have knowledge to contribute to political discussions.[11] If childhood's meanings are socially constructed, if children's skills and knowledge depend on their social contexts, if both children and adults are agentic and subject to socialization and social constraint, then why are children so frequently excluded from political life? Why don't they get to participate in the many decisions that affect them and their communities? Why do most social movements not include children as meaningful participants? And is children's ongoing exclusion from democracy and political life just? Peru's movement of working children effectively demonstrates that children can, in fact, be critical political actors and activists, if they are given the right opportunities and supports. Against the assumption of exclusion, this book argues for the value of children's meaningful participation on the grounds that it is good for kids, good for society, and far more ethical.

THE POWER ASSUMPTION. As a social group, children consistently have less power than adults.[12] Differences between children and adults are not merely differences of age and generation, but also differences of access to power and resources. Age categories are laden with power and inequality, creating dynamics and structures of marginalization and oppression that scholars have named ageism or adultism.[13] This inequality is often invisible and normalized; it is taken for granted in most intergenerational contexts that adults should be the ones who are "in charge." Even spaces that challenge children's political exclusion and argue for children's right to participation frequently still leave adult power and authority unquestioned.[14] In contrast, the movement of working children seeks to significantly increase children's power across multiple contexts, including families, schools, municipal governments, the Peruvian national government, and international human rights organizations and institutions. In addition to arguing for children's dignity, power, and full citizenship rights, they directly challenge adult domination and power within the movement itself by theorizing and enacting horizontal intergenerational relationships—relationships rooted in a belief in children's fundamental equality with adults and in practices of non-hierarchical collaboration between children and adults. These relationships of collaboration are an example of prefigurative politics, with the movement "prefiguring" the social relations it would like to see in the wider society. These two political approaches—prefiguring horizontal relationships that challenge age-based hierarchies and advocating for increases to children's power in other institutions—complement one another and make up the movement's two-pronged political strategy. This challenge to the assumption of adult authority is one of the most profound and unique contributions of the Peruvian movement of working children.

In challenging these five commonsense ideas about childhood, I am not trying to say that they are entirely false or definitively prove them wrong. Many other scholars have done excellent work that presents the philosophical and ethical arguments against some of these assumptions and have provided systematic data and evidence regarding the cultural and social influences upon children's developmental trajectories and capabilities.[15] I name these five assumptions here so that they are made visible, and I ask readers to treat them with some suspicion rather than taking them for granted as truths about children and childhoods. Questioning commonsense assumptions is precisely the purpose of critical scholarship. *The Kids Are in Charge* therefore adds to the critical scholarship on childhood by ethnographically exploring an emergent version of childhood otherwise—a version of childhood where children demand their collective rights, expect adults to treat them as capable and knowledgeable subjects, and seek to act as equal partners with adults in the collaborative pursuit of their political visions.

Childhood studies scholars have consistently argued for treating childhood as a social construction whose meanings are produced through discourse, practices, and institutions, and are actively negotiated by children. Much of this work has focused on illuminating the dominant or hegemonic models of childhood. In contrast, this book focuses on an alternative vision and emphasizes that childhood, as a social construction, is open to change. This notion of the potential for intentional transformations of childhood is often implicit within childhood studies rather than directly addressed. The movement of working children reminds us of one of the key features of a socially constructed category: such categories can be reconstructed and remade, and these remakings may emerge from large-scale structural changes (such as digital cultures or new economic imperatives), but they may also be the result of social movement activity and political struggle. Childhood and its meanings can be actively contested, debated, and challenged by children themselves.

When I speak in public about this work and my interest in intergenerational equality and horizontalism, some adults are quick to express their discomfort with the idea of having children take on a greater role in decision making of all kinds. In some of these interactions, I encounter a stubborn refusal to consider alternative ways of thinking about childhood. But many other adults, and certainly most children and youth who I talk with about this work, are excited about the prospect of at least discussing the (il)legitimacy of the profoundly unequal power relations between children and adults. This is a discussion that provokes, and a discussion that I mean to provoke. In arguing for reimagining childhood as a space of greater political and social power, neither I nor the movement of working children is suggesting that adults do not have responsibilities for caring for children or protecting them from harm. Children's particular dependencies and vulnerabilities are real and need consideration in any redefinition of adult-child relationships. And, as the example of the criminalization of children of color in the United States makes very clear, sometimes being treated like adults is not in children's best interests. However, these complexities should not prevent us from questioning children's marginalization from political life.

In addition to challenging these five commonsense ideas about childhood, Peru's movement of working children also challenges the dominant approaches of many programs and organizations for children. It offers readers a vibrant and viable alternative model for how to increase children's democratic participation, inclusion, and collective power, whether that be in the context of educational institutions, after-school programming, children's organizations, social movements, or the ever-expanding landscape of spaces designed to involve children in formal politics. Since the drafting and ratification of the United Nations Convention on the Rights of the Child in 1989, children's participation has come to be seen as a kind of policy common sense in many parts of the world.[16] Article 12 of the convention requires that signatory states "assure to the child who is capable of forming his or her own views the right to express those views freely in all matters affecting the child, the views of the child being given due weight in accordance with the age and maturity of the child." Governments, NGOs, and schools loudly and frequently proclaim the value of "including children's voices" in decision making.[17] However, the vast literature on children's participation has identified notable limits to this particular formulation of children's democratic power, including the ease with which children's voices can be dismissed.[18] Many participatory programs for children tend to be "tokenistic, unrepresentative in membership, adult-led in process, and ineffective in acting upon what children want."[19] These programs also often function primarily as educational opportunities that aim to prepare children as future citizens and treat them as citizens-in-training, rather than fostering children's meaningful political power in the present.[20] In contrast to these more widely practiced approaches to "children's participation," "student voice," or "youth engagement," the movement of working children has developed theories and practices that are rooted in building collective power, rather than the framework of individual rights. *The Kids Are in Charge* therefore provides concrete ideas for improving programs aimed at children's political inclusion and participation.

While it is undeniable that childhood in Peru is distinct from that found in other national contexts, the alternative vision of childhood developed in this movement is still highly relevant to conversations about childhood elsewhere, including the United States. Whether it be in the various discussions of "helicopter parenting," parents being punished for letting their children walk alone around their neighborhood, or frequent adult reminiscences about their own childhood independence and freedom, there is a clear sense that many contemporary US childhoods are heavily supervised, organized, and managed by adults.[21] But

US childhoods are also diverse and uneven, with poor and working-class children and children in immigrant families taking on substantial responsibilities and acting with far more independence and autonomy than their more socially and economically privileged peers.[22] And while white children continue to be primarily imagined and treated as innocents by both media and public discourse, children of color are regularly criminalized, judged, and treated as adults by police and the criminal (in)justice system.[23] With only a little bit of probing, the image of childhood as a time of safe, protected, and responsibility-free play is revealed as a racialized and class-specific myth. But it is a powerful myth, and one that continues to play a role in how individual adults and social institutions treat children. The United States is also the only United Nations member state to not have ratified the UN Convention on the Rights of the Child, reinforcing a continuing approach to treating children as objects of protection, intervention, or punishment rather than as subjects of rights. By offering a striking contrast to these dominant narratives of childhood, the Peruvian movement of working children raises the possibilities for thinking about childhood differently.

But elements of the movement's vision of childhood are also not entirely unfamiliar: many parents, teachers, and children's advocates aspire to enact more egalitarian and horizontal forms of relating with children. "Democratic parenting" websites and manuals offer advice to parents on giving children choices and decision-making power in their family relationships. The Sudbury schools and other radical schools run by direct democracy sometimes describe children and adults as equals, and give students control over their own learning.[24] In the realm of politics, articles and blog posts offer tips for how to talk to kids about social and political issues, including racism, war, and other injustices. High school and middle school–based youth activist organizations, kid-friendly spaces within larger social movement events, youth participatory action research projects, and a small handful of political groups for younger children, like the widely celebrated Radical Monarchs, also aim to engage kids as citizens-in-the-present rather than citizens-in-the-making.[25] These all suggest some popular interest in expanding children's democratic power and political engagement, and an openness to reconsidering intergenerational hierarchies. The movement I analyze in this book offers insights for adults who are already reimagining childhood through these kinds of spaces and practices, but it also enters into new territory: a model for horizontal intergenerational activism that is explicitly committed to expanding children's power in economic, social, and political life.

The Kids Are in Charge presents the movement of working children as a model for including children in social movements, increasing their political power, and creating more egalitarian intergenerational relationships, but it also illuminates the very real difficulty of this work. I don't romanticize the movement or gloss over the challenges of trying to disrupt age-based hierarchies and adultism. Peru's movement of working children has a forty-year history of reimagining childhood and practicing horizontal intergenerational collaboration, but still struggles to make its vision real in both the daily life of the movement and the larger society. The movement is not a utopian space free from the constraints of the larger social context. We live in age-stratified societies in which adults have far greater power, privilege, and resources than young people. This power differential is particularly heightened when we are talking about children, and not just youth (teens or young adults). The reverberations and consequences of the five assumptions above continue to appear within the movement, and children and adults do not easily shake off their habits of hierarchical intergenerational interaction. Further, there are some serious theoretical and conceptual complications that emerge in the process of trying to envision intergenerational equality. Therefore, the challenges involved in transforming childhood and adult-child relationships are also central to my analysis.

To be clear, in presenting the movement's struggles to achieve its political visions, I am not suggesting that it has "failed" or that it is "not successful." Instead, I treat the movement's struggles as an opportunity to explore the messy and always unfinished nature of transforming social relations. My discussion of the difficulties is not so much a criticism of the movement as an acknowledgment of how much this endeavor is *always* an incomplete process. There are no easy answers to these challenges, and so my task here is not to try to "solve" them, but to draw them out so they might be more deeply understood and discussed. The movement is not perfect, but we should not expect perfection of it, or of ourselves. By showing how the pursuit of intergenerational equality is always partial and in process, I invite all of us into this political project, no matter how distant the ideal may seem from our own current practices. Instead of saying, "Look at this flawless model; you should be just like them," I ask adults, including those who are already doing this work in this specific movement or in other intergenerational spaces, to continually reflect on how, where, and when we are engaging with children in ways that amplify their collective and individual power, and how, where, and when we are engaging with children in ways that diminish that power.

My approach to thinking through adult-child relationships relies heavily on the work of US feminists of color and transnational feminists who have written extensively about creating meaningful political coalitions across lines of difference and inequality, most notably gender, race, class, sexuality, and nation.[26] This body of work highlights the complexity of solidarity and alliance in the context of inequality, emphasizes the importance of leadership by those most marginalized in the wider society, and argues for the need for ongoing reflection about internal power dynamics in social movement contexts. The scholarship on horizontalism and participatory democracy similarly underscores how the pursuit of more egalitarian relationships and democratic interaction is shaped by larger social and cultural expectations and is therefore always unfinished.[27] Sociologists of social movements have also written extensively about the intersecting differences of gender, race, class, and sexuality among activists,[28] and a growing number of authors have begun to write about adult-youth dynamics in social movements.[29] All of this theoretical and empirical work emphasizes the value of collaboration across difference *and* the need to take seriously the fact that inequality is never entirely erased, but must be regularly confronted.

The Kids Are in Charge adds to these conversations by focusing intensively on the dynamics of age, which have generally been under-studied by scholars of social movements.[30] But age also always intersects with other lines of difference, including gender, class, racial and ethnic identity, ability, and sexuality. Therefore, while my argument foregrounds age as the primary object of analysis and study, I address other identity categories, most especially gender, class, and racial/ethnic identity, when they emerged in my fieldwork in ways that interacted with the movement's age dynamics. In devoting primary analytic attention to age, I am not suggesting that age is more important than these other lines of power in children's lives, or that it is fully separable from these other dynamics, which of course transform children's experiences and how age categories operate in their lives. Instead, I choose to focus on age because age dynamics remain under-theorized and because age is the most central category in the discourses, identity frameworks, and politics of this particular social movement.

In exploring age as an axis of identity and inequality, this book emphasizes childhood and adulthood far more than other age-based social categories, such as youth and adolescence. Even though movement frameworks discuss working children and adolescents (*niños, niñas y adolescentes trabajadores*, or NATs) as a combined social group, the movement's political discourse centers primarily around *infancia* and *niñez* far more than *adolescencia*. Further, even many older adolescents in the movement regularly refer to themselves as *niños* or *niños trabajadores*. Therefore, I refer to the young people in this movement as either "NATs" or "kids." I use the term "children" when discussing the abstracted social group, but primarily use "kids" when I'm discussing actual living, breathing young people. Although some find the term "kid" to be demeaning or diminishing, I appreciate its informality and the fact that it is language often used by young people themselves. Of course, the specific young people in this movement are Spanish-speaking and so don't use either of these English terms. However, my perspective is that "kids" better captures the more casual spirit of their self-understanding than "children." Finally, it is worth noting that the term "youth" (*juventud*), both in Latin America in general and in the specific context of the movement of working children, generally refers to young people who are older than those found in this space. The NATs are never described by either themselves or adults as *jóvenes*. While youth is frequently linked to political change and social movements, childhood has a very different symbolic and material relationship to the political, requiring its own consideration apart from the discussions of youth activism. It is also a far more salient concept for this specific intergenerational movement.

In the chapters that follow, I pose a number of questions: How are childhood and adulthood being conceptualized in this unique social and political space? What does intergenerational equality mean to this movement? How are children's political power and equal citizenship made possible and impossible? *Can* children and adults interact in a horizontal fashion in political space? What do these interactions look and feel like? When and under what conditions do these collaborative political partnerships flourish and when do they falter? What are the discourses, practices, and institutionalized organizational structures that facilitate and/or produce barriers to more egalitarian intergenerational partnerships in the context of social movements? How do children and adults in this movement challenge age-based hierarchy, and how do they replicate it? In addressing these questions, I attempt to go beyond simplistic binaries of children as either active or passive, liberated or oppressed, and independent or manipulated. I explore the subtle and not-so-subtle dynamics of what I call age-based power, or the construction, distribution, and deployment of differential authority, influence, status, or value on the basis of chronological age.[31] I treat power as pervasive, relational, and dynamic, and see its presence not only in practices of authority and control, but also in discourse and the processes of subjectification and subject making (how people's identities are produced and regulated).[32] The power relations that exist between children and adults are constituted via material conditions, institutional structures, organizational and individual practices, habituated social interactions, and discourses about what it means to be a child or an adult. Focusing on this unique social movement context, I offer a textured understanding of how age-based power and hierarchies operate and, more importantly, how they can be undermined through horizontal intergenerational activism.

Chapter Outline

The Kids Are in Charge traces how adults and children in the movement of working children conceptualize children's place in public life, how they envision horizontal and egalitarian relationships between kids and adults, how they put these ideas into practice in the movement, and how they advocate for them in the wider society. Chapter 1 introduces the movement of working children and the Peruvian context and discusses my research methods and practices. In chapter 2, I look at the range of conceptualizations of childhood that circulate in and around the Peruvian movement of working children. I outline several of the more pervasive and dominant paradigms of childhood in contemporary Peru and then consider how the movement of working children responds to and directly challenges these paradigms, radically redefining childhood as a space of social, political, and economic subjectivity and engagement. Chapter 3 maps the movement's multiple interpretations of, and arguments for, horizontalism and intergenerational equality, expanding further on the movement's theoretical contributions and imaginative challenges to hegemonic understandings of childhood and adulthood. In chapter 4, I shift attention from discourse to practice and look at how the movement creates a collaborative intergenerational political community by focusing on the relationships between the NATs and their adult *colaboradores*. I highlight the tension between horizontalism and teaching that is embedded in the role of the *colaborador* and explore different ways *colaboradores* seek to manage or minimize this tension. In chapter 5, I take a more critical stance and look directly at issues of power, outlining multiple modalities of age-based power in order to consider how adult authority is reinforced or disrupted in the movement. I also look at the key role of adolescents in the movement and the ways that their power and presence complicate the child/adult binary. Chapter 6 takes a wider view in order to address the diffuse impacts of the movement on Peruvian childhood and on working children's lives outside the movement context. Each chapter ends with a three-part conclusion that highlights how the movement of working children undermines widespread assumptions about childhood, explores some of the difficulties of this work and what those difficulties tell us about how age-based power operates, and identifies ways the movement can serve as a model for intergenerational politics and the inclusion of children as full participants in their communities.

PART I

Alternative Visions of Childhood

1

Learning with the Peruvian Movement of Working Children

Norma has been an active participant in the movement of working children for decades. She began participation as a twelve-year-old in 1979 and has continued her involvement through adulthood, taking on new roles and responsibilities over time. Immensely proud of the movement's accomplishments and deeply committed to sharing its approach, Norma invited me to participate in a meeting of working children from her neighborhood on one of my first days in Lima. As she gave me the address, Norma explained that the group was in a housing cooperative that had been founded by the municipal workers' union in the district of Surquillo. A plaque labels the concrete maze of small houses Barrio Obrero, and the small working-class community has a long history of labor activism. Adults in the barrio are often very active in their union, several youth are part of the Juventud Obrera Cristiana, and many of the kids who live in the barrio participate in MANTHOC, one of the central organizations in the movement of working children. Norma has been the *colaboradora*, or adult supporter, for this base group of MANTHOC for many years, and she plays a key role in the neighborhood, building and sustaining its localized culture of collective political engagement and community organizing.

When I arrived at the Surquillo Barrio Obrero for my first visit, Norma was playing a game of cards with four kids until it was time for their weekly meeting. As the daylight faded and the meeting time approached, all six of us went out into the neighborhood to gather the others. We headed into an open courtyard in the center of the houses, and Norma and the kids called out, yelling names to different windows and asking whether they were coming to tonight's meeting. As kids trickled out of the houses, they would each run up to Norma and give her a hug. Having gathered about a dozen kids, the much larger group then returned to Norma's place to begin their weekly meeting around her kitchen table. Lili, the oldest of the small group, was thirteen and helped to organize the younger kids, all between the ages of five and ten, but mostly eight- and nine-year-olds. She asked them to go around and introduce themselves to me and to tell me about their work. As they shyly said their names, most of them told me that they work helping their families around the house; a few added that they help at the market or sell things at school or on the streets. Lili described what they do together, as a base group of MANTHOC. As she explained it, they meet every Friday to make plans, to learn, and to discuss different issues related to the children's work and children's rights. They also get together on some Saturdays to go to the library or on other trips together, have fun social events and parties, and participate in larger movement activities like the annual May 1 march to celebrate the day of the worker. They sometimes make things together that they then sell in order to raise money for their activities, and they send a delegate to the regional, Lima-wide meetings of the movement in order to plan larger activities and political campaigns.

Watching the Surquillo group meeting that evening, very early in my fieldwork, I was struck by the strong emotional and personal connection between Norma and the kids, by the longevity of Norma's participation and the depth of her commitment to fostering children's social movement leadership, and by the group's historical relationship to other working-class organizations. And, in listening to the kids talk about their work, I was surprised to learn that many of them identified as "working children" when all of their labor was familial and unpaid. While some worked occasionally as vendors and in nearby markets, none of them fit the stereotypical image of the child laborer that circulates in most stories about the subject published in the Global North. Finally, while the group described some time spent on political campaigns directed at large-scale, institutional change, many of its activities were less explicitly political in the traditional sense; the prefigurative politics of trying to build a new kind of intergenerational relationship was central to the group's approach to social change. All of these things, I would later learn, are common patterns in the movement of working children.

Peru's Movement of Working Children: A Brief History

Peru's movement of working children was founded at a meeting of the Peruvian Juventud Obrera Cristiana (Young Christian Workers) in 1976. The JOC, one of two youth wings of the larger Catholic Action movement, has been active in Peru since 1935.[1] In the mid-1970s, many union members and labor leaders, including youth labor leaders in the JOC, were being fired from their jobs as part of a wave of repression of popular movements that came with the transition to the government of Francisco Morales Bermúdez.[2] In order to plan for the general strike called for July 19, 1977, around eighty JOC youth leaders held a national gathering. At this meeting, however, the JOC youth were not interested in talking about the problems that they were facing as unemployed workers, but instead wanted to discuss the future of the country and the future of organized youth. They had been organizing in the factories, but now felt that the future of young people's work was not going to be in the factories, and if there were no youth in the factories, they needed to organize outside workplaces, in the neighborhoods. They were concerned that without the context of the factory, young people would not understand the concerns of workers or their identities and interests as part of the working class. This, some of the JOC youth argued, meant that they needed to begin organizing at a younger age. They argued that if their movement, the JOC, was concerned with the working class, they needed to also be concerned with working-class children. And, remembering their own experiences working as children, they articulated the position that having an organization like the JOC, but for kids, would have made a positive impact on their lives from an early age.

This 1977 meeting marked the initial founding of MANTHOC, the Movimiento de Adolescentes y Niños Trabajadores Hijos de Obreros Cristianos (Movement of Working Kids and Adolescents, Children of Christian Workers), although they would not take on this name until a group of kids themselves came up with it a few years later. The project was an incredibly new idea; the JOC youth had no models and no one to ask for advice about how to go about organizing kids. They started with five "intuitions" about how this new organization should operate, based in their own experiences as working children and as organized youth.[3] The first of these was that the organization should be autonomous—not

Figure 1.1. Working children gathered in 1979 in Surquillo for a meeting of the organization that eventually became MANTHOC. Photo courtesy of Movimiento de Adolescentes y Niños Trabajadores Hijos de Obreros Cristianos—Nacional.

part of or dependent upon any adult or youth organization. Second, the kids themselves must be in charge of and represent the organization. Third, an organization is not an end in itself, but a tool for addressing the needs of those workers and children beyond and outside the organization—the masses, if you will. Fourth, the organization should be both national and international because the issues of workers are not merely local, but also linked to national and international political and economic conditions. And finally, members should not assume that what works in organizing and educating youth will also work with kids and should therefore develop a new methodology and pedagogy for this work. With these ideas in mind, the JOC youth from around the country began to immediately organize base groups of kids in different neighborhoods and parishes.

Throughout the late 1970s and 1980s MANTHOC grew slowly, with new bases emerging as individual JOC members, friends, and allies among both clergy and laity started to create spaces for working children in their own parishes and communities. MANTHOC kids were part of the larger popular movements taking place at the time around the country, but most especially in the *pueblos jóvenes* or *barriadas* on the outskirts of Lima. As waves of migrants moved to the city from the countryside, they created collectives and organizations that would take over and occupy empty land, building homes and communities nearly overnight.[4] In Lima, this land is primarily coastal desert, with sand, dust, and little else. The work of building these communities and organizing for essential services was work that engaged whole families. As many other constituencies and groups had spaces for self-organization in a diverse and growing organizational landscape, the kids had MANTHOC.

MANTHOC was also closely tied to the development of liberation theology, a religious movement that emerged in Latin America in the 1960s that sought to refocus the Catholic Church on the liberation of the oppressed and the pursuit of economic and social justice.[5] Alejandro Cussianovich, a Salesian priest and an active participant in ONIS, a group of clergy around Lima who were discussing and developing liberation theology, was the JOC's advisor during the period in which MANTHOC was formed.[6] Alejandro, or Chito, as the kids continue to call him, had written several texts on liberation theology, one of which eventually led to his expulsion from his order, and he had worked with young domestic workers involved in the JOC for several years prior to the founding of MANTHOC. Although he was originally skeptical of the JOC proposal to create a children's organization, Alejandro is now an important theorist of childhood in Latin America, and he continues to be the intellectual and spiritual heart of the working children's movement in Peru. He has written numerous books and essays on working children, pedagogy, and children's *protagonismo*, a concept I discuss extensively in the next chapter. Alejandro also teaches courses on childhood and social policy at the Universidad Nacional Mayor de San Marcos and at IFEJANT, the movement's training institute for adults. He is regularly asked by the organizations in the movement to lead discussions and workshops for both children and adults. Just over eighty years old, he is a beloved figure in the movement of working children, and his writings serve as the philosophical inspiration and ideological core of the movement. When he is not himself leading training sessions and discussions, his writings are used as resources, and his definitions and words, which are informed by his theological approach, circulate throughout countless movement materials and conversations.

MANTHOC's roots in the vibrant popular movements of the 1970s and 1980s and in liberation theology continue to shape the movement's culture, practices, and ideology, but the movement was also substantially transformed during the 1990s and 2000s, as three larger political shifts encouraged participants to focus increasingly on working children *as children*. First, the movement had to navigate and survive the period of internal conflict between Sendero Luminoso (Shining Path) and the government. The escalation of Sendero's guerrilla violence and the government's authoritarian and violent response led many grassroots organizations, including those that made up the movement of working children, to de-emphasize some of the more class-based politics of their work. Speaking in the language of Marxism became less feasible and less desirable as the government failed to distinguish between different movements and Sendero frequently targeted leftist groups and parties in Lima's *barriadas* for intimidation, harassment, and assassination.[7] With base groups in many of the *barriadas* that experienced significant Sendero violence, the movement of working children re-focused organizational attention on children's issues and distanced itself a bit from the dangerous and deadly space of adult-led popular left organizations. At the same time that it distanced itself politically, the movement also geographically expanded into some of the mountain zones most affected by the violence, because it saw its work as protective: by organizing with poor and indigenous children in the region, the movement was giving them a sense of their potential power and collective capacity to improve the world without resorting to Sendero's violent tactics.

From the mid-1980s through the 1990s, the movement was also increasingly drawn into a new set of relationships and conversations centered more in Peru's growing "children's rights" community. In 1984 various NGOs in Lima formed the COTADENI, or the Coordinadora de Trabajo por los Derechos del Niño (Working Group for Children's Rights). While MANTHOC eventually left the COTADENI due to the network's difficulty including kids as participants in the meetings and decisions, the departure was fairly amicable and the movement continued to have a relationship with this larger children's rights body.[8] In the following years,

MANTHOC was involved in a few large-scale events on children's rights and continued to build its relationships with other child-focused NGOs and to participate in Peru's conversations about the Convention on the Rights of the Child and the drafting of the Peruvian comprehensive national law on children and adolescents (Código de los Niños y Adolescentes). This connection with the larger children's rights community in Peru continues to be a central feature of the movement today.

The 1990s were also a period of increased conflict over "child labor" as the International Labor Organization's International Program on the Elimination of Child Labor (ILO-IPEC) increased pressure on nations to ratify ILO Convention 138 on the Minimum Age. Originally drafted in 1973, Convention 138 aims for the abolition of work done by children under the age of fifteen, with the exception of some "light work" for those between the ages of twelve and fourteen. However, ratification of this convention was very slow up until at least 1989, increased steadily through the 1990s, but was even more heavily adopted during the early 2000s as countries also began to ratify Convention 182 on the Worst Forms of Child Labor. Convention 182 prioritizes ending the most harmful and dangerous forms of children's work, but Convention 138 instead assumes that *all* work done below the minimum age is harmful to children, despite a lack of compelling evidence to prove such harm.[9] With the growing investment of the ILO's program to end child labor and the changes in Peruvian law that prohibited work, Peru's working children in the 1990s found themselves facing criminalization, including the threat of being removed from their families, and increasing stigmatization as they were discussed as a visible marker of both poverty and national "underdevelopment." The movement thus needed to defend children's work as morally and legally legitimate, a need that had not really existed during the first fifteen years of MANTHOC's work. Previously, movement participants had been primarily focused on working children's status as workers and as members of the popular classes. Now, their status as children was far more significant. Age-based inequalities and the idea of an "adult-centric society" became increasingly central to the movement's discourse. Thus, the movement's focus shifted to defending children's right to work and challenging the "abolitionist" approach to child labor offered by the ILO.

MANTHOC and Movement Structures Today

In the forty years since it was founded, MANTHOC has grown significantly, generating an array of additional organizations and institutions,
and inspiring working children's movements in multiple countries
around the world, including Bolivia, Paraguay, Colombia, Ecuador,
Nicaragua, India, and Zimbabwe, as well as support organizations in
Germany, Belgium, and Italy. Today, MANTHOC itself involves around
two thousand kids in twelve different regions of the country: Puno,
Arequipa, Ayacucho, Lima, Pucallpa, San Martín, Cajamarca, Piura,
Amazonas, Iquitos, and Cusco. Kids participate primarily in base groups
of ten to thirty kids that meet weekly, biweekly, or monthly depending on the group. In Lima, there are currently seven base groups. One
is connected primarily to a parish, two to specific small neighborhoods, including the Surquillo housing cooperative, and the other four
to two different community centers operated by the movement. Each
base group elects delegates who participate in regional meetings. These
regional delegates must be approved by the entire region at biannual
regional assemblies. In Lima, the regional coordination meets twice a
month and plans city-wide events and activities. The regional assemblies also propose delegates to the national coordinating committee, and
those delegates have to be approved by the national assembly, which
meets every two years. The national coordinating committee members
thus serve a two-year term and meet regularly via Internet conference
calls as well as two or three times a year in person. The national committee plans larger movement strategies and generates national activities,
campaigns, and goals. At each of these levels of organization (base
groups, regional coordinating committees, and the national coordinating committee), one or two adults serve as supporting *colaboradores*.
In the case of the regional and national groups, these *colaboradores* are
elected by the delegates at the assemblies. The *colaboradores* of the base
groups, on the other hand, are not elected and often serve as *colaboradores* for a base for many years, providing substantial organizational
continuity and keeping the bases alive and active. Norma, for example,
has been the *colaboradora* in Surquillo for over twenty years.

In 1996 MANTHOC members, along with several other working
children's organizations and organizations of street children, launched

MNNATSOP as a more inclusive, expansive, and overarching national movement for working children's rights.[10] MNNATSOP, the Movimiento Nacional de Niños, Niñas y Adolescentes Trabajadores Organizados del Perú (Peruvian National Movement of Organized Working Children and Adolescents) incorporates close to ten thousand working children from around the country and has its own organizational structures and practices. In some regions, MNNATSOP is more active than MANTHOC, while in others, the situation is reversed. Technically, however, MANTHOC is a "base," or subgroup, of MNNATSOP. Like MANTHOC, MNNATSOP hosts regional and national gatherings and assemblies that bring together the different base groups for large-scale events and activities. At these events, members also elect regional and national delegates. However, one of the important features of its structure has been the existence of a national headquarters in Lima. Every two years, three of the elected national delegates are chosen to serve two-year terms in the headquarters.[11] These three national delegates, from three different regions of Peru, all move to Lima to live together in the headquarters and to work together coordinating the movement's national activities. During the first year of my fieldwork, these three teens could be found at nearly every event related to children's rights in Lima. They were important leaders in the national movement and were recognized as such by adults and by their peers.

Much as MANTHOC is a "base" of MNNATSOP, MNNATSOP is also a "base" of MOLACNATs, the Latin American and Caribbean Movement of Working Children. Like MNNATSOP, MOLACNATs emerged out of a large gathering organized primarily by MANTHOC. In 1988 working children's organizations from Argentina, Brazil, Bolivia, Chile, Ecuador, and Paraguay came to Lima for the first Latin American Meeting of Working Children. Meetings in 1990 (Argentina) and in 1992 (Guatemala) followed. Today, MOLACNATs continues to host biannual international gatherings, as well as smaller working meetings. I was able to attend one of these smaller meetings in Lima during my second year of fieldwork. At that meeting, working children from Bolivia, Colombia, Ecuador, Mexico, Paraguay, Venezuela, and Peru, as well as adult allies from these nations plus Argentina, came together to discuss long-term strategies and to develop an action plan for the next several years. While MOLACNATs is certainly the most significant international organizational space for the kids involved in the Peruvian movement, it is worth noting that the Peruvian working children have also had the chance to meet and collaborate with working children's movements from Asia, Africa, and Europe.

The movement of working children is also part of a broader children's rights movement in Peru. Members of MANTHOC, MNNAT-SOP, and other smaller working children's organizations in Lima serve as delegates to, and active leaders in, the RedNNA (National Network of Children and Adolescents). The RedNNA incorporates both working and nonworking children's organizations to address issues of children's rights. During my time in Lima, it was focused on proposed changes to the Código de los Niños y Adolescentes (the national law on children and adolescents), was an active participant in a national campaign for the positive treatment of children, and was part of an international campaign for the ratification of the third optional protocol to the Convention on the Rights of the Child.

All of these organizations and movements of children are supported by a small handful of adult-led institutions. INFANT (Instituto de Formación de Adolescentes y Niños Trabajadores, or Training Institute for Working Children and Adolescents) provides support, education, and training for the kids involved in the movement of working children. It publishes a variety of materials, facilitates research, and leads many educational events and workshops for kids. IFEJANT (Instituto de Formación para Educadores de Jóvenes, Adolescentes y Niños Trabajadores, or Training Institute for Educators of Child, Adolescent, and Youth Workers) does many of the same activities as INFANT, but with a focus on the education and training of the adult *colaboradores* who support the movement. IFEJANT offers courses in childhood studies, children's rights, and critical pedagogy. It also provides support and training for several schools that primarily teach working children and has been the organizational home for the PROMINATs program, a micro-finance program for working kids to start their own businesses, either individually or in collectives. Both INFANT and IFEJANT publish many excellent scholarly and practical resources on working children's issues and children's rights. Finally, the adult *colaboradores* who support the movement of working children also have their own movement organization: MOVICOLNATs. In this space, *colaboradores* gather together to provide each other with support and feedback and to consider how they, as adults, can further the goals of the working children's organizations. The movement of working children is thus a complex multi-organizational field, but the organizations are extremely closely linked to one another through interlocking memberships and through long-lasting personal and institutional relationships, making for a very tightly knit social movement.

The *colaboradores* are a fairly diverse group. Many, like Norma, were once child participants in the movement who have decided to stay involved in a new role. Others are teachers, youth workers, or religious people who encountered the movement initially as shorter-term volunteers but became long-term participants. A few are family members of participating NATs who enter via their children's participation, but this is fairly unusual. Many of the *colaboradores* have been working with the movement for decades, but there are also some newer *colaboradores* who have stepped into the role in the past five to ten years. In Lima, about three quarters of the *colaboradores* are women and a quarter are men. Most of these adults primarily understand themselves as urban mestizos,[12] but a few individuals who grew up in Quechua-speaking communities in the Andes articulate and claim a more explicitly indigenous identity, describing themselves as *andinos*. Similar to the intercultural activists described by María Elena García, identifying as *andino* was a way to "signal the importance of their connection to the Andes, rather than accept the assimilationist implication of mestizo as they understood it."[13] The adults are generally part of the urban working class, although a few have worked their way into new professional class statuses, in some cases at least partly due to the support they experienced as kids in the movement. The most notable exception to this ethnic and class composition is Alejandro, who is both white and from a middle-class background. A very small number of *colaboradores* make a living through their work with the movement, paid as staff members for the movement's different centers or institutes, but most are volunteering their time. Being a *colaborador*, as I'll discuss in later chapters, is seen as a vocation that requires ongoing training and reflection, and the adults who take on this role are incredibly dedicated to the movement.

The overall goal of the movement is, according to MNNATSOP's official declaration of principles, to "aim for a society in which all human beings, and specifically children, are not only recognized and have their rights respected, but also in which children become protagonists . . . in the development and enjoyment of a full life." Further, the movement, "at every level, wants to be an experience of a new relationship between generations as a concrete sign of our vision for a world in which children and adults can all exercise our rights to be protagonists, with no one excluded." Or, as it is stated in MANTHOC's official materials, the movement aims to "develop the *protagonismo* of NATs [*niños y adolescentes trabajadores*, or working children and adolescents] and NNAs [*niños, niñas y adolescentes*, or boys, girls, and adolescents] for the exercise and defense of their rights and to improve the conditions of their work, health, education, and quality of life." The movement is guided by three central commitments: a deeply held belief in children's ability to be full participants in economic, social, and political life; the pursuit of children's right to dignified work without exploitation; and the value of horizontal intergenerational collaboration. In arguing strongly for children's rights, self-determination, and capacity in all realms of public life, the movement aims to improve the material conditions of working children's lives and to radically redefine children's place in the world. As I'll discuss throughout this book, the movement challenges children's frequent exclusion from politics and social movements and provides a model for engaging with kids as capable and critical political subjects.

In order to pursue these goals, the movement uses a wide variety of strategies and practices, most of which are implemented in base groups. Some base groups, like the Surquillo group, have no particular infrastructure beyond the kids and their *colaborador*, while others are also part of more comprehensive social service centers. The MANTHOC base group with whom I spent the most time was the group at one of those centers, the Casa Franco Macedo Cuenca in Yerbateros. Run via donations from international organizations and individuals, the brightly painted, multilevel house sits just off a busy street near several major markets and at the base of a few steep-sided, dusty hills covered in small houses. The center is open six days a week, providing before- or after-school care, meals, homework support, and a variety of workshops and activities. On a typical weekday, a few dozen kids will pass through the house to hang out, play games, be tutored and assisted in their homework by both Peruvian and international volunteers, and participate in

Figure 1.2. NATs and *colaboradores* from MANTHOC at a march organized by MNNATSOP-Lima in 2015. Photo by Gabriel Cohn.

ongoing workshops on topics ranging from nutrition and mental health to participatory budgeting and local governance, as well as economic activities, like making greeting cards to sell. The house is most crowded right around lunch time, when kids who attend both afternoon and morning school line up and pay a few *soles* to get a bowl of soup and a healthy, filling meal. The kids themselves keep track of who has paid and who owes money, with one or two of them sitting at a ledger, collecting coins, and writing notes at the start of every meal. They also serve the food, and then all the kids sit down at long tables with colorful benches and eat together. After the meal, the kids take their own dishes to the outdoor sink, wash them, and set them to dry. Then rotating teams of kids clean the dining area (and chase after each other with brooms). On weekdays, much of what happens at the house in Yerbateros could be occurring at any number of organizations that support and care for children, but there are some important differences: the kids self-organize many of the activities, they take on much of the responsibility for implementing the rules of the house, and the content of some of the workshops is politically oriented. Furthermore, on Saturdays, at the weekly assembly, the social movement dimensions of the base group become much more evident. At the assemblies, NATs develop and practice their skills of facilitation, political discussion, organization, and mobilization. They have important discussions about issues of children's rights and child labor politics, and they plan their campaigns, including recent campaigns to raise awareness of gender-based discrimination, challenge violence against children, and promote more environmentalism and ecological care in their neighborhood. They also plan and implement cultural events and group activities, and organize fundraisers for their projects. At the weekly assemblies, the house's delegates from the regional and national coordinating groups share regional and national movement projects and campaigns and ask the house to participate in different kinds of advocacy work and activism to address working children's issues at the local, national, and international levels. Unlike a union, the movement does not organize children and adolescents in specific workplaces, nor does it regularly confront employers. Instead, it provides an organizational structure that encourages working children's individual and collective development as political, economic, and social subjects, helps them to confront various challenges in their lives, and supports them as they pursue respect, dignity, and full inclusion in Peruvian society.

The parents of the NATs may sometimes have a small role in the movement, although this varies quite a bit. In some base groups, *colaboradores* organize programs and workshops to discuss children's rights or their vision for intergenerational relationships with the NATs' parents. In others, they ask parents to help out with specific tasks and events, or may try to meet regularly with parents individually. But, while many parents are highly supportive of the movement and speak about how much they appreciate how it has helped their child develop confidence, participation in the movement can also sometimes lead to family conflict as parents' and kids' expectations about appropriate behavior and what is respectful diverge. I'll discuss some of these dynamics in chapter 6, but it is worth noting here that the movement's goals of transforming intergenerational relationships and remaking childhood have implications for kids' interactions with the other adults in their lives, most especially their parents.

There are elements of these organizations, their daily practices, and their structures that would suggest that they could be described primarily as an interlocking group of children's rights NGOs. However, I write about this terrain as an intergenerational *social movement* for a few key reasons. First, unlike most children's organizations, the objective is not simply to support, empower, or even transform the lives of the specific children who participate in the group but to impact the broader social and political context, and thereby change the lives of other NATs and NNAs. Second, unlike many children's rights NGOs, the organizations that make up the movement of working children explicitly frame their work as political, with overt critiques of structures of power, colonialism, and inequality: they do not traffic in the more "neutral" languages of humanitarianism or child saving. Third, their activities include what scholars of social movements refer to as "extra-institutional tactics" for social change (marches, boycotts, proclamations, rallies, alternative cultural practices, autonomous community building, and so forth). They therefore fit a common sociological definition of social movements: "sustained, intentional efforts to foster or retard broad legal and social changes, primarily outside the normal institutional channels endorsed by authorities."[14]

The NATs and Their Economic and Educational Contexts

The working children in the movement are between the ages of eight and seventeen, and they are recruited into base groups informally through networks of family and friends. Some participate for only a short period of time, while others become long-term organizational members, continuing their involvement into adulthood. Unfortunately, there is no registry or comprehensive survey of movement participants, meaning there is no demographic data available on organized working children. My ethnographic observations suggest that, in Lima at least, movement participation and leadership are fairly balanced in terms of gender, with perhaps slightly more girls taking on roles as regional and national delegates. There are more kids participating between the ages of eleven and fourteen, with somewhat smaller numbers of participants in the upper and lower age categories (eight to ten and fifteen to seventeen). They are poor and working-class, but the work they do varies a great deal. Most of the kids work alongside their families in the household or in small enterprises. This includes work on family farms in the countryside and work in restaurants, market stalls, and shops, or as street vendors in the cities. Some primarily do domestic labor, helping care for younger siblings, cooking, cleaning, and other reproductive labor for immediate and extended family members. Other NATs work for employers outside the family, but in similar contexts. Some run their own very small businesses, some of which are funded partly through the movement's micro-lending program. As a few more specific examples, I met kids who sell homemade candies in their schools and on the streets, who help their grandmothers and aunts at their market stalls, who work in family-owned juice stands, who carry fruit for buyers at a wholesale market, who work as babysitters, and who serve food or bus tables in restaurants. Some children in the movement say that they did not identify themselves as "working" until they entered the movement and began to see their "helping out" at home or in family enterprises as a form of labor. All of the kids in the movement also go to school, so they are usually balancing schoolwork, family labor, paid work, and their movement participation, not to mention involvement in other clubs and hobbies, from volleyball to folkloric dancing.

In Lima, the kids who participate in the movement mostly live in the few neighborhoods where there are active base groups: Villa El Salvador, Surquillo, Rimac, Yerbateros, and Ate-Vitarte. While a few kids come from families that have been in Lima for generations, most are either the first generation in their family to be born in Lima or were themselves part of the migration process. Their families were often part of the great waves of rural to urban migration that occurred in the 1990s. Very few of the movement kids had family roots in Peru's Amazon region, but many had ongoing connections to villages and towns in the Andean highlands. I met only a handful of kids who had lived in Peru's rural areas or smaller cities long enough to have significant memories of these places, but many of them would go visit family, especially grandparents, living in other parts of the country during school holidays. A few came from families where they spoke at least some Quechua at home, and more were part of different community projects designed to help children maintain stronger connections to their families' Andean roots through activities like weaving or dancing, but none of the NATs really self-identified as indigenous or Andean.[15] While many of them are likely to still confront racism in their daily lives due to their physical appearance, their clothing choices and language practices generally mark them as mestizos or *citadinos* (city kids), and both of these are terms that they would use to describe themselves. However, while the NATs may not describe themselves as indigenous, the movement explicitly draws on Andean indigenous perspectives, embracing these as counterpoints to a Western model of childhood, and encourages the NATs to value their individual and collective indigenous (usually Andean) roots. In comparison, the movement does not often discuss Afro-Peruvian experiences or perspectives, despite the fact that a few kids in the movement in Lima have at least some connections to an Afro-Peruvian identity.[16]

There are no systematic data kept on the participants in the movement, so it is difficult to provide quantitative summaries of the conditions of their lives, their family income levels, or their school experiences. However, thanks to the extensive and long-term Young Lives research project, which includes Peru as one of its four national sites, there is fairly substantial data available on poor and working-class Peruvian children in general. Taken as a whole, the Young Lives data highlight noticeable inequalities among Peruvian children in regard to health, education, and overall well-being. Much of this inequality is mapped onto the linked divisions of rural/urban and indigenous/non-indigenous, as well as onto family wealth and income. Poverty is substantially higher in rural areas in Peru: 54 percent of the rural population lives in poverty, compared with 19 percent of the urban population.[17] In 2009, among the child participants in the Young Lives study, 55 percent of children whose mother's first language was an indigenous language were living in poverty, compared with 37 percent of children whose mother's first language was Spanish.[18]

Primary school enrollment is nearly universal in Peru, with some statistics indicating that 98 percent of primary school–age children are enrolled.[19] Secondary school enrollment is somewhat lower at 78 percent.[20] At the secondary level, there are again significant urban/rural differences: 85 percent and 69 percent enrollment, respectively.[21] Further, many local and international education experts express substantial concerns about the quality of rural education, the distance children must travel to arrive at school, and the lack of resources and teachers for rural schooling.[22] Qualitative data from the Young Lives study also identify various problems in the educational system, including physical punishment, teacher absenteeism, and a lack of learning materials.[23] Government investment in public education is quite low, with expenditures hovering at around 3 percent of GDP during the time of my research, compared to the OECD average of 6 percent. Additionally, the educational achievement outcomes are much higher for children in urban schools and for children in private schools.[24] The Young Lives school study finds that "private schools tend to enroll children with better-educated parents (which is not a surprise, given that they have to pay for their schooling). Among the public-school students, indigenous children and their families have worse infrastructure at school and worse educational outcomes."[25] In short, as with many other nations, the educational system does not generally operate as an equalizing force but reinforces other inequalities.

Peru has also been the site of significant international research and intervention regarding child labor. This is, in part, due to the fairly high incidence of children's participation in work compared to other nations with similar levels of economic development.[26] According to a 2015 national survey on child labor, 27 percent of children ages five to seventeen are reported as involved in some form of economic activity for at least one hour per week, down from nearly 42 percent in 2007.[27] However, as I will discuss in greater detail in the following chapter, there are numerous competing definitions regarding what should be included in the different statistical categories of "work," "child labor," "hazardous child labor," and "the worst forms of child labor." The movement of working children has one set of answers to these questions, while the researchers who produce both the national and international statistics on child labor use quite different definitions. Furthermore, researchers have changed their definitions over time and are often working with quite limited data.[28] All of these issues make it difficult to come to definitive conclusions about rates of "child labor" in Peru or to make systematic comparisons between organized and unorganized working children. There is a general consensus, however, on the fact that much of the work done by children is done in the context of the family, including work in subsistence and small-scale agriculture and in small family businesses.[29] Further, as should be clear from the statistics on primary school enrollment, nearly all of the children in Peru who are engaged in various forms of work combine that work with school, although this declines somewhat among adolescents.[30] In at least these two ways, working children in the movement do not appear to be very demographically different from those who do not participate, except that anecdotal evidence suggests they are more likely to continue their schooling beyond secondary education.

Officially classified by the World Bank as an "upper middle income country," but at the lower GDP end of this category, Peru has experienced substantial and rapid economic growth over the past twenty years, with much of this growth occurring in just the past fifteen years. After the intensely difficult and deadly period of the internal armed conflict, which continued through the 1990s, Peru has also had significant improvements on many of the basic human development indicators. For example, life expectancy has increased to seventy-four (from fifty-three in 1970 and sixty-six in 1990), and the under-five mortality rate was reduced by 76 percent between 1990 and 2011.[31] Ranked 84 out of 188 countries on the 2014 Human Development Index, Peru is now near the middle of the Latin American and Caribbean nations. Poverty has also decreased substantially, with the percentage of the population living below the poverty line dropping from 54.5 in 1991 to 31.3 in 2010.[32] However, most macro-analyses of Peruvian development data find substantial inequality to be a persistent and long-standing problem.[33] The Gini coefficient, a measure of economic inequality, has remained largely unchanged, with only slight declines in the past few years.[34] Growth, particularly under the neoliberal model being pursued by the Peruvian government during the "boom," has not led to reductions in inequality.

The kids who are part of the movement of working children in Lima live in a context of substantial and highly visible economic inequality, and they face significant challenges and injustices. Poverty, economic precarity, and poor-quality schools are pervasive in their lives. However, their identities and experiences are not well captured by the popular images most often associated with the term "child labor" in the Global North. They are not the sad-eyed factory workers who stare silently out from photos, or the desperately hungry street children who turn to theft, drugs, or prostitution and who feature prominently in documentaries and news stories. While some working children in Peru encounter these forms of violence and exploitation, these one-dimensional images of child laborers are regularly criticized by the kids in the movement, as well as by the local organizations for street children. Instead of seeing working children as passive and tragic victims, as dangerous threats to public safety, as kids who have "grown up too soon," or as symbols of "underdevelopment," the NATs ask that those who are concerned about "child labor" get to know them as individuals who work in a range of contexts and conditions and who are not entirely defined by their work. They are far more than just workers: Diego is a huge fan of K-Pop, Patricia dedicates any free time she has to playing volleyball, Carmen is a serious and diligent straight-A student, and Andrea loves to draw. Learning about these NATs, with all their personal interests and quirks, as well as their activist engagements and visions, significantly destabilizes the stereotypical image of the working child.

Learning with Social Movements

Working children's movements have been extremely well studied, with especially large bodies of literature published in Latin America and Europe.[35] Much of this research focuses on the movements' perspectives on children's work as they relate to children's rights and/or childhood studies, or engages with the movements primarily as contexts for studying working children themselves, analyzing their work conditions, social relations, geographies and use of space, or their development and learning.[36] I enter these abundant and rich conversations from a very different angle as a scholar of social movements and young people's political practices; my focus is not on children's work per se or how working matters in their lives, but on the dynamics of children's activism and their political relationships with their adult allies, the *colaboradores*.

This book is rooted primarily in ethnographic participant observation, but also draws upon document analysis and in-depth interviewing with both children and adults. Analyzing the extensive collection of websites, publications, flyers, pamphlets, training manuals, and other relevant materials of movement organizations allows me to trace organizational discourses regarding intergenerational collaboration and to analyze the movement's collective narratives about children's political identities. But organizational discourse, of course, is not identical to organizational practice. Therefore, I rely most heavily on extensive ethnographic observation, conducted on four research trips to Lima between

June 2012 and May 2017, with the longest being a five-month stay in 2013. In total, I spent over twelve months attending local, regional, and national meetings, workshops, assemblies, gatherings, panel discussions, strategy sessions, meals, celebrations, and field trips.

Rather than spread out across all of Peru, I chose to spend my time focusing on the movement's activities in Lima. This allowed me to build closer relationships and get a more detailed picture of the dynamics and practices within a few groups. The base groups in Lima are somewhat different from the bases in the other parts of the country because they are inevitably more closely connected to national policy debates. As the capital, Lima is the site of much of the more explicitly policy-oriented actions of the movement, and so is a particularly good place to look at the organization's political advocacy. Staying focused on Lima also allowed me to see the movement at multiple levels because many of the national and international gatherings take place in Lima. I was able to attend dozens of base group meetings, but also some regional, national, and international meetings. When in Lima, I participated in as many movement events and activities as possible (generally at least one per day), and was an especially consistent participant at the Saturday morning assemblies at the Yerbateros house and at the biweekly meetings of the RedNNA. I also spent significant time at one of the schools that was connected to the movement through IFEJANT and attended a few multi-day movement retreats. In addition to spending time with kids and adults in the context of the movement, I spent several days in 2015 following individual children through their daily routines, moving with them through home, work, the movement, and other activities. I had hoped to also go with them to their schools, but I found that most kids were uncomfortable with this idea and that both kids and adults felt that gaining official permission to attend school with them would be incredibly difficult, if not impossible. While this is a slight disadvantage in terms of my ability to speak to how the movement shapes kids' experiences in other parts of their lives, my intellectual interest (and thus the bulk of my ethnographic engagement) was with the movement itself.

I conducted semi-structured, in-depth interviews with fifteen children and nine adults who are involved in the movement. The adults and children who were interviewed were all active participants in the movement and were purposively sampled for range (of age, years of experience, base group, leadership role, and gender). The interviews focused on individuals' discourses about and experiences with intergenerational collaboration and their understandings of the social and political significance of age differences. During the interviews, participants were asked about their initial entry into the movement, their interest in intergenerational collaboration, their perspectives on the challenges, values, and dynamics of adult-child partnerships, their thoughts about the differences and similarities between children and adults, and how they think participation in this intergenerational collaboration has impacted their organizations and their own individual experiences. These interviews allow me to examine how individuals, both children and adults, interpret and make claims about the meaning of childhood, adulthood, generational difference, and egalitarian collaboration. I also conducted five interviews with key individuals in the Peruvian government and civil society who interacted with the movement on a regular basis. These interviews were intended to give me a picture of the larger political context and how outsiders to the movement who were engaged in issues of childhood, children's rights, or child labor perceived the movement and the children in it. All of the individual names have been changed, with the exception of these public officials and of Alejandro Cussianovich, who also agreed to use his real name because of his distinctive role as the author of numerous books articulating the movement's positions and theories.[37]

From my very first email in 2012 until today, I have been astounded at how much my research interest has been supported and welcomed by the movement. IFEJANT, the movement's research and training institution, has been a home base for me when in Lima, with the organization's director consistently helping me to make new contacts, get connected with hard-to-reach individuals, and generally smoothing the process of gaining access to the many different movement groups and spaces. In order to give something back to the organization, I have done some Spanish-to-English translation work for them, helped with some evaluation research that they were doing on the micro-finance program, and led several requested workshops for movement participants on my research itself and on research methods. When introducing myself to new people in the movement, I would often say that I was "working with IFEJANT" or "connected to IFEJANT." This relationship granted me a kind of legitimacy in the eyes of both kids and adults. During my longest stays in Lima, in 2012 and 2013, I was also a regular volunteer at the Yerbateros house, where I provided some tutoring support and English language lessons for the kids at the request of their *colaboradora*.

Adults and kids in the movement are used to interacting with the many foreign visitors, volunteers, and international children's rights advocates who come to Lima for short periods of time in order to learn about MANTHOC and MNNATSOP. I was, at first, treated as just another one of these many outside observers. With each additional trip, however, as people saw that I had a longer-term commitment to engaging with them and to participating in their struggles, I was increasingly described, introduced, and treated as a "friend of the movement" rather than as a visitor. Becoming a "friend of the movement" meant that kids and adults started to relax more around me, doing less explicit promotion of the movement and its perspectives. It became assumed that I was on their side and did not need convincing of the legitimacy of children's work or their rights to political participation. On the one hand, this was beneficial as it meant that people started to also express their doubts, concerns, and thoughts about some of the complications of the work being done. On the other hand, they also began to stop explaining themselves and what they meant by different terms or ideas unless I asked.

My role as a "friend of the movement" was distinct from that of a *colaboradora*. I was seen as another adult who would support the kids, who respected their knowledge and capability, and who valued their voices, but not very much was expected of me. Unlike the *colaboradores*, I could be fairly passive at meetings and events, watching, listening, taking notes, and occasionally asking a few questions. Over time, observing my tendency to scribble things down, both kids and adults began to ask whether I was willing to take minutes at meetings, and this became one of my common responsibilities. My tendency to be seen as a listener or a learner was also amplified by my imperfect Spanish. Having learned the language through both academic classes in the United States and intensive fieldwork in other countries (Mexico, Argentina, and Venezuela), I have full listening comprehension ability (although sometimes had to ask for explanations of local slang), but I would occasionally make grammatical errors or use terms and phrasing from other locations. This would usually lead to giggles and corrections from the kids. Being slightly inexpert linguistically, I was made "less adult" and treated as someone who had things to learn.

Both kids and adults in Yerbateros and elsewhere also worried about my safety, and kids often took on the role of teaching me about where to walk and where not to walk to get to the buses I needed. While I have dark hair and dark eyes and don't instantly stand out in a crowd in some of the wealthier parts of Lima, I am also identifiable as a white foreigner, especially in the poorer areas where the movement operates. For kids, my foreign status meant that I was someone who needed guidance, but also someone whom they could question about life in the United States and ask to translate song lyrics from English to Spanish so they would know what they were singing. For adults, and for kids with longer histories in the movement and more strategic visions, my position as a US citizen meant that I could be a useful ally by bringing the movement's perspective and ideas to a new audience.[38]

People in the movement often asked what I was studying, and I would tell them that I was interested in the interactions and relationships between the *colaboradores* and the NATs. They were therefore aware that I was paying attention to these dynamics when I was in the meetings and events. While this may have changed their behaviors, I think that I was at enough events to eventually become a fairly normal and accepted part of the social landscape, with my specific research interests mostly forgotten. However, it is also impossible to know the extent to which my involvement and presence in these spaces changed how kids and adults engaged with one another. This was especially a concern for me after a presentation, late during my 2013 research trip, on some of my initial findings and analysis. IFEJANT had asked me to share what I was finding with some of the *colaboradores* and NATs. I agreed to do so, but with some trepidation as I knew that both my own status and the movement itself might change somewhat after I presented what I described to them as a "friendly critique" of some of the ways that adults continued to dominate movement spaces. On the other hand, this was a great opportunity to hear participants' responses to my ideas. I got some very useful feedback, but also noted that while some *colaboradores* affirmed my analysis, others responded with defensiveness. Immediately after this event, several *colaboradores* told me that they were trying to be more aware of these dynamics, or that they had been thinking a great deal about what I had said. The movement is, as they frequently say, very interested in self-critique and reflection, and my presentation was taken seriously as part of this process. Therefore, my argument about how both children and adults continue to replicate adult-dominated social relations in many moments led to some changes in these relations. When I came back to Lima in 2015, many *colaboradores* told me that they had discussed my ideas quite a bit in some of the gatherings of *colaboradores* and that they were striving to pay greater attention to the habituated operations of power within the movement. I had also, at this point, published an article (in English) on this subject, which Alejandro told me he had read and had been discussing with some of the NATs as well as the *colaboradores*. Thus, my research engagement became part of the movement's own ongoing internal conversation about intergenerational power and equality—a conversation that I continue to study. While some might interpret this as a disruption of the "natural" state of "the field," I instead see this as a recursive and dynamic process of collaborative knowledge creation. Thinking alongside this movement, I was also a part of its theorization, and not a neutral outside observer. I observed patterns and then discussed them with my interlocutors, with all of us engaging together in the very challenging project of reimagining childhood, adulthood, and intergenerational relationships.

Anthropologist Arturo Escobar has described an approach to the study of social movements that begins from the insight that "social movements should be seen as knowledge producers."[39] This approach ethnographically engages with activists' knowledge practices in order to build bridges between the theories and vocabularies of the academy and the theories and vocabularies of social movements. *The Kids Are in Charge* engages in this conceptual bridge building, but centers the activist knowledge produced by marginalized children and their allies in the Global South, frequently locating the related academic and scholarly debates in the endnotes. Further, social movements are important sites for imagining alternatives and for expanding our ideas about what is possible, or how the world could be otherwise. The participants in the Peruvian movement of working children articulate complex, nuanced, and textured arguments about children's place in the world and about intergenerational power relations, challenging commonsense ideas about childhood. They also put these arguments into practice, making them into embodied political projects. Therefore, in addition to bridging academic and movement discussions, the chapters that follow also present the movement's contributions in a manner that is meant to be accessible and useful for adults interested in rethinking their assumptions about children and collaborating with children as political partners in the pursuit of social justice, equity, and dignity.

2

Protagonismo and Work

Reimagining Childhood

William, a tiny ten-year-old boy with rumpled hair and a baggy t-shirt, stood in front of a group of about twenty-five children and youth to offer an analysis of a set of proposed changes to Peru's Código de los Niños y Adolescentes (the national law on children and adolescents). The kids, all active members of working children's organizations or other allied children's groups, had come together for a two-day workshop to kick off an advocacy campaign around the Código. William emphasized that his group was concerned that the new Código "still only protects adolescent workers and doesn't talk about work done by boys and girls." His co-presenter, Graciela, a sixteen-year-old with many years of experience in the movement, explained that the new Código calls for replacing the newly formed children's consultative councils (CCONNAs) with a council of adults who work in children's organizations and therefore "represent" children. Other kids were outraged at this news, saying, "But they [the government] just started the CCONNAs!" "Adults don't think the way we do." "They can't just stop letting us participate—it is our right." William explained to his peers that his group thought that this particular change implied that "the people who wrote this think that adults know what is best for us, and that we kids can't speak for ourselves."

Later in the day, after a lunch break, a staff member from Save the Children Peru, Tanya, led the whole group in an extended discussion of the "visions of childhood behind the different versions of the Código." She told the kids that before the ratification of the United Nations Convention on the Rights of the Child, it "took many years to convince adults that children were subjects of rights." She then asked the group what they thought were some of the older ideas about childhood. As participants in children's rights organizations and the movement of working children, many of them had discussed these ideas previously, and they were quick to respond and call out other approaches to childhood: "we were objects of protection," "the property of adults," "incapable," and "excluded from citizenship." Nodding, she then asked the group, "Do you think these ideas still exist?" There was a resounding and definitive "Yes!" called out from all across the room. Tanya then went on to say that many of the older ideas about children were being brought back in this set of proposed revisions to the Código. She asked the group whether they could think of examples of this, based on their analysis of the documents. Graciela mentioned the fact that many of their rights were now limited by the phrases "under the supervision of parents," or "with their parents' permission." A boy called out that this meant "they are taking away our rights." Tanya agreed, confirming their view that this version of the Código had "mother and father everywhere: supervising, watching, authorizing," and that it placed them "under the power of their parents at all times." This was, she noted, against the spirit of the Convention on the Rights of the Child, which gave them rights as individuals, no matter what their parents thought. Yolanda, a sixteen-year-old leader in MNNATSOP, then brought up that they, as kids, had also not been consulted at all in the drafting of this law because "the authorities think that a group of adult experts know what should be done, that we don't have the ability to be involved. But we are part of this society!" Another girl added, "and they think we can't make decisions, that adults are more capable of deciding about childhood." William spoke up to say, "They also don't think we should be involved in work." Overall, the kids concluded that the adults who had drafted this new Código did not see kids the way that they saw themselves: as capable citizens with the right to actively participate in political, social, and economic life.[1] The kids involved in this workshop articulated a profoundly different understanding of childhood than the one that was operating in the national legislature. Their critiques of the Código were rooted in their alternative perspective, developed through their participation in movement organizations.

The critical scholarship on identity categories, such as gender and race, has consistently shown that denaturalizing these social categories is a fundamental element in challenging inequality and oppression. Feminists critique the idea that gender differences are inherent, and critical race scholars highlight how race is made and given meaning through social processes of racialization. This chapter is part of a critical tradition in childhood and youth studies that engages in a similar intellectual and political project of denaturalization by highlighting how discourses about what it means to be a child are both wildly divergent and often in conflict with one another. Scholars working in such diverse fields as history, literature, philosophy, sociology, and anthropology have all argued that childhood is a socially constructed and changeable category.[2] Being a child does not have the same meaning across time and space. Further, as this story indicates, paradigms of childhood, or sets of ideas about the meaning of childhood, are highly contested and multiple paradigms can operate within the same historical and social space. This chapter outlines the competing discourses about childhood that circulate around and within the movement of working children, explicitly challenging the idea of childhood as a natural category with inherent characteristics.

Before turning to the movement's own alternative perspective, I will focus specifically on four major discourses on childhood that are external to the movement: the colonial model of children as unruly and in need of control; Andean child-rearing approaches that position children as members of an interdependent community; the increasingly globalized narrative of children as priceless objects of protection and affection; and the international institutional model of children as rights-bearing individuals. The first two paradigms are more thoroughly rooted in Peru's own national and local histories, while the latter two paradigms are more recent transnational interventions. Each of these four paradigms circulates in the narrative landscape in Lima, shaping adults' expectations of children, family relationships, schooling practices, state institutions, and public policy, as well as NATs' own understandings of their identities, providing the context in which the movement of working children seeks to reimagine and redefine childhood. My discussion of these four paradigms is not meant to provide a comprehensive picture of the long histories and trajectories of childhood in Peru.[3] Scholars of Peru and historians of Latin American childhood will certainly find this overview to be cursory, oversimplified, and unsatisfying, but my objective here is to briefly outline the key discourses of childhood with which the movement itself engages. I specifically address the ideas that are most frequently taken up in the movement's own discussions of childhood and are either criticized, embraced, or reworked by movement participants. This is not a full delineation of Peruvian cultures and histories of childhood, but a schematic mapping of some of the discursive elements that most directly inform the movement's framework.

Colonial Influences: Children as Unruly Subjects in Need of Moral Guidance

The figure of the child has played a substantial role in colonialist discourse. As art historian Carolyn Dean writes, "Colonizers commonly compare the people they have conquered and colonized to children. In the viceroyalty of Peru, for example, Hispanic authorities—both state and ecclesiastical—frequently characterized native Andeans as childlike or even childish. Infantilizing ideologies not only justified paternalistic attitudes on the part of the colonizer but also legitimized political domination."[4] These discursive linkages were used to dehumanize indigenous communities, but this oppressive function depends on children also being seen as not fully human. As such, these narratives both illuminate the deep racism of colonialism and draw attention to colonial assumptions about childhood. The child being invoked and imagined in these claims was a particular kind of child: irrational, incapable, and in need of management. According to Dean, "in early-modern Catholic Europe, the notion that a child was naturally inclined to misbehave was articulated in the doctrine of infant depravity, which held that childhood folly was a manifestation of original sin."[5] To be childlike, in the Spanish colonial mindset, was to be both unruly and sinful, and therefore in need of religious education and moral guidance. This deeply negative vision of children was used to justify racialized colonial rule and facilitated the development of state and church institutions that would teach "good Christian behavior" and punish "disobedient" Andean children and infantilized adults.[6] Infantilization works as a method for marginalization only if children are marginalized; otherwise, the claim that a group is "childlike" would have less impact. White supremacy, colonialism, patriarchy, and ageism have, in this way, historically functioned as mutually supporting frameworks that position the white, European, modern adult male as the epitome of human development over and against the supposedly irrational, incapable, and less fully human other.[7]

Colonial powers across the Americas (and elsewhere) not only infantilized indigenous populations, but engaged deeply with children and childhood as a strategy for expanding and solidifying colonial control over territories and communities. The important scholarship on boarding schools, mission schools, and the forcible removal of children from indigenous communities traces the violent process of indigenous children's insertion into the colonial project. Drawing on comparative analysis of Australia and North America, Victoria Haskins and Margaret Jacobs note that while "reformers and government officials touted child removal as a means to 'uplift' and 'civilize' indigenous children," such schools were "part of the strategy of warfare" that aimed to fragment and destroy indigenous communities and sever ties to land.[8] In the colonial Peruvian context, although "education among Andeans was a privilege limited to the Indian elite,"[9] schooling these young elites was an explicit strategy for managing the indigenous population. As Pablo José Arriaga, a Jesuit missionary who created several schools in the early seventeenth century, wrote, "The only way to make the curacas and caciques behave . . . is to begin at the beginning and instruct their children so that from childhood they may learn the Christian discipline and doctrine."[10] In these schools and those founded later by other missionaries and intended for a wider population, children's lives were highly regimented, with substantial regulation and control of daily behavior. Children were to be taught not only Christian doctrine, but also good Christian comportment, including obedience to authority and honesty, traits that they (and indigenous adults) were seen as lacking.[11]

The logic of punishment and control that was deployed against children and indigenous communities in the early colonial period continued, but was somewhat transformed, in the development of the early modern juvenile justice system. Tracing the history of the structures of punishment for street children in Lima, historian Bianca Premo argues that by the late eighteenth century, "enlightenment ideas, emphasizing education and elevating childhood to a stage in life during which social values and practices become imprinted on human beings, began to steer judges toward a philosophy of reform."[12] Children and youth, especially those who were poor or working, were still seen as problems, and as potentially dangerous, but they were also reimagined as objects of socialization whose early years would have a lasting impact on their adult lives. During this period, attorneys who were defending juvenile offenders emphasized children's "lack of malice, limited forethought (*menos advertencia*) and imperfect comprehension."[13] Children's wayward and disorganized nature, therefore, needed to be controlled. They needed to be made into particular kinds of adult subjects by way of hard work, discipline, and obedience to authority. Thus, children and youth who had not been properly disciplined and raised by their families were to be "corrected" by the controlling interventions of the state. In this framework, children's misbehavior is not seen as inevitable, but is instead blamed upon bad or absent parents. And, notably, the label of "bad parent" is something that was, and continues to be, weaponized and used against primarily poor, working-class, and indigenous families.[14]

Of course, the idea that children are willful, troublesome, and in need of strong discipline is not unique to Peru. An emphasis on order, control, and adult authority over children is a common feature of many understandings of childhood. Local iterations of this paradigm, however, are shaped by distinctive contexts and histories, relying on particular models of authority and power to manage children. Peruvian historian and feminist scholar Maria Emma Mannarelli argues that Peruvian childhood has been indelibly marked by three distinct hierarchical models of adult-child relationships: the hacienda (with its combination of paternalism, servitude, and obedience), the Catholic Church (with its preoccupations regarding the control of sexuality and moral order), and the Republican nuclear family (with its emphasis on submission, protection, and a division of labor).[15] According to Mannarelli, this history of hierarchy and authoritarianism enables the ongoing legitimation of patriarchal control and physical punishment in parent-child relationships and in the various institutions that interact with children today, including schools. Across these analyses of childhood in Peruvian history, scholars emphasize how children, especially poor and nonwhite children, were understood by the colonial and early modern state as unruly subjects who need to be controlled, managed, and disciplined into appropriate behavior as part of a racialized project of civilization, modernization, and national development.[16]

This paradigm of childhood continues to reverberate through Peruvian political and social life in both overt and subtle ways.[17] The argument that children need a strong and powerful guiding hand was precisely one of the "older" ideas of childhood that movement participants saw reemerging in the legislature's discussion of the Código. Many of the proposed changes to the law limited children's rights by saying that they had these rights only with the authorization or supervision of their parents. They also proposed to diminish the protections that prohibited humiliating physical punishment. These suggested changes coming from the legislature, according to one of the adult presenters at the workshop, assume that "children are a mess and they need strong laws and strong hands to control them. . . . They think kids now have too many rights and are trying to restore adult power and authority." Children, in the view of some legislators, needed to be resituated under adult control.

In addition to criticizing the potential return of these ideals in the Código, movement organizations were active in a multi-year public awareness campaign against the physical punishment of children in schools and families, acknowledging that these ideas also sometimes emerge much closer to home. Movement participants, both NATs and adults, talk regularly about how these older ideas about children continue to influence many of their own family members, including their parents, grandparents, aunts, and uncles. Conversations about home and school highlight how many adults often want them to be more submissive, silent, and obedient to adult authority. The NATs understand that many adults in their lives have good intentions and sincerely believe that strict rules and punishments are in children's best interests. When confronting institutions, like schools and the government, the NATs' rejection of this paradigm of childhood is explicit and direct, but it is generally much more difficult to challenge its tenacious hold in their own lives, among adults whom they love and respect.[18]

The idea that children are either immoral or amoral and therefore need adult control and guidance often justifies children's exclusion from politics.[19] If children are troublesome, unruly, and naturally wild, then the primary role for adults in their lives is to manage, control, and contain them. This paradigm of childhood understands children as passive recipients of intervention and action, rather than moral agents deserving of power in social and political space. Children, understood in these terms, are certainly not worthy of inclusion as active participants in democratic community life. Unfortunately, many well-meaning adults and policy makers, in Peru and elsewhere, are still influenced by this and similar views of childhood. It continues to be a substantial barrier to increasing children's citizenship and to engaging with them as political subjects in families, schools, social movements, and state institutions.

Andean Paradigms: Children as Part of Networks of Care

The hierarchical colonial vision of disciplining unruly childhoods stands in powerful contrast to how movement participants and some scholars describe indigenous Andean approaches to childhood and child-rearing. While Peru's indigenous communities are highly diverse, movement participants primarily reference Andean rather than coastal or Amazonian indigenous practices and communities when discussing their ideas about childhood. Activists in the movement, as well as many childhood studies researchers of Quechua-speaking communities, argue that Andean communities have frequently understood children to be growing and developing community members who are situated within mutual relationships of responsibility, respect, and care. This emphasis on mutuality and reciprocity can sometimes be romanticized, over-stated, or essentialized by scholars and movement participants in ways that replicate many of the problems anthropologist Orin Starn has iden-tified with "Andeanism," but there is also some empirical ethnographic support for these claims.[20]

In her ethnography of child-rearing in one village in the Peruvian Andes, anthropologist Inge Bolin argues that children are generally given a great deal of free rein and are raised in a highly permissive man-ner, with minimal punishment. This permissiveness relies upon the fact that "at a young age they are introduced to the unwritten law of reci-procity, the hallmark of Andean life."[21] Vidal Carbajal Solís, a scholar of Andean indigenous language practices, also emphasizes that the Que-chua idea of providing care should be understood as mutual rather than hierarchical—a relation between interdependent equals. For example, he notes that people regularly say that they take care of the alpacas and the alpacas take care of them, that they care for the earth and the earth cares for them, and that this model also applies to how many indigenous Quechua-speaking communities think about the care of children.[22] Children are seen as deserving of care and concern, but are not viewed as passive recipients of this care. Instead, they are considered to be capable of contributing to the family and are expected to provide as well as receive care in a reciprocal relationship of respect.

According to Peruvian education scholar Fernando García, children show respect in some Quechua-speaking communities by "behaving modestly and quietly, especially in the presence of adults" in order to listen, observe, and pay attention.[23] García notes, however, that this respect and careful listening should not be understood as submission or as counter to children's autonomy. Instead, children are expected to listen carefully to adults not in order to submit to them and their rules, but in order to learn how to participate in community activities. By listening, observing intently, and participating alongside adults in a quiet and calm manner, children are learning how to be active community members.[24] Anthropologist Patricia Ames also identifies this type of learning process in multiple Quechua-speaking communities. She notes that infants and toddlers accompany parents in their work, and that from the age of four or five children begin to take on their own autonomous activities while continuing to learn other skills by observing their older siblings and the adults around them.[25] Importantly, as they learn agricultural and productive skills, children are also learning moral and sociocultural lessons regarding the communities' values of reciprocity and collective responsibility.[26] From this perspective, children's participation in work is a way to learn skills and develop as a member of a community. Childhood is thus understood as a period of learning, growth, and development, but this learning is not separated from community contributions or located only in a separate institutional space for children (the school). This view of children and their role in social and economic life is not only influential in rural areas, but is also present in the experience and meaning of childhood in Lima, as both people and ideas in Peru travel back and forth between the cities and rural communities.[27] While kids in Lima do very different work than in rural communities, many working children and their parents in Lima emphasize children's potential contributions to the family and their shared responsibility for care.[28]

Participants in the movement of working children regularly invoke these ideas of mutuality and the integration of work, learning, and play as a foundational part of the movement's approach to childhood. More importantly, they name these ideas as either "Andean" or "indigenous" and they position them as something to be defended against Western, globalized, or neocolonial incursions. For example, Enrique, a former NAT and now a *colaborador* for MANTHOC, described his own childhood to me by emphasizing how, in his rural community near Lake Titicaca, "when we were working, we were also playing, and also learning." This, he said, "was our indigenous culture." And, at a workshop for *colaboradores*, Nico, one of the IFEJANT staff members, presented a detailed argument about how Andean visions of childhood were being attacked by the Western perspective: "With the context of globalization, Western perspectives on childhood are radiating everywhere. This is what Aníbal Quijano calls the colonization of ideas." He continued by saying that "this is control by way of control of thinking. The model of the ideal child that is used by those who want to eradicate child labor also eradicates the ideas of indigenous Andean culture regarding work—it is eradicating a culture." While this invocation of indigenous culture homogenizes diverse and changing communities and practices, it is also a powerful symbolic political resource that activists draw on when articulating their own approach. Nico's framing highlights how ideas about childhood are multiple and contested, rather than natural or universal, and how the struggle over the meaning of childhood has much larger social and political implications—ideas about nation, culture, progress, and development are all bound up with the figure of the child.[29]

In the movement's articulations of indigeneity, the NATs are all, no matter their own personal racial and ethnic family histories, invited to connect to an imagined shared indigenous ancestry. For example, the 2011 Declaration on the World Day for Dignity for Working Children, written by child and adolescent delegates of several movement organizations, stated, "We value work because it allows us to be active protagonists in the economy of our families and of our society. We see it as our historical and cultural inheritance from our ancestors." On the one hand, movement participants here might be read as participating in a version of the Peruvian nationalism where "the legacy of *indigenismo* facilitates the shallow uptake of indigenous signifiers by outside parties."[30] But not all movement participants are "outside parties," as some NATs and adults, especially from the base groups outside Lima, self-identify as indigenous, and many of the Lima participants are also not necessarily very far removed from their families' indigenous and rural roots.

Further, by referencing the similarities between "indigenous culture" and their own vision of childhood, movement participants also seek to legitimize their position and align themselves with decolonial activism and indigenous resistance, as they also regularly articulate support for specific indigenous movements and struggles for self-determination. These alliances, however, are largely symbolic, as there are only a few actual political relationships between the movement and indigenous organizations in Lima.[31]

When compared to discourses of colonial childhood, this paradigm of childhood makes a much stronger case for children's inclusion in political life (as well as their inclusion in work), but it does not see children as simply the same as adults. By recognizing children as developing and growing subjects within an interdependent community, it bridges ideas of children as "becoming" and "being." Children are still "becoming" in the sense that they are on a developmental trajectory toward greater knowledge and skills, but they are also regarded as already making valuable contributions to the community—as already "being."[32] This idea of children as both developing *and* participating has clear implications for children's political inclusion. It suggests that children need some adult support in order to participate as political actors, but that, when they do, their contributions are real and not merely practice for the future. Children, situated in mutual relationships of responsibility and care, are included as active members of communities even as they are expected to be particularly quiet and respectful in order to learn from elders and improve their participation.[33]

Globalizing Norms: The Priceless Child

In his presentation to *colaboradores*, Nico argued that the paradigms of childhood rooted in Peru's history of Spanish colonization and Andean child-rearing practices are both increasingly being challenged by the expanding global circulation of another paradigm of childhood. As historian Elizabeth Kuznesof writes, "Globalization has produced a common vision of what the experience of childhood should be, and what children should do, a kind of global 'morality.' . . . However, this 'global notion' really constitutes an elite vision, and does not coincide with what the experience of childhood has been in Latin America."[34]

In this vision, childhood is marked off as a separate time and space, in which children, in the words of anthropologist Elizabeth Chin, "are domestic, part of families, primarily unproductive, and dependent."[35] In the movement of working children, this globalizing paradigm is most often summarized by the catchphrase "treating children as objects of protection."

The image of a child in need of protection from the dangers and threats of the public sphere draws upon earlier Romantic notions of children's innocence and purity, articulated by Rousseau and others.[36] Viviana Zelizer's now classic analysis lays out the economic, social, and cultural imperatives behind this powerful narrative. Children, she argues, were transformed from useful and capable economic actors into useless, but priceless, objects of sentimental value. Focusing primarily on the United States, she writes, "The expulsion of children from the 'cash nexus' at the turn of the past century, although clearly shaped by profound changes in the economic, occupational, and family structures, was also part of a cultural process of 'sacralization' of children's lives."[37] Childhood became increasingly separated from utility, economics, and the public and moved into a private, emotional, and romanticized vision of the patriarchal nuclear family.

The ideal of maintaining children's innocence by way of their protection and exclusion from the public sphere has created a powerful set of sentimental and moral imperatives about what constitutes a "good childhood." A good childhood, in this discourse, is understood to be a sheltered childhood defined by play, schooling, and family. This is the vision of childhood that undergirds the international calls to end child labor. Work is automatically assumed to sully or destroy childhood. International development and foreign aid institutions regularly present working children, street children, and many other kids who fall outside the boundaries of this idealized childhood as tragic victims of circumstance.[38] Represented as passive, helpless, and inevitably damaged by living childhoods "out of bounds," these children find both themselves and their parents being criticized and stigmatized.[39] Working children are seen as a marker of "underdevelopment" and as a social problem partly because they are children "out of place," living some of their childhoods in public rather than private space, doing tasks that do not mesh with this increasingly powerful set of globalized ideals about what childhood is supposed to be.[40]

Through the influence of globalized media, popular culture, and international development agencies and organizations, this is a view of children that has increasingly taken hold across Latin America,[41] including Peru, where many middle-class urban Peruvians see "the child's daily life as being geared exclusively to education and play."[42] If one is to be modern, developed, and respectable, one's children should not work. Both individual families and the Peruvian state promote an image of themselves as cosmopolitan and in-step with global norms by criticizing children's work and those "other" families that allow their children to work. Working children become symbolically associated with poverty and backwardness, which are highly racialized and associated with indigeneity in Peru.[43] As a point of contrast, when children in the United States work, whether as actors, babysitters, or digital coders and designers, their work no longer carries the stigma of "child labor" or the assumption that their families are culturally deficient. It is only in the context of the colonialist and racist imaginaries about the "developing world" that children's work continues to be marked as inevitably anti-modern. By proudly claiming their identities as working children, the NATs position themselves against the ideals of the modern Peruvian mestizo citizen, and directly criticize the discourse of the priceless child for stigmatizing them, their families, and their labor.

In addition to excluding children from labor and work, the discourse of the priceless child supports the assumption that children should be excluded from politics. The innocent, priceless, sacred child is not a particularly capable, competent, or agentic child in that he or she is not imagined as having any real contributions to make to the social, economic, and political life of communities. When children are primarily seen as objects of protection, it is assumed that adults are the source of that protection, and that adults can and should speak for children, without needing to explicitly invite or listen to children's opinions. When childhood is seen as a natural and sacred state of innocence, properly located in the sphere of the family, rather than as a social category produced through political and economic relations, children's issues can be treated as if they are apolitical or private concerns. Further, as many feminist theorists have noted, the logic of a public/private divide sustains patriarchal control over both women and children.[44] This influential global paradigm of childhood thus removes both children themselves (as subjects) and childhood (as a category) from political debate and discussion.

International Institutions: Children's Rights

In the almost thirty years since the adoption of the UN Convention on the Rights of the Child (CRC), scholars and practitioners around the world have debated what it means to think about children as subjects of rights.[45] The children's rights perspective is often contrasted with that of child protection and emphasizes children as "social actors, as active agents and autonomous, independent human beings in constructing their lives."[46] On the one hand, this view of childhood is a profound departure from the ideal of the privatized priceless child, in that children who are subjects of rights are situated as public citizens and participants. On the other hand, scholars have argued that the Convention on the Rights of the Child is ambiguous, in that a protectionist view of the vulnerable child who is incapable of making his or her own decisions continues to appear alongside the image of a speaking, active, rights-bearing child.[47] Furthermore, the paradigm of children as rights-bearing subjects has often been invoked to argue that all children have a right to a specific kind of "good" childhood (no work, no responsibilities, and so forth) that is assumed to be natural and therefore universally desirable.[48] Children's rights discourses can sometimes be used to support the ideal of the priceless child, despite their many differences.

The Convention on the Rights of the Child has also been critiqued for being rooted in Western ideas about what it means to be a person, and Western models of psychological growth and development. Sociologist Berry Mayall notes that "the Convention refers to a universal, free-standing, individual child: a child who is on a particular developmental trajectory. It implies that biologically-based relations between parents and children are more fundamental and natural than other sorts of family or community relations."[49] Psychologist Colette Daiute also offers a thorough analysis of the vision of development embedded in the CRC:

The general model of human development embedded in the CRC—although not explicitly discussed—is one of a gradually maturing organism—expressed in terms like "evolving capacities of the child" and "will be given weight in accordance with age and maturity." Characteristic of the CRC discourse is its reference to "the child," implying that "child" is a universal category. The related discourse of maturation suggests that this universality is biological.[50]

This view of children's development as a primarily biological process of universal maturation is profoundly challenged by sociocultural development theory, which argues that "the mind is shaped through symbolic interaction in cultural systems."[51] This latter approach to development suggests that children do not *necessarily* have particular capabilities at particular biological moments, but that what children learn and are able to do is shaped by the social opportunities for their development. Therefore, giving children greater opportunities for participation, critical thinking, self-expression, and self-determination increases their cognitive skills and capacities in these areas. Daiute notes that without this sociocultural perspective on development, it is quite easy for states and other institutions to limit children's rights by simply asserting that children of a given age do not yet have "the developing capacity" to exercise those rights. She also argues that states often assume that children's capacities are substantially less than what social science evidence would indicate to be the case.[52] The child in the CRC, while a subject of rights, is therefore also still often imagined and treated as a not-yet-capable subject, or a subject who is, in fact, still an object.

Peru signed and ratified the convention in 1990, with only minimal public debate or fanfare. Today, as human rights scholar Mikaela Luttrell-Rowland notes, the Peruvian government's "discursive commitments to the concept of children's rights are notable," and Peru's children's rights initiatives have received substantial international praise and recognition.[53] In my own observations, I too was struck by the depth and breadth of governmental and civil society attention to children's rights. When one enters government spaces devoted to children or families, there are often murals and posters with images of children proclaiming, "We have rights!" The strength of the children's rights paradigm in Peru is also evident in the extensive institutional landscape for children's rights, including the *defensorías* for children's rights, where children (or their representatives) can take their complaints of rights violations. There are *defensorías* that exist in a variety of institutions, including community organizations, schools, churches, and within the structures of municipal governments. The municipal *defensorías*, or DE-MUNAs, are the most widespread and see the largest number of cases.[54]

Alongside institutions for the protection of children's rights is a set of much newer governmental institutions that invoke children's rights discourses and are designed to encourage children's political engagement and citizenship. The most significant of these spaces are the CCONNAs (Consejos Consultivos de Niños, Niñas y Adolescentes). The oldest of these CCONNAs was founded in 2008, and there are now a few dozen CCONNAs that have been created in municipalities around the country, including one for Lima. Each CCONNA operates slightly differently, but all are designed to be spaces where children and adolescents can express their opinions on local policy issues to the appropriate authorities. Children are also increasingly included in participatory budgeting processes in many municipalities in Peru. Participatory budgeting, which began in Brazil in the 1980s and has since spread to many cities around the world, is a democratic process by which community members make decisions on how to spend a portion of the local budget.[55] In Peru, the participatory budgeting process primarily involves individuals who serve as representatives of organizations, rather than as independent citizens. Children's organizations are among the organizations included in the process in some of the municipalities that engage in participatory budgeting.

The formal, state-based opportunities for children's political participation in Peru are partly the result of the presence of an extensive civil society and social movement landscape that has advocated for children's participatory rights. There are many national and local groups of organized children and adolescents. In Lima alone, my fieldwork brought me into contact with at least a dozen different social change organizations led by children and adolescents. Furthermore, large international NGOs and foundations with an emphasis on childhood and children's rights, like Save the Children, WorldVision, Terre de Hommes, and Plan-International, all have a significant presence in Peru, as does UNI-

CEF. Children's rights are certainly not always actualized or made real, but the children's rights framework has had a substantial *discursive* impact in Lima, with many people both within and outside the movement of working children using rights-based language to talk about children and childhood.

The movement of working children regularly draws on this rights-based approach to childhood. In July 2013, for example, several movement organizations helped to organize a Festival for Children's Rights in Villa El Salvador, one of Lima's former *pueblos jóvenes* with a rich history of community and political organizing. At the festival, there were colorful signs and banners proclaiming, "Our opinion matters in the family, in school, and in society," a clown walking around on stilts, and speakers for music and announcements. Each base group from MANTHOC, as well as youth from several other organizations, had a tent canopy with a table for providing information about their group and had organized a fun activity designed to teach about children's rights. There was a memory-style card game with different rights written on the cards, a game where kids would "fish" to catch little cards with different rights written on them, and a giant board game where players would roll a big fuzzy die and then move themselves forward along the colorful path, answering questions about their rights along the way. In each of these stations, movement kids shared their knowledge about the Convention on the Rights of the Child and about children's rights more broadly with both adult and child members of the community who were passing by. The event MC also made several statements about the proposed changes to the Código and played a radio announcement that the movement kids had recorded that criticized how the changes would curtail their rights. Rights-talk is pervasive in the movement, and both kids and adults are very comfortable referencing the CRC, even as they critique and contest this paradigm in some important ways.

Children's rights frameworks are often lauded for their embrace of children's agency and their inclusion of children's political rights, including rights of association, participation, and expression.[56] In this sense, the CRC and the children's rights paradigm is the most widespread and visible challenge to the assumption of children's exclusion from politics. However, the children's rights paradigm is thoroughly rooted in a liberal model of civic participation, emphasizing individual participation and voice, often at the expense of collective action and the creation of social contexts that can facilitate and enable meaningful participation. Further, it leaves wide open the possibility of placing substantial limits on children's political participation if such participation is deemed to be beyond their "natural" developmental capabilities. The idea of children as individual rights-bearing subjects is also frequently depoliticized, in the sense that it doesn't engage with questions of power or inequality, either in terms of adult-child relations or global political economy.[57] Finally, the children's rights framework has been used to both challenge and justify children's exclusion from work, underscoring how its conceptual ambiguities allow it to be deployed for a range of purposes.[58] Although it is a highly influential global discourse (except, perhaps, in the United States) that can be productively used by children and their advocates to increase respect for children's capacities and expand children's roles in public life, the children's rights paradigm also has notable limitations for the more ambitious political project of challenging age-based hierarchies and amplifying children's power.

Protagonismo: Children as Social and Political Actors

The movement of working children actively responds to the four discourses of childhood just discussed, either through outright rejection or through engagement and incorporation, but it also offers its own distinctive theory of childhood. Movement participants call their way of thinking about children the "paradigm of children's protagonismo." Part of the discursive landscape of the movement of working children since its beginnings in the late 1970s, the concept of protagonismo emphasizes children's collective agency in political and social life. Numerous essays, articles, and books written by participants and published by movement institutions discuss protagonismo, and the concept is frequently referenced by adults and kids in movement events and daily conversation. When encouraging kids to speak up and take more leadership in the movement, colaboradores remind them to "practice protagonismo." When kids speak in public at rallies, seminars, or public lectures, they tell the audiences that they, working children, "are protagonists." The slogans, chants, and banners for the movement also frequently proclaim things like "Our *protagonismo* is a right and a responsibility" and "We are protagonists, listen to us!"

Multilayered and complex, the concept of *protagonismo* is practically impossible to translate into a single English word. While some authors have translated it as leadership, empowerment, participation, or advocacy, the movement and its key theorist, Alejandro Cussianovich, have rejected each of these descriptors for different reasons. Each one of these English words fails to capture some of the dimensions of the concept, and Alejandro has argued that all attempts to translate it are bound to erase the historical lineage and distinctive contextual contributions that give it its complexity and depth.[59] I have written more extensively elsewhere about *protagonismo*'s intellectual genealogy, its shifting meanings over time, and its relationship to a variety of Latin American social movements and critical theories,[60] but here I focus primarily on how the concept has been used by the movement to redefine childhood as a social and political collective identity (against the natural assumption) and to argue for children as active subjects who deserve full participation in political life (against the exclusion assumption).

In Latin America in the 1960s and 1970s, social scientists and analysts referenced *protagonismo popular* when discussing the ways that poor people, neighborhood groups, women's groups, unions, indigenous groups, and others were claiming space as protagonists, or central actors, in the national political scene. Alejandro writes that when these analysts spoke of *protagonismo*,

> everyone understood what they were saying, that it was the popular organizations, the women in the barrios, the youth who were supporting the unions, who were involved in this, the public sector workers, the teachers. . . . But if someone asked, "But what is the definition of *protagonismo*?," you would say, "It is this—look how the people who had been more or less shut out were now standing up, coming forward."[61]

Rooted in this history, the idea of children's *protagonismo* explicitly acknowledges children as a social and political group, not simply individuals in a natural developmental stage. The movement "put the category of generation on the table,"[62] alongside those of class, ethnic group, and gender. Or, in other words, the idea of children's *protagonismo* signals that "we see children as a social phenomenon."[63] This perspective is also realized through IFEJANT's published materials and workshops, which frequently outline the development of different institutional and cultural approaches to childhood and draw heavily on historical, anthropological, and sociological analyses of the category. And, as the opening to this chapter indicates, kids in the movement also understand that childhood is a contested, socially constructed category, with multiple meanings. They certainly see the movement's view of childhood as "better" than others, but they don't treat it as obvious or inevitable. Because the movement's perspective is so clearly unusual and unlike more dominant ideas about childhood, NATs are aware that the idea of children as protagonists doesn't describe an asocial reality, but is one of many potential ways of seeing themselves. In short, compared to the paradigms of childhood outlined above, the movement's discourse much more directly challenges the idea that there is a "natural" meaning to childhood.

However, despite a widespread agreement among movement participants that childhood is a social category that is only given meaning in social life, the discourse of children's *protagonismo* still asserts some ideas about children's essence or inherent qualities. But this essence is understood to be shared with adults—children's nature is simply human nature and not necessarily different from adult nature. Most notably, drawing from the organization's deep ties to liberation theology, the concept of *protagonismo* invokes each individual's God-given ability to be the decision maker for their own life, the protagonist of their story. In a 1997 essay, Alejandro wrote, "*Protagonismo* is simply recognizing the vocation of all social groups to think, suggest and act with their own imagination, their own identity, with the capacity for self-determination."[64] To not have this recognized is "a problem of dignity. No one was born to not be the protagonist of their own life. This is the vocation of human beings. . . . Those whose *protagonismo* is negated are also having their dignity injured."[65] Drawing from liberation theology's commitment to every individual's dignity and freedom, the movement of working children argues for children's full humanity and therefore their rights to liberation as subjects. In this view, children are no less deserving and no less capable of self-determination than adults. At a regional assembly, one of the adult *colaboradores* reminded the kids that "here, your age doesn't matter to your humanity. We can all act, we can all move for what we want." A teacher who had experience working with the movement of working children and who had received training from IFEJANT told me that this has transformed how she sees her students. "They are not just students, but they are people, with their own issues, lives, concerns, and we should think about them this way." *Protagonismo* affirms children's inner lives, their capabilities, and their complexity as they are, rather than simply treating them as partial, developing people. It emphasizes their "being" rather than their "becoming."

Protagonismo refuses older ideas of children as passive objects of socialization, protection, and intervention, and "transforms NATs from simple beneficiaries or target groups of social policies into true social partners, into active subjects rather than objects."[66] Both children and adults involved in the movement talk frequently about how kids are "social actors" and "active social subjects." In interviews, kids defined *protagonismo* as "being able to be part of the construction of a better world," "being a social actor," "expressing your opinions without fear," and "feeling capable, like you can do whatever action you are involved in and develop as a person." For many NATs, *protagonismo* is primarily understood as being able to make decisions, express yourself, and act on your beliefs and desires. While the children's rights framework also positions children as (somewhat) capable agents with full humanity, the movement's articulation of children's *protagonismo* recognizes far fewer limits upon children's capabilities by challenging the assumption of universal and natural development and by claiming that children can "realize a principal and determinant role in their lives."[67]

In a further expansion of the children's rights paradigm, *protagonismo* does not just recognize the individual agency of children but highlights organization, collective agency, and the question of social and political power. In his 2010 book on the subject, Alejandro sought to warn readers and movement activists against turning *protagonismo* into merely a celebration of the autonomous, responsible, self-actualizing individual found in the children's rights framework and celebrated by neoliberalism.[68] Against this potential diminishing, movement participants continue to reference the concept's roots in social struggles for liberation. The historical lineage of the concept highlights children's unjust exclusion from public life and implies a redefinition of power relations and an assertion of authority by those who have been marginalized. As Alejandro writes, to "be a subject of rights, we also have to have social presence, and be recognized as true social actors. This requires changing the dominant culture from an adult-centric society."[69] Further, "although *protagonismo* is an individual right, its practical exercise actually depends on the extent to which working children manage to occupy local, regional, national, and international spaces (within the family, school, community, etc.)."[70] Or, as fifteen-year-old Joaquín put it, "From the beginning of my involvement I knew that kids are capable of doing many things and of contributing to making a better world, a more just world. . . . But I've learned that we are social actors. . . . And more than this, we have to make ourselves part of the public." For Joaquín, the pursuit of children's *protagonismo* isn't just about acknowledging children as individual agents, but requires transforming how children are seen and understood in the wider society so that they are included as legitimate actors in the democratic public sphere. In these statements, we can see that *protagonismo* is, at least in part, understood to describe a social relationship of power, where the *protagonismo* of a group is dependent on its members' position in social structures and institutions. *Protagonismo*, as a critical concept, is not synonymous with individualized agency and "empowerment," although this is one of its features.

The difference between a children's rights approach to agency and *protagonismo* can also be seen in how these two paradigms seek to enact children's political inclusion. Article 12 of the CRC and most spaces for children's participation emphasize children's rights to express themselves, but don't necessarily consider the actual impact and power of children's voices.[71] Having children speak, in many of these spaces, is "good enough," and whether or not and how authorities respond to those voices is largely considered irrelevant. In contrast, the movement's vision of children's *protagonismo* incorporates questions of "decision-making, the education of children, and organization" into an analysis of whether or not children's participation is actually meaningful.[72] Marco, a fourteen-year-old, noted that "*protagonismo* means that we are the ones who make the decisions, we are the ones who advocate, socially and politically, we create our own activities, our own projects." *Protagonismo* is not simply evidenced in the ability to express oneself or to have a voice within the confines of a prestructured participatory opportunity, but must be assessed by the impact of that self-expression and the extent to which a social group does, in fact, have a role in shaping the story or impacting the political and social world.

In order to push back against more individualized approaches to children's agency and political participation, the movement again turns to indigeneity as a discursive and cultural resource. For example, Alejandro writes, "In Andean culture, the individual is not the main actor, and everything has a collective connotation, including personal lived experiences, which are collective experiences, in relationship with everything."[73] Here too we can see an essentializing tendency, but also the movement's more recent engagement with some of the larger conversations happening in contemporary Latin American social movements about indigenous cosmopolitics and decolonial activism.[74]

The movement's theory of children's *protagonismo* clearly draws upon its interpretations of indigenous Andean childhood as well as international children's rights discourses. The former inspires a belief in children's active roles and responsibilities within interdependent communities, while the latter highlights children as agentic subjects. The movement then combines elements from these paradigms with the more critical, political frameworks found in liberation theology and working-class social movements to illuminate children's status as a marginalized and oppressed social group, and to draw attention to questions of power and inequality. The movement also actively engages with childhood studies theories and sociological and anthropological scholarship in order to argue against the natural assumption. By bridging these very different intellectual traditions, movement thinkers have articulated a distinctive paradigm of childhood that explicitly challenges the assumption of children's political exclusion and argues that this exclusion is an injustice rooted in adult-centrism.

Working Children and Valued Childhoods

Protagonismo redefines children as legitimate but marginalized social and political actors. The movement of working children's analysis of "child labor" adds to this by arguing that children should also be seen as legitimate economic actors. In stark contrast with the International

Labor Organization's desire to eradicate, abolish, or "end child labor," the movement argues for a "critical appreciation" of children's work. By arguing that children have a right to participate in work, the movement again redefines the place of children in the public sphere and pushes back against an increasingly hegemonic global common sense about the separation of childhood and work, rooted in the ideal of the priceless child.

To understand the movement's arguments on this issue, we need to step back from assumptions based on the pervasive public images of factories full of child laborers and consider the range of children's work experiences. Children work in a variety of contexts and conditions—not just in highly dangerous, damaging, or exploitative workplaces. The widespread media images of child labor tend to simplify and distort the issue, making it seem as if all work done by children is brutal, unjust, and harmful. In contrast to the tendency to assume that all work done by children is of this type, social scientific research (in English) often uses a distinction between the terms "child work" and "child labor," to separate work that is safe for children and ethically acceptable from work that is not.[75] However, there is substantial conceptual slippage between the negative "child labor" and other forms of children's work in a great deal of policy, as well as public discussion, and the definitions being used for these terms vary greatly.

The International Labor Organization and its International Program on the Elimination of Child Labor (ILO-IPEC) is a powerful political force on this subject, but is also a source of conceptual collapse as organizational rhetoric tends to lump together many kinds of children's work, despite the organization's multitude of terms, definitions, and statistical categories. The most extensive recent data set on children's work in Peru comes from a survey funded by the US Department of Labor and done in collaboration with the ILO, the Peruvian Labor Ministry, and Peru's Instituto Nacional de Estadística e Informática (INEI) in 2015. This report finds that 26.4 percent of Peruvian children are involved in some form of economic activity, or some kind of work, on a regular basis.[76] In this report, the category of "economically active" children includes children who work in family enterprises for at least one hour a week, whether they are paid or not. This survey, however, distinguishes between the family-based work that is part of "economic activity," which has some potential relation to the market, and family-based domestic work, or what a classic Marxist feminist analysis would identify as reproductive labor. Work that is reproductive in nature (cleaning, cooking, caring for siblings) is not considered in the national survey to be part of "economic activity," but is instead classified as "domestic chores." In contrast to this definition, the movement of working children tends to see reproductive labor within the family as a form of work, including children who work in their own homes without pay in the movement's collective identity of "working children." As one girl told me, "I used to think of what I did as just helping out, but in MANTHOC I came to see its value as work." Already, then, we can see that the movement considers a larger population of "working children" than even the standard survey's most expansive category. Work, according to the movement, encompasses a very wide range of activities. To call for the abolition of all of these activities, from the movement's point of view, is patently absurd.

The ILO would argue that it does not in fact criminalize children for doing "chores" or even for being "economically active." But, according to both the movement and critical scholars, the ILO's tendency to not talk about acceptable forms of work obscures these important distinctions.[77] The ILO's global reports and the Peruvian report mentioned above generally make distinctions between the category of "economically active" children and the category of children involved in "child labor." "Child labor" is a normative category that identifies working children who, from the ILO's perspective, should not be doing the work in which they are currently engaged. In their framework, this includes *all* children who are involved in any economic activity between the ages of five and eleven (below the minimum age in ILO Convention 138), plus any twelve- to fourteen-year-olds who work beyond the acceptable "light work" of two hours per day, plus any children who are involved in "hazardous work." However, as children's work experts Bourdillon, White, and Myers argue, this definition makes no distinction between "child labor" defined as such on the basis of actual harm experienced by children and child labor defined as such only on the basis of not meeting a minimum age criterion, which many researchers have found is not necessarily harmful to children at all.[78] In the case of Peru, for example, an eleven-year-old who is engaged in the "economic activity" of helping out in a small family business for one hour per week is now defined as a "child laborer," doing work that should be abolished according to the ILO, even if there is no evidence of children being harmed by this work. Further, the elements that make work "hazardous" according to these surveys deserve scrutiny; in the Peruvian survey, hazards include contact with trash, including animal residues (manure), any work done after 7:00 p.m., and any domestic work in the homes of other people, but the report does not tell us which of the various hazards were most prevalent. It is certainly possible that many of the children identified as "working in hazardous conditions" are children who care for family animals and are therefore exposed to animal residues. The movement has roundly rejected this survey, arguing that the list of hazards is far too extensive and that it represents a neocolonialist judgment of traditional ways of life.

The final category deployed in the International Labor Organization's various statistical reports is that of the "worst forms of child labor." This category includes the above category of "hazardous work," but also adds an additional group of practices that are considered the "absolute worst forms of child labor": slavery or forced labor, prostitution and pornography, and drug trafficking. The ILO global reports and the Peruvian report acknowledge that data on these "absolute worst forms" are quite difficult to obtain. Therefore, very few statistics beyond the statistics on hazardous work are offered. In contrast to the ILO definitions here, the movement of working children argues that the things the ILO considers the "absolute worst forms of child labor" belong to an entirely different category of activity. They argue that these things are *not work* but are instead crimes against children. They cannot be addressed by the kinds of programs and policies the ILO advances but instead require international police investigation and action. Building from this, the movement claims that the ILO uses the example of these crimes against children in order to justify its actions and policies against child labor and children's work in general, despite the fact that these crimes are obviously very different from the vast majority of the work done by children.

The ILO's method of defining "child labor" as opposed to "children's work," according to the movement of working children and other critical scholars, is not adequately based on evidence of harm to children. Instead, it is based on potentially dubious lists of "hazards" and the assumption that any work done before the age of twelve is always inevitably "harmful." Furthermore, by including major crimes against children (slavery, forced labor, sex trafficking, and so on) in the same general category (child labor) as the economic activity of people under the age of twelve, the ILO's rhetoric erases crucial differences in the experiences of working children. This collapse, however, then lets the ILO rely upon the horrific and shocking examples of the "worst forms" to justify its arguments for a broader politics of abolition. The "worst forms" of child labor come to represent and stand in for the whole of the category, even though they represent the experience of a very small percentage of working children.

In contrast to the deployment of the abstract and slippery category of "child labor," the movement of working children focuses its analysis on the social group of working children and their lived experiences and well-being. It is child-centered, rather than concept-driven. The movement's emphasis on the lives, experiences, and needs of working children has led to its deep critique of the ways that the abolitionist approach has harmed working children through stigmatization and criminalization.[79] Graciela was ten years old during a major wave of police intervention in working children's lives. In our interview, she told me about how, during this period, children were being taken from the streets and markets where they were working and put into detention facilities and orphanages. Parents, kids, and the movement were all intensely worried about children being removed from their families and put under state control for doing no more than helping out a few hours a day in a family market stall. Graciela described her own fears, her mother's fears, and her moral outrage at the fact that her government was claiming that working children were "abused" by their parents. The movement gave her a way to challenge that claim. Reflecting back on that time, she said that this was when she came to see how important the movement was and what it meant to defend the rights of working children.

The movement of working children does not naively assume that all work is positive for children. By focusing on working children's well-being, it also identifies instances in which work is harmful to children. It argues strongly against the exploitation of children and seeks to promote working conditions that respect children's rights and dignity. Kids and adults in the movement make a distinction between exploitative work and *trabajo digno*, or dignified work. The kids in the Yerbateros base group spent several of their weekly assemblies doing activities to develop their collective and individual analysis of this distinction. They drew pictures, created skits, and talked together about what kinds of conditions they thought made work dignified and what conditions were unjust and exploitative. As a group, they created a poster, which they kept on the wall for several weeks, which listed their ideas about these two categories. Under *trabajo digno*, the group wrote the following: they pay you well, they don't mistreat you, good bosses, you are there voluntarily, it gives you benefits in your life, it looks out for your health, you are treated with care, you like what you do. They described exploitation, on the other hand, as work that is against your will, doesn't respect your rights, when you are obligated to work, when you are yelled at, when it is dangerous.

While these lists of dignified versus exploitative work are fairly straightforward, the NATs' discussion of these ideas was far more complex, with kids taking up different positions about which specific working conditions should be understood as acceptable for kids and which should not. When the *colaboradora*, Mónica, asked the group about how much they thought kids should be able to work each day, the NATs shouted out numbers ranging from two to six. They discussed this a bit, with some kids sharing that they have plenty of time to work six hours, that school and homework are easy and don't take much time, and other kids responding that they don't think kids should work quite that much, that maybe they should have time for other things too. They also discussed specific jobs and work conditions; Mónica asked a thirteen-year-old boy what he does: "I cut fabric," he replied. She then asked him, "What do you think of this? Are you ashamed of it?" "No," he said, "it is good work!" Mónica nodded, then asked a younger girl about her work. She smiled shyly, and said, "I work in the market. It is also *trabajo digno*." Mónica then asked the group whether there were any jobs that they thought were not dignified, or not safe, or not good for kids to have. One kid raised his hand and said, "washing windshields!" A few others began to shake their heads in disagreement. Mónica asked him to expand, to say why he thought washing windshields was not good for kids. He said it can be dangerous, you are out on the street, it might not be safe. A girl raised her hand and said, "I know someone who does this, and they are really careful. They get to choose where to work and how to work, and so I think it is good, it is *trabajo digno*." Another boy agreed: "I've done this a little, and I think it is okay as long as you are careful and go to safe places to do it. Like in a parking lot." In discussing their various opinions on the issue, the kids did not come to a unified definition of exploitation or a concrete set of requirements for what counts as *trabajo digno*, but they developed tools for analyzing their own working conditions and for thinking about how those conditions could be improved. Through these conversations, NATs learn to think about their work and the work of their peers in new ways so that they can, as Mónica reminded them at the end of the meeting, "reach out to kids we know are being exploited, talk to them about their rights, and help improve everyone's work situations." Discussing what makes work exploitative or dignified encourages kids to see themselves as workers with rights to dignity, rather than as total victims of a practice (child labor) that is assumed to be always negative.

The movement of working children promotes kids' greater access to *trabajo digno* by supporting kids' creation of their own businesses and cooperatives in a training and micro-finance program, PROMINATs. Juan, the *colaborador* who coordinates this program at the national level, explained, "We were talking about *trabajo digno*, but what could we offer them? This was what we were missing, so we talked about creating small businesses, or even a larger business where the NATs could work. So we began this project in order to hear what ideas the kids had for these businesses so that they could improve their working conditions and their quality of life." Kids involved in PROMINATs learn how to make a business plan, how to set prices for their commodities, and how to work together, as well as the skills of each particular business: baking empanadas, designing greeting cards, making jewelry, and so on. They also improve their math skills: adding and subtracting, figuring out loan percentages, and balancing their budgets. PROMINATs, according to many of the kids and adults, is an alternative to work in exploitative conditions, an example of what dignified work for kids can look like, and shows how work can also be a site of substantial education and learning.

Work's positive relationship to education and learning is one of several reasons that the movement of working children argues that children's work should not simply be abolished but should, instead, be appreciated and valued. Adults and kids both spoke extensively about the things that kids learn through work, whether it be how to do the var-

Figure 2.1. NATs involved in a movement bakery cooperative. Participating kids learn a variety of skills and have an opportunity to earn money in dignified working conditions. Photo courtesy of Instituto de Formación para Educadores de Jóvenes, Adolescentes y Niños Trabajadores.

ious agricultural tasks that have been passed down through generations, or balancing a budget with a computer spreadsheet. As Joaquín said, "Work is a tool for learning, for relationships, for communication, a tool for personal development and citizenship." In the schools with relationships to the movement, this idea of learning via work is practiced as an intentional pedagogy. For example, I observed one class of fourth graders who were practicing their multiplication skills by tripling the written recipe for *alfajores* (cookies) that they would bake and then sell in their neighborhoods. Notably, similar practices are also enacted in schools in the Global North under the frameworks of "project-based learning" and seeking "real-world applications," but they are not usually identified as involving children in work, even when children engage in economic activity during these projects. For the movement of working children, emphasizing the educational potentials of work allows them to draw on and reference more widely accepted discourses about childhood as a time of learning while also suggesting that learning and education can happen beyond the boundaries of formal schooling and can happen via participation in work, rather than being antithetical to work.[80]

The movement makes a parallel set of claims about the relationship between work and play. Responding to the argument that child labor prevents children from living what should be happy and playful lives, the movement of working children often emphasizes the fun that kids have in their work, and the pleasure that work gives them. Play and work, they suggest, do not have to be seen as entirely separate activities. Many kids told me about how they liked playing with their friends when they were working in the markets, and several adults who grew up in the mountains explained how the tool used to harvest potatoes was fun to use as a kid since you get to jump on it. Playing while working, and having fun at work, according to kids and adults, are two of the things that define *trabajo digno*. Importantly, in the case of both learning and play, the movement discourse continues to situate these activities as central to childhood and as part of what it means to be a child. In this way, it draws on and repeats more widely held ideas about what children should be doing. However, movement participants argue that these activities of childhood are not necessarily threatened by work, but can happen through and alongside work experiences. Work becomes incorporated into the domain of childhood through its connection to two "child-appropriate" activities.

In addition to making child-specific arguments, or arguments that focus on how work is valuable for children *as* children, the movement also makes claims about children's right to work based on children's general humanity. In these instances, movement discourse identifies work as a fundamental human activity and a source of dignity and fulfillment. Work, in the sense of producing, creating, and acting to meet one's material needs, they argue, is a central feature of what it means to be human. Movement leaders regularly argue that Andean culture sees work differently than Western frameworks. In the same workshop for *colaboradores* where he discussed indigenous Andean approaches to childhood, Nico argued that pre-conquest Andean communities did not have a separate word for "work": there was simply activity of various kinds, and that doing the activities where you accomplish things was not seen as separate from other kinds of activity, such as socializing. Work, he said, "was happiness, dance, community coming together to achieve things, sharing with others." Whether or not this is historically or anthropologically accurate is not my concern here—rather, the important point is that the movement's narratives about indigeneity support a vision of work as a humanizing, fulfilling, and collective experience. These narratives imagine a form of work very different from the alienated labor of capitalism.

The idea of work as a positive experience is also reflected in how participants talk about the work of children. Elena told me about a conversation with several PROMINATs participants who told her that they "like the feeling of being a producer—they have a desire to be useful and there is pleasure that comes from making something that matters in the world. It isn't just that they are motivated by the money, but that they get pleasure from this." NATs also regularly told me that they work because it is a way to contribute, and that making these contributions to the family economy gives them a sense of pride, pleasure, and accomplishment. Work is satisfying because it situates the individual in a larger social web of interdependence and care, which clearly articulates with the movement's conceptions of indigenous Andean perspectives on childhood.

It is from this perspective that the movement of working children argues that work is both a right and a vital form of participation in the public sphere. Through work, an individual becomes an active, engaged, contributing member of a family and community. Work becomes seen as a potentially positive experience for children in that it can be fulfilling, support their education, and be fun. The movement's arguments about children's work simultaneously draw on more widely accepted ideas about childhood (as a time of learning, as a time of play, and as part of community networks of reciprocity) and present a profound challenge to the increasingly global ideal of protecting children from work and economic responsibilities. And, most importantly for the focus of this book, the movement's framework of a critical appreciation of children's work, like the concept of *protagonismo*, positions children as legitimate and valuable participants in public and community life.

Children as Political, Economic, and Social Subjects

This chapter has outlined the major discourses about childhood that circulate in and around the movement of working children. From this discussion, we can see that the movement of working children offers a distinctive and counter-hegemonic understanding of childhood. Returning now to the larger themes of the book, I consider how this conception of childhood challenges the five assumptions I identified in the introduction, helps us to identify some of the sticky and persistent features of age-based power and inequality, and offers a set of practices and principles for how to engage in intergenerational politics that includes children.

Challenging Assumptions about Childhood

Concepts of childhood are invested with strong moralistic and normative dimensions: the ideas of a "good childhood," of "lost childhoods," or "children without childhood" all imply substantial moral judgment not just about what childhood *is*, but about what childhood *should* be like. For example, when I tell kids and adults in the United States that I am writing about working children, they often immediately conclude that these children must not have a "good childhood" and that the research must be "very sad." Work is assumed to be incompatible with children's happiness and well-being. A good childhood, according to the dominant view in the Global North, is a childhood that is sheltered from work and other responsibilities, usually including politics. On the other hand, kids and adults in the Peruvian working children's movement know that the United States is the only UN member state that has not ratified the Convention on the Rights of the Child, and they express concern that kids in the United States are treated as passive objects to be protected by adults, and therefore *they* do not have a "good childhood." A good childhood, to them, means a childhood with rights, agency, and the opportunities to participate actively in community life both as individuals and as an organized group. This example, and this chapter more broadly, clearly indicates how childhood is a contested social category, challenging the assumption of it as a natural or universal state of being.

This does not mean that all versions of childhood are equal, or that we shouldn't discuss what is good for children. But, instead of making claims that "children should not work," or "childhood is a time of play" simply because "that's what childhood means," we need instead to ask questions about children's lived experiences and the impacts of those experiences on their well-being, as well as larger ethical questions about justice, rights, and respect for children's full humanity. The first type of question is much easier to grapple with, as it can be answered through empirical social science: what happens to kids' relationship to authority when they are subjected to strict rules and regulations? How does working alongside family members matter for kids' sense of belonging in their communities? How does increasing kids' decision-making power and influence in their schools impact their educational outcomes? There are significant data and evidence to conclude that children's work is not always harmful, and that children can benefit from inclusion in both work and democratic political life. Research demonstrates that participation in work and politics isn't automatically antithetical to kids' well-being, but can improve their lives, both in the present and in the future.[81]

But the question of what constitutes a "good childhood" is not just an empirical one; it is also an ethical and political one. For the movement of working children, children's exclusion from community life, in the form of both work and politics, is an injustice that must be challenged because it does not respect children's subjectivity and human dignity. And paying attention to the principles behind the arguments for children's inclusion is vital; this book's principles are entirely distinct from a recent set of narratives in the United States that reject the logic of protection because it makes children weak or coddled or prevents them from "growing up." This position is well represented by Republican senator Ben Sasse in his widely discussed book, *The Vanishing American Adult*, which argues that the current generation of American youth is spoiled, self-centered, and irresponsible, and that one part of the solution to this perceived problem is having children do more chores and "hard work" at a young age. Sasse's arguments for children's work are rooted in the values of self-reliance, responsibility, independence, and individual toughness.[82] In contrast, the critique of children's exclusion found in the movement of working children is based in a commitment to children's equal belonging within interdependent, mutually supportive, and caring democratic communities. While we might agree that children do not necessarily need to be excluded from some kinds of work, these are fundamentally different understandings of the reasons for their inclusion. And as this contrast emphasizes, ideas about what constitutes a good childhood convey political and ethical beliefs about what makes a good citizen, a good community, and a good society. For this reason, debates about childhood and what is good for children are always already political.

The Persistence of Age-Based Power

Public debates on what children can do, what children need, how children "should be," and what constitutes a "good childhood" are pervasive. The cultural landscape is full of disagreement about childhood and children, whether expressed as anxieties about how children's ways of thinking are being changed by digital media, as critiques of a coddled generation that can't handle adversity, or as conflicts over whether or not children need strict rules or more freedom. Given this obvious diversity of ideas about childhood and the extent of our public disagreements about childhood, I often feel surprised that there is *not* a more widespread questioning of the assumption of childhood as a natural phenomenon. How is it that, despite all this debate about the meaning of childhood, many people continue to act as if they themselves know the absolute and universal truth of childhood, or as if the category simply describes a natural identity? Statements like "Of course children can't understand that topic," "Everyone knows children need strict rules," or "Childhood is a time of play, not work" continue to be commonplace. Adults and adult institutions regularly acknowledge that childhood has changed over time, indicating a willingness to accept some challenges to the natural assumption, but we still continue to naturalize at least some beliefs about how children *really* are and what children *really* need. This all suggests that consistently engaging with childhood as a social construction is actually very difficult, and that simply pointing out a multiplicity of discourses about the category isn't sufficient for undermining the power of the natural assumption.

Transforming discourses about childhood specifically to acknowledge children as capable social, political, and economic subjects is also notably thorny. In part, this is because most calls for protecting children from "the outside world" emerge from adults' deep emotional ties to children and their feelings of concern and love. Adults who seek to prevent children's engagement in both work and politics do so because they think it is in children's best interests, not because they intentionally want to limit children's power and agency. Of course, not all children are protected from hardships, dangers, and injustices, but the ideal of childhood as a time of innocent and carefree play, which is often used to justify children's political and economic exclusion, is particularly hard to challenge because it appeals to deeply felt desires for children's happiness.

These difficulties in questioning both the natural assumption and the assumption of children's exclusion illuminate two interlocking dynamics in the operation of age-based power: paternalism and the centrality of emotion. As political theorist Elizabeth Ben-Ishai writes, "Paternalism refers to interventions in individuals' lives, often against their wills, that are justified on the grounds that they promote the individuals' welfare."[83] Not all systems of oppression and inequality operate paternalistically, although paternalism has historically been deployed against marginalized communities, including women, people of color, and disabled people, and is usually justified by claims that these individuals have reduced capacity and are "childlike."[84] As a method for defending unequal power relations, paternalism has proven to be quite effective, and children are the quintessential subjects of paternalism. Paternalism is an everyday feature of children's lives as they are told that adults are only "doing what is best for them." Paternalism's hold over children hinges upon ideas about their lack of capabilities and the belief that the adults act in children's best interests because of their emotional ties to these children. The emotions of the parent-child relationship, which is assumed to be loving, caring, and affectionate (despite examples of abuse, violence, and harm to children from family members), give license to adults' protective control over children. And, as with gendered power, the intimate and familial relationships between children and adults make it so that age-based power dynamics are infused with complex feelings. Adults' strong emotional responses to their own childhood memories, whether they be nostalgic or traumatic, as well as their feelings about the children in their lives, profoundly shape their relationship to the category itself and play a role in how children's ongoing exclusion from work and politics is understood, experienced, and justified as natural.

The Movement as a Model for Intergenerational Politics

Denaturalizing social categories is one of the primary goals of both critical sociology and many movements for social justice. Acknowledging categories as socially produced, rather than natural, opens them up to change and transformation. Social movements are counter-hegemonic forces that encourage us to ask, "Does the world have to be like this? Might it not be different?" This is precisely what is taking place in the movement of working children. By discussing multiple discourses of childhood, and by articulating its own distinctive and oppositional perspective on childhood, the movement engages children and adults in rethinking the meaning of this category. Children, participants argue, don't have to be passive objects of protection or punishment, but can instead be protagonists in their communities.

The method of challenging the naturalization of childhood through a critical analysis of different competing discourses is one that could certainly be taken up by groups of adults and children in other organizational and institutional contexts. What, for example, might happen if teachers and students in US schools discussed the ideas about children embedded in their classroom practices? Or if kids and adults in a community center collectively analyzed the way that police and other state agents talk about kids in poor neighborhoods as being "at risk"? And what might happen if these same groups also talked about an alternative discourse of children as social, political, and economic subjects? The model of the movement of working children suggests that engaging kids and adults in this kind of critical conversation about childhood is not only possible, but also potentially transformative.

These conversations about the contested meaning of childhood are important not just as thought-experiments or because they would be stimulating discussions, but because discourses matter. Discourses produce particular kinds of subjects: when children are told that they *are* a certain way, they are far more likely to actually also be that way. Children may contest or reject elements of these discourses as they are navigating between conflicting claims about what it means to be a child, but discourses generate particular kinds of identities. Further, as the example of the debates over the Código shows, discourses about childhood inform public policies, which then profoundly impact children's lives. Ideas about childhood also inform culture and the social dynamics of how adults and children interact with one another. Transforming ideas about childhood, according to movement participants, is meant to transform everyday practices and adults' ways of relating to children, which is also a form of political action: a prefigurative politics that models how the world might be otherwise.

When we denaturalize childhood, the question shifts from "What are children?" to "What do we want children to be?" The movement of working children answers that question with the idea of children as engaged social, economic, and political subjects. By conceptualizing children in this way, it opens up important discussions about how to actualize this possibility, and how to better include kids in social movements and in the construction of deeper, more inclusive, and more participatory democracies. This transformative vision of childhood raises vital questions about how kids are treated by the state, by activists, and by social movements, as well as by parents, teachers, and other adults in their everyday lives. Thinking about children in this way should encourage us to not only consider how we can better engage with children as citizens and political agents, but also reflect on our own everyday relationships with children and the extent to which those relationships respect children as decision makers, community members, and protagonists.

3

Equality and Horizontalism

Reimagining Intergenerational Relationships

Graciela was only fifteen when I met her, but she had already been active in MANTHOC for seven years. She began working in her parents' market stall at the age of six, and was first invited to attend a workshop at the Yerbateros house when she was eight. She remembers that first visit to MANTHOC fondly, and also remembers her initial surprise (and pleasure) in learning that it wasn't just a place for recreation and play, but that it was also a place where kids learned how to organize and stand up for themselves. MANTHOC became her home away from home: "I basically grew up in the Yerbateros house!" In the movement she has learned "to value myself as a person, to value myself as a student, as a daughter, as a worker." In 2012 and 2013 she was one of two elected national delegates for MANTHOC from Lima. In this leadership role, Graciela has taken on a great deal of responsibility in the movement. She is comfortable speaking to the press and in front of the national Congress and often facilitates the meetings of the RedNNA. A powerful presence in any gathering, Graciela has round cheeks, bright eyes, and a warm smile that always seems to include the entire room. She takes charge easily, but also often steps back and encourages other (younger) kids to take on more responsibility in meetings and events.

In our interview, she explained that "in society there isn't equality between adults and kids because the adult is seen as being above, seen as knowing more, and the kid is seen as below, as not being able to make his or her own decisions—the kid should just think and do what the adult says. But when you are in the movement all this changes, it goes away." The movement is a space where kids and adults practice a different kind of intergenerational relationship, but, she continued, "it is complicated because in the movement we have structures where we see equality between kids and adults, between boys and girls, and everyone. But if we are talking about society, then we can see that there isn't equality between kids and adults. So, when we want to do something out in the society, we sometimes can't, because it isn't allowed, or it isn't expected." The movement, from Graciela's perspective, provides an important counterpoint to her experiences in her family, at school, and in other interactions with adults. In the movement, she feels respected and valued, and that she is an equal to the adult *colaboradores*.

This idea that children and adults are equals was a sentiment I heard many times from NATs and *colaboradores* in the movement of working children. However, the meaning of this equality is not unitary or entirely straightforward, and equality between children and adults can be quite difficult for many people to imagine. Indeed, even critical scholars of childhood who have argued for paying attention to children's agency and subjectivity have not offered many intellectual tools for thinking through the dynamics of age-based power relationships.[1] More specifically, scholars of childhood have often struggled with how to understand children's relationship to social and political power outside the paradigm of children's human rights, which has been criticized as individualistic,[2] or earlier models of children's liberation, which have been criticized as overly romantic and simplistic.[3] Recent work on children's participation and children's place in democratic life, however, has tried to move beyond this impasse by drawing on feminist, poststructuralist, and radical democratic political theory in order to challenge children's ongoing economic, social, and political marginalization and exclusion.[4] These writers draw on various theoretical traditions to collectively imagine what it would take to include children as full and equal citizens in contemporary social and political life. In this chapter, I show how these concerns have been central to the movement of working children for many years, highlighting the movement's contributions to theories of children's equality and power. In doing so, I also identify how these contributions challenge three core assumptions about childhood: the assumption of binary difference, the assumption of children's passivity and lack of critical agency, and, most especially, the assumption of the rightfulness of adult power over children.

Referring sometimes to the concept of *igualdad* (equality) and sometimes to *horizontalidad* (horizontalism), movement participants expressed deep ideological commitments to transforming and equalizing the power dynamics of adult-child relationships. In the analysis that follows, I disentangle four different dimensions of this commitment, which I name equality of dignity, equality of capacity, equality of insight, and horizontalism. The first three dimensions represent core beliefs about children and adults that are articulated by many in the movement: beliefs that children and adults are equal in these three ways. Horizontalism, on the other hand, is expressed as the movement's goal and objective for intergenerational relationships. It is the prefigurative aspiration that emerges from the three beliefs about children's fundamental equality and is the concept that is often used to question age-based hierarchies and to address dynamics of age-based power on the ground, in social life and organizational practices.

In using the language of equality, I am cognizant of its various conceptual burdens, including the connotations of sameness and a narrow juridical approach to justice, both rooted in its historical links to liberalism. Indeed, in progressive and radical US social movement contexts, "equality" is sometimes a maligned term. For example, a widely circulated meme depicts three people, of different heights, standing on boxes of the same size in front of a fence, making it so that only the tallest of the individuals is able to see over the fence; this scenario is labeled "equality." An image in which the shortest person, probably a child, is standing on a taller box so they can also see over the fence is labeled "equity," and the final image, named "liberation," removes the fence entirely. However, the vision of intergenerational equality offered by the movement of working children is *not* at all the same as this image of different individuals all receiving the same treatment despite their different conditions and needs. For the movement of working children, equality does not reference how people's relationship to injustices or obstacles (the fence) should be addressed, but instead references a fundamental state: the idea that children and adults *are* equal. And, importantly, this idea that children and adults are equal also does not, for them, mean that children and adults are the same. Participants in the movement construct versions of both intergenerational equality and horizontalism that do not deny or ignore children's differences, dependencies, and distinctive vulnerabilities.

In the analysis that follows, my goal is not to prove that children and adults are equal in each of the ways that the movement suggests, but to explore the ideas of the movement in relation to the complex questions of children's equality with adults, age-based power dynamics, and horizontal intergenerational relationships. I am also not trying to resolve the complications, contradictions, or tensions in these ideas; rather, I aim to illuminate them in order to push forward a discussion of age-based stratification, inequality, and alternative visions for organizing adult-child relationships. By exploring ideas about children's equality and intergenerational horizontalism in the movement of working children, I invite readers to consider the distance between these visions and their own experiences either as children or as adults interacting with children. In what ways do our (adults') habituated ways of engaging with kids deny them their dignity, underestimate their capacities, or ignore their insights? Why is thinking about children as equals so unsettling for many adults? How would the social and political institutions that structure adult-child interactions be different if we recognized children's equality?

Equality of Dignity

The most straightforward and potentially least controversial set of beliefs about children's equality with adults emphasizes their equal dignity and equal humanity. Put simply, this vision of intergenerational equality states that children and adults all have inherent human dignity and therefore deserve to be treated with respect and to be seen as ends in and of themselves, rather than as means to someone else's ends. As children's participation expert Harry Shier notes, this understanding of equality hinges upon seeing children and adults as having equal worth.[5] Equality of dignity is not fully actualized in either the movement of working children or in the larger society, but this version of articulating intergenerational equality raises the least public skepticism and is, in some ways, easier for movement actors and others to imagine implementing than those visions of equality and horizontalism that will be discussed in the following sections. The assertion of children's equal humanity, while not necessarily widely recognized or realized in many contexts, is nearly axiomatic both in the children's rights landscape and in childhood studies.[6] The idea that human rights apply to children, codified in the UN Convention on the Rights of the Child, hinges upon the philosophical assertion of their equal dignity as human subjects. The convention, in fact, begins with the "recognition of the inherent dignity and of the equal and inalienable rights of all members of the human family."

Equality of dignity and humanity flows seamlessly from the movement's redefinition of childhood. By emphasizing children's status as active social subjects and contributors to economic, social, and political life, the movement suggests, as childhood studies scholar Nigel Thomas puts the point, that "children do belong to the class of morally responsible persons and are entitled to respect."[7] Numerous movement pamphlets, booklets, and analyses argue for the fundamental equality and dignity of all human beings, including children. Alejandro writes that the movement "opens up a new approach for claiming children's status of equal belonging in the human species, as members of society of which they are a part."[8] And, in his analysis of MNNATSOP, Anthony Swift also highlights that "the kids say everyone is equal, but this does not mean that children, adolescents, and adults are the same. It means that they have the same value as human beings."[9] Articulations of children's equal dignity and humanity are rarely justified or explained in movement texts—instead, this vision of intergenerational equality of dignity is understood to be a moral imperative and serves as an ethical foundation for many movement practices.

Valuing each other and seeing each other as equally deserving of respect, according to many of the kids and adults in the movement, are absolutely basic to the process of creating collaborative and horizontal intergenerational relationships. Juan, a former NAT who is now a *colaborador*, explained how before becoming involved in the movement, he had thought that disagreeing with an adult showed a lack of respect, but that the movement taught him that it was, in fact, the other way around: having deliberative and open discussions between kids and adults is a demonstration of their respect for each other as equals. He continued, "There is another way for kids and adults to relate to one another. We don't always have to have the adults above and then the kids." Juan emphasized how, when he was a new member of the organization, seeing how deeply adults listen to and respect kids was "the moment when I realized the importance of this movement."

One way that movement participants signal their commitment to equality of dignity is through naming practices. *Colaboradores* have the

NATs call them by their first names to show that they value more horizontal relationships and that they are not deserving of the extra respect or authority implied in a formal title simply because of their age. Alejandro, the movement figure who would be most likely to be treated with deference on the basis of both his importance to the movement and his age (nearly eighty), is always referred to by his playful, casual nickname, Chito. As he tells the story of this nickname, he worked in Callao, the working-class port city just outside Lima in the 1970s, and there were so many different young people who came to the youth center there that he would playfully call all of them "Chito" until he learned their names. "Chito," he says, at the time, was common slang for thief, and something many kids also called each other, teasing one another about how they were perceived by the larger society. The kids also took up calling him "Chito" in response, which he clearly loved for the ways it diminished his authority and included him in their circles. The nickname has stuck for decades. The movement's founding figure is therefore still called a petty thief by everyone in the movement. While a small detail, it also signals that age does not necessarily or inevitably require greater deference in the movement.

This issue of having and demonstrating equal respect for one another, regardless of age, can also lead to some challenges for kids when they first enter the movement. Juan, the *colaborador* quoted above, reflected on how different this can be from kids' norms. "In Peruvian society, from our families even, they say that 'he is older so you have to respect him; if he is speaking, you have to be quiet.' In my family it was like this. . . . It is different calling adults 'sir' there, but here, in the movement, it would be 'hello Jessica,' 'hi Juan.'" Juan says that this renaming reshapes the adult-child relationship and that it "is the beginning of how you will relate to one another, of a relationship of warmth and trust. It is important." However, this can be difficult for kids at first, and is complicated by the kids' parents sometimes telling them to use the more respectful and formal titles of *señor, señora,* or *señorita* for their *colaboradores.* To solve this problem, kids learn to switch back and forth, using *colaboradores'* first names only when their parents are absent. I am not suggesting that formal titles for adults *necessarily* position children as "less than," or that the parents of the NATs do not see their children having equality of dignity, or that using first names always makes for a more egalitarian relationship. Rather, my point is to highlight one way that movement practices make real the discursive commitment to challenging age as a basis for respect and dignity.

Children's equality of dignity may not be a radical departure from the discourse of childhood found in children's rights frameworks, but there are also countless social practices and institutions in Peru and around the world that implicitly reinforce children's lesser status, and many children do not experience themselves as being treated with equal dignity. Withholding important information from children, lying to children, not giving them explanations for why they should act in a particular way ("because I said so"), not listening to children, and dismissing their feelings as temporary and therefore illegitimate ("you'll get over it") are all examples of common practices that don't respect children as full human beings with interiority and dignity. The movement of working children intervenes in this landscape by consistently and explicitly reminding children of their inherent equal worth, and by regularly signaling everyone's equal rights to being treated with respect and honor.

Equality of Capacity

No one is born knowing how to facilitate a meeting, how to organize a press conference, or how to write a proclamation. The skills of political organizing and activism have to be learned by all who participate in social movements. According to the movement of working children, kids and adults are equally capable of learning these skills. One movement booklet argues, "If the future of our society is to be defined by increasing participation of everyone in civil society, then all groups need to be taken into account equally, and considered to have the same level of competence to participate in the organization of society."[10] However, while movement participants believe that age does not define an individual's ability to contribute, learning how to participate in social movements is a process that takes time. Age is therefore not entirely irrelevant to political capabilities, complicating the movement's vision of intergenerational equality.

At times, the belief in equality of capacity is articulated as a belief that children and adults are truly the same, particularly in terms of their potential to be effective participants in political life. For example, when

I asked Joaquín, who was fifteen at the time, whether he thought there were any differences between children and adults, he definitively stated, "No, I don't think so." I pressed a bit: "Any differences at all?" He replied, "No, I don't think there are differences. We all have the same capacities." He went on to explain, "We [kids] are capable of contributing, having an impact, being strategic, and achieving many of our goals. So, in the end, I think that while there is a legal difference, there is no difference in our thinking or our actions." Or, when I asked Guillermo, an eleven-year-old, the same question, he said, "No, we all have the same ability to vote and to give our opinions." In these statements, the NATs not only deny the relevance of age as a criterion for the potential to contribute, but also argue strongly that age does not matter for one's political abilities.

This rejection of age-based criteria is also found in movement actors' discussions about children's work and the problems with the minimum age framework. Alejandro described how he first learned to question age-based definitions of capability from a young girl from Cajamarca during a discussion of Peruvian laws. A proposed law at the time would give those over the age of twelve the right to work, but outlaw all work done by children under twelve. According to Alejandro, a young girl stood up and took the microphone to say, "I don't agree with this. I'm a working child, and I'm twelve years old, and I work with my brother and my sister. He is eleven and she is nine. Why can I work and they cannot? We live in the same house, we have the same parents, we go to the same school, but I can work and they can't? I don't think this makes sense." In telling this story, Alejandro emphasized that this girl did not see age as an important criterion for rights, but as an arbitrary distinction—in her view, she was not particularly different from her brother and sister. This, according to Alejandro, was an important learning moment for him in that it led him to question the validity of age-based criteria for many kinds of participation.

Tom Cockburn, a British sociologist who focuses on children's citizenship, has also persuasively argued against seeing children as necessarily less capable of political participation simply because of their age. He writes,

All our experiences in the public world of politics, communities and workplaces are ones that are evolving, irrespective of how old we are: yet this does not seem to offer any theoretical obstacles to adult participation. It must not be assumed that children are necessarily underdeveloped for citizen participation, as experience is more important for maturation than chronological age. Indeed, today some children have wide and extensive experiences of decision-making processes, such as in school councils, youth parliaments and research consultations. Yet still we are concerned with identifying age cutoff points.[11]

Like Cockburn, many participants in the movement of working children emphasize that an individual's experiences are more important to their participatory abilities than their chronological age. There are twelve-year-olds with nearly four years of experience attending movement assemblies and meetings, and fifteen-year-olds who are entirely new to the process. Presuming that the fifteen-year-old is more capable of facilitating the next assembly would just not make sense.

The movement's critique of chronological age as a defining feature of capability is also supported by psychological research. The work of critical developmental psychologists like Barbara Rogoff demonstrates that children's knowledge, capabilities, and skills are dependent on the contexts in which they are immersed.[12] The more commonplace assumption that capabilities are directly tied to age is rooted in a narrow cognitive approach to children's development that ignores these important interventions. Rogoff persuasively argues that what children know and can do depends very much on what they have had a chance to learn, to experience, and to participate in. Children's capabilities at a given age are thus not inevitable or universal, but are quite context-specific.[13] Rejecting age as a marker of what individuals can do not only undermines the assumption of a binary difference between two distinct categories of people (children/adults) but also raises questions about the logic behind a variety of age-defined policies, including the minimum age for work and the minimum age for voting.

Instead of using chronological age to define political capabilities, *colaboradores* and NATs emphasize how experience, time, and opportunities to learn help strengthen people's political skills, knowledge, and confidence. In difficult meetings, at moments of disagreement, or even simply in the face of a shy group of kids, participants often reiterate this point, reminding each other that being full and equal participants in political space requires learning, practice, and growth for both children and adults. Kids talk about their own process of learning, and adults mention that they too are always working on becoming better *colaboradores* by learning from the NATs. Yolanda, a sixteen-year-old national leader, remembers her own process of learning in the following way:

> We didn't know how to organize, how to participate. . . . The teachers and adults who accompanied us made it so that I was able to participate. At first, I couldn't really express myself, maybe because I was afraid to speak in public. Later, and this is a really beautiful moment and memory for me, I began to speak up, participate, and learn about the movement, about the organization, and how to organize ourselves as kids and how we can also speak to the public.

While neither adults nor kids immediately know how to organize in the context of an intergenerational social movement, both groups are understood as having the capacity to develop these skills.

In the movement of working children, learning how to participate is not automatic, but is a process that is carefully structured and intentionally guided by both adults and more experienced NATs. The process begins with entry into the movement via a base group. Some base groups meet only once a week, but the larger and more vibrant bases are tied to the different community centers run by the movement. Many kids in these bases come to the centers nearly every day for a hot meal, homework help, and educational workshops. In order to continue to be part of the center, kids are required to attend weekly assemblies that introduce them to the process of organizing and encourage their political knowledge and skill development. The weekly assemblies that I attended at the Yerbateros center happened every Saturday morning, and usually involved around twenty to thirty kids. Seated on fading and chipped but once brightly painted wooden benches that were pushed into a circle in the main room, the kids at the assembly were a rowdy, chaotic, and easily distracted bunch. The assembly would hold their attention only sometimes—boys would get into minor shoving battles over bench space, girls would lean over and braid each other's hair, and whispered side conversations were pervasive. The teenage facilitators who led these meetings were constantly trying to remind the kids that this assembly

Figure 3.1. NATs at a base group assembly meeting. Photo courtesy of Movimiento de Adolescentes y Niños Trabajadores Hijos de Obreros Cristianos—Yerbateros.

was for their own benefit, so that they could exercise their rights and have more voice in the center. Each assembly started with a discussion of recent news that children had heard about or read, and getting the kids to contribute required significant coaxing from the facilitators. Large-group discussions only rarely developed into full community conversations, but small-group drawing or theatre activities in which kids discussed and presented their ideas about *trabajo digno*, children's rights, or health and well-being, for example, all provided kids with engaging opportunities to think together about some of the conditions of their lives. There were also some moments in the larger assembly when the kids would become focused on the topic at hand and engage one another in discussion, usually in relation to making changes to the activities or regulations of the center.

While the assemblies were clearly frustrating at times for the facilitators, and clearly boring at times for the newer NATs, they were also valuable spaces of political and organizational learning for both groups.

Over the course of several months, I watched as some of the teen facilitators developed both patience and new strategies for getting the assembly to talk and as new assembly members developed their understanding of the space and became more confident contributing to discussions. The facilitators and the *colaboradores* would regularly use the space to remind the newer participants that they wanted to hear their voices, that participation and speaking up are highly valued. For example, at one assembly after a recent visit to the center by members of the international movement of working children, the adult *colaboradora*, Emilia, was helping debrief the visit. She asked the whole group a few basic questions about the visitors: "Who were they? Why did they come?" A few kids answered these questions and then she asked the group, "Did you tell them about your experiences? Did you talk to them?" Many of the kids shook their heads. Emilia nodded and said, "No, it was just Graciela and Julio. I know that it can be hard to talk in front of a group of people, but these people were other NATs, and this is something to work on, something to practice, to learn, to develop." Emilia reminded the kids in the assembly that their voices are valued by the movement, but also reminded them that they have the capacity to contribute, to grow, and to become more comfortable in these spaces. The weekly assembly therefore socializes the newest members of the movement to the ideas and practices of children's participation, signaling that adults and older kids want them to contribute, to share their perspectives, to listen to one another, and to make democratic decisions about the movement. Amidst their noise, their play, and their boredom, the kids learn more about the movement and learn how to participate in its political and organizational activities.

Being part of a base group and its weekly assemblies is just the first step in what, for some kids, becomes a much more extended process of political skill building and education. In addition to learning how to develop the agenda and facilitate the meetings of a base group, some kids go on from the base groups to participate in regional, national, and international organizational spaces. In each of these spaces, they continue to develop new knowledge, skills, and confidence for political organization. In these spaces, they learn more about national policy processes, the various players in the government and how to lobby them, how to mobilize their peers from across the country, and how to increase their skills of political argumentation, writing pronouncements for major events and holding press conferences. In the winter of 2013, I watched as one girl, Lili, began to take on national leadership. Representing MANTHOC-Lima in the national council of MNNATSOP during a period in which MNNATSOP decided to phase out its national secretariat, Lili was being asked to take on several new responsibilities as the only MNNATSOP national delegate who lived in the capital. After a meeting in which several other NATs and adults listed all of the spaces in Lima where the secretariat had previously been active, and where they hoped Lili would begin to participate, I asked her how she was feeling about these changes. She smiled at me, shrugged her shoulders a bit, and then said, "It seems like a lot, but it is part of my growth and development as a delegate." Over the next few weeks, I saw Lili in several of these other organizational spaces. She was working hard to learn the landscape, took diligent notes at every meeting, but admitted that she was feeling overwhelmed by how much she had been asked to take on. While this transition to greater responsibility was difficult, she was supported in this process by two different *colaboradores*—one from her base group, and one from MNNATSOP. Lili regularly turned to each of them for support, information, or advice about how to relate to each of the different organizational spaces. Lili and her *colaboradores* all acknowledged that she was growing and learning, and that they did not expect her to already know exactly how to navigate this new responsibility and the new organizational and political landscape.

Kids themselves also try to encourage their peers' political learning and skill development. At a regional meeting in which the group was dividing tasks for the upcoming anniversary celebration of the movement, Luisa, a twelve-year-old, suggested that they assign Manuel, another delegate from her base group who had not yet arrived at the meeting, to a task by himself. She was concerned that he was not yet taking on enough responsibility and was relying on other NATs to do too much of the regional group's ongoing work. If he were given a task of his own, she argued, he would become more motivated and more engaged in the regional group, and he would learn new skills. Similarly, at a meeting of the RedNNA, Graciela and two of the younger participants discussed a recent conversation with Alejandro about an upcoming campaign. Graciela took this as an opportunity to push the two younger participants a bit:

Chito asked you about the campaign and you were quiet. We have asked you to read the material on the campaign, and we asked you this not so you would memorize it, but so you would understand it, and develop your own ideas, and be able to talk about it. Chito likes to ask questions; this is good for us. And when we don't know what to say, we need to be self-critical. You both need to not get so distracted, and need to be more focused in the meetings. . . . I understand that you are young. I also had a phase where I was very distracted in meetings and wanted to play, but you need to work on this, to develop in order to grow in the movement.

Graciela's comments here show that the movement does not entirely ignore age, acknowledging that these things can be challenging for younger children, but she also demonstrates the movement's belief that young children can (and should) develop and grow as political participants.

The movement's belief in equality of capacity is not just articulated as children's ability to learn, but also as adults' need to learn new skills and approaches in order to become *colaboradores* and effective movement participants. IFEJANT is dedicated largely to the project of educating, training, and supporting the learning of *colaboradores*, and offers regular workshops, discussions, and training sessions for them. Graciela also described how the movement organizations hold feedback sessions in which the group discusses "how well we are all fulfilling our roles, the NATs, the delegates, the *colaboradores*." When I asked her whether she thought the *colaboradores* listened to the feedback they got and improved over time she said, "Yes, many listen and we can see the change that they make, but there are some . . ." She paused, unsure about whether or not she should be explicit in her critiques of those *colaboradores* who don't seem to be improving, and instead concluded, "Well, this is also a process." The feedback sessions provide a clear space in which the NATs directly try to educate and improve the intergenerational collaborative political skills of the *colaboradores*, but this is not always easy for adults to hear. What is perhaps even more interesting, though, is that Graciela describes the adults' political participation in much the same way that adults describe that of the NATs. Adults regularly reiterate that the NATs are "in a process" of learning how to take up their own *protagonismo* and participate. Graciela reminds us that this is also true of adults—they also have their struggles, challenges, and things that they need to learn. In these moments, we can see how the movement's ideas about intergenerational equality not only reimagine childhood, but also reimagine adulthood and undermine the assumption of a binary difference between the two groups. Sameness is asserted as both children and adults are defined as "still learning."

Equality of capacity, in the context of social movements and political organizing, emphasizes that all people, no matter their age, are capable of learning how to be activists and engaged protagonists. This is quite distinct from the commonplace assumption that kids are just "not ready" for this kind of activity. Rather than operating from the idea that children just can't do something, and therefore excluding them from social movements, the movement takes a pedagogical approach, offering tools, resources, and experiences so that children can develop their capacities and realize their potential as activists. Recognizing children's equality of capacity invites us to reconsider our ideas about what children can and cannot do and instead ask, Why do I think they can't do this? And how might I support their learning so that they can do this thing that I think they cannot do? Further, in describing both *colaboradores* and NATs as developing political subjects, the movement undermines the assumption of a binary difference between children and adults in which children are growing, while adults are "complete." They emphasize that all people, no matter their age, are still learning and changing. Treating both groups as simultaneously capable *and* developing helps to level their positions within the movement and encourages kids and adults to see each other as equal participants in political space.

Equality of Insight

The movement's third core belief about intergenerational equality also takes seriously the importance of learning, but does so in a different way. This third belief, which I am calling equality of insight, emphasizes that both children and adults have important knowledge and ideas to contribute to social and political life, and that the two groups should learn from each other. While equality of capacity highlights everyone's ability to learn to be a protagonist and political actor, equality of insight draws attention to everyone's ability to add to collective analysis and political understanding, and therefore everyone's right to democratic inclusion, recognition, and voice. Pushing back against the passivity assumption and the idea that adults are critical thinkers while children are merely passive sponges who soak up adult-created ideas, the movement's articulation of equality of insight re-values children's critical interpretations of the world around them as legitimate and important sources of knowledge.

In the movement of working children, equality of insight often draws upon assertions of the distinctiveness of children's perspectives, based on their particular social locations and experiences. Many movement participants consider the knowledge of the NATs to have important differences from the knowledge of adults. In some instances, this different knowledge is seen as resulting from differences in terms of one's place in the life course, while in other moments it is discussed as differences of generational identity. Elena noted both of these dimensions when she stated, "We are equal, but we are from different generations who come from different times. And we might have different problems or difficulties in our families, in our homes, in our lives." Or, as a presenter at a workshop on revisions to the national law on children and adolescents told the group, "Kids today, their world has changed and there are new social models and paradigms. They know things that I don't know." Most often, children's distinctive insights are seen as the result of their particular lived experiences. This is frequently discussed in relation to the subject of child labor. Working children, according to the movement, are the real experts on this topic because they are the ones who are currently living and experiencing it. Countless examples of this argument can be found in the movement's publications and documents, especially those that chastise the International Labor Organization for making policies about child labor without contributions from working children who live with the consequences of those policies and therefore understand the issues deeply. Several recent movement publications and proclamations have emphasized this point with the phrase *nada de nosotros sin nosotros*, or nothing about us without us.

This argument about working children's expertise on the subject of child labor is also expressed in daily practice. For example, I attended a panel discussion on working children's movements and political advocacy work that included several NATs as well as an international visitor and supporter of the movement of working children. Before the panel, the moderator, twelve-year-old Andrés, asked the adult visitor, Gustavo, for a bit of information about himself so he could introduce him. Andrés asked Gustavo, "What have you done?" Gustavo then replied, with a smile, "I haven't really done anything." Andrés tried another approach: "Your name placard for the table says you are an expert on working children." Gustavo shook his head and said, "No, no, not so much an expert as you." And, in another workshop, Gustavo, a professor with a doctoral degree, carefully referred to all of the participants, both children and adults, as *doctor* and *doctora*, playfully highlighting everyone's equal status as a contributor to the discussion. In these kinds of practices, as well as in their discursive emphasis on working children's rights to contribute to the debates and policy discussions on child labor, the movement reinforces the idea that NATs possess vitally important but often marginalized knowledge.

Some NATs talk about how children and adults have different kinds of knowledge to offer the movement. Even Joaquín, whom I quoted earlier rejecting the idea of age-based differences of any kind, says that kids and adults *might* think differently. He said, "I don't believe that there are differences between us, but I do think that the only small difference is that we may think slightly differently. We have the same capacities, but the perspective of an adult, the point of view—not all of them, but some—may think differently than us in that they think that we can't do certain things." Here, Joaquín references slight differences in perspective, but the main one he sees is adults' doubt about kids' capabilities, not about truly different ways of seeing the world or types of knowledge. Of all the NATs, Joaquín tended to take the strongest position regarding adult/child similarities in both capacities and insights. Much more common was Anabella's position:

> Our [NATs'] perspective can be a little more practical—we give our opinions, we make proposals, and we decide. The adults ask us to step back and reflect a little bit more on what we say; they augment our conversations based on the experiences that they have had, and times when something similar has happened. So, I think both sets of opinions, both perspectives are equally valuable.

Adults' ideas, according to Anabella and others, are rooted in historical knowledge developed over time, while children's ideas come from their current lived experiences. Anabella's position, in contrast to Joaquín's, highlights substantial differences between the knowledge of kids and the knowledge of adults, but she also clearly articulates intergenerational equality of insight. While kids may not necessarily know the details of national and international laws (although they can and do learn these details in the movement), they often have strong ideas about what things they like and dislike in their lives, and about what is just and what is unjust. I often heard NATs say, "No es justo" (It's not fair) in relation to numerous social problems, including the criminalization of children's work, instances of violence against women and girls, or examples of gender or ethnic discrimination. While they don't have the vocabulary of democratic political theory, they do know that they have a stake in many policy decisions and that they should be included. And while they don't have decades of experience planning social movement events, they do know what kinds of activities would be engaging and fun for other kids. According to Anabella and other NATs, kids' knowledge may be incomplete, but it is still valuable.

In making claims about the value of children's perspectives, movement participants echo claims made by other marginalized groups regarding subjugated knowledges and the importance of listening to those who speak from a marginalized standpoint.[14] However, poststructural theorists have criticized standpoint theory for assuming that experiences of oppression *necessarily* produce good, accurate, or critical perspectives on that oppression, arguing instead that all knowledge should be seen as constructed and partial.[15] But this debate between standpoint theory and a more poststructuralist stance does not, I would argue, need to be resolved in order for us to recognize children's knowledge as legitimate knowledge. Whether children's insights are to be especially valued because of their distinctive social location and direct experiences (as standpoint theory would suggest) or simply should also be included because all knowledge (including that of adults) is perspectival and influenced by one's context, experiences, and communities of discourse, both epistemological approaches can provide support to the movement's belief that children's differences do not preclude them from having knowledge. However, children's contributions have often been ignored because of the long history of recognizing only some kinds of knowledge and some kinds of speech as worthy of inclusion in political and democratic life. In particular, as childhood studies scholar David Oswell writes, we continue to "conceptualize the political as logocentric (or overly rational) . . . to the exclusion of children and others."[16] Children's knowledge, Oswell argues, may not sound like adult knowledge, but this should not prevent us from taking seriously children's ideas, insights, or ways of seeing the world. Whether we take up the claims of standpoint theory or a more poststructuralist approach to epistemology, both perspectives' critiques of the idea that there is one true and accurate picture of the world provide theoretical support for the movement of working children's core belief that children's insights deserve full consideration in democratic life.

Claiming children's equality of knowledge and insight does not, of course, mean that children are the only source of knowledge; nor does it mean that everything they think is "right." Rather, movement actors are quick to point out that both kids and adults have important ideas and that both groups need to learn from each other in a mutual and equal relationship. As Alejandro writes, "Our movements have the historical responsibility to be a symbol and an example for a society that has redefined social roles and relationships and that has broken from two things: adult-centrism and child-centrism. . . . Not a society that revolves around adults, where adults set the direction, and not a society in which a child's sneeze is the word of God."[17] Or, as Luis, a *colaborador* with nearly twenty years of experience, put it, "Neither of us are the owners of reason—not the adults, not the kids. We have to learn together, from each other." Enrique also stated that "we learn from them, and they learn from us. It is reciprocal and horizontal." Knowledge, then, does not belong only to one social group, but is seen as produced in an open dialogue between and among individuals with different life experiences, perspectives, and ways of seeing the world.

Rooted in the movement's long connection to Freirian pedagogy, the belief in children as, in Alejandro's words, "producers of knowledge, not just recipients of knowledge," deeply shapes organizational practice. Children are not told what to do and how to do it, but are asked to take on leadership and authority in the movement by sharing their thoughts, opinions, and suggestions with each other and with adults. Assemblies, meetings, and workshops all rely on a pedagogy that asks kids to share what they think about any topic being discussed, whether it be how the movement should respond to a recent newspaper article decrying child labor, or the best location for the movement's annual anniversary celebration and party. As I'll explore in chapter 5, kids don't necessarily step up and take the lead in some discussions, and adults sometimes dominate conversations, but kids are *always* asked to share their thoughts and ideas on any issue that is on the table. In my many months with the movement, I can think of no instance in which adults simply made pronouncements or decisions without inviting kids to respond and give their own perspectives.

The movement's belief in equality of insight does not mean that children are expected to communicate their knowledge in the same way as adults. Instead, *colaboradores* and NATs in their teens will often talk about needing to develop fun and child-friendly ways for kids to express their views. This often involves drawing, as when the kids in an assembly drew pictures of their ideas of a "healthy and happy childhood" and pictures of an "unhealthy childhood," in order to kick off a wider discussion on heath and nutrition. Or it may involve performance, such as when kids were asked to develop skits for their peers showing what they think of as dignified work versus work in conditions of exploitation. By using these "kid-friendly" approaches to expression, the movement seeks to acknowledge some of children's differences from adults and create venues for even the youngest children to articulate their opinions about their experiences and their analyses of the larger social and political contexts in which they live.

Adults involved in the movement of working children express deep commitments to taking children's insights seriously. Indeed, they would often remind me that they not only support the NATs but also learn from them. This requires being radically open to perspectives and ideas that may be different from their own views on the world. As the facilitator in a workshop for adult *colaboradores* emphasized, "In order to work with kids in an equitable, horizontal, and radical fashion, we have to ask questions of ourselves, have doubts, and not be sure of what we think we know." In an interview, Juliana explained that this is the real meaning of collaboration:

> When we talk about *colaboradores*, or about collaborating, it is in the sense that both of us can help each other. It is mutual. He collaborates

with me, and I collaborate with him, and not just in doing things, but also in learning. Because he is collaborating with me from his experiences, and he shares them with me, and so I continue to learn more, I continue to take in more of the reality of children today.

Similarly, as Juan described it,

It is important to be with them [the kids] and not to really believe yourself—at times you might feel like an adult and think that you are the best, that you've already arrived, and everyone has to listen to what you said and follow, but thinking like this is an error. This is where problems begin. Yes, kids are different from us and from each other, but it is from their differences that we learn together.

As each of these adults indicates, creating horizontal relationships means taking children's knowledge very seriously and being open to being changed by that knowledge.

In practice, being responsive to children's insights requires adults to really listen and consider changing their views when children disagree with them or articulate alternatives to their ideas and proposals. In my observations, I found that kids did not often disagree with adults' larger ideological points, although this did happen occasionally. For example, one national delegate stopped a presenter to say that he felt like the presenter was not making enough of a distinction between different types of political participation and that the movement was getting too caught up in lobbying and formal participatory activities and needed to return its focus more to organizing other NATs into the movement, struggle, and activism outside state channels. More often, kids' disagreements with adults centered around *how* they should organize, or on the specifics of a given event. For example, when a *colaborador* suggested that a group of NATs who were meeting to work on writing a proclamation in response to the proposed changes to the Código also draft the script for a radio spot to be produced and aired, one girl immediately disagreed and said it needed to be a separate committee. And when choosing where to hold an annual social event for the NATs, the delegates rejected the *colaboradores'* advice regarding a more affordable location. In these not uncommon instances, kids feel empowered to disagree with their

Figure 3.2. Small-group discussions like the one pictured here create spaces where children and adults listen carefully to one another's ideas and perspectives, engaging in meaningful political conversations. Photo courtesy of Instituto de Formación para Educadores de Jóvenes, Adolescentes y Niños Trabajadores.

adult *colaboradores* and to articulate ideas, proposals, and perspectives that are distinctive from those presented by the adults. The *colaboradores* don't dismiss these ideas, but engage in dialogue with the kids about the point of disagreement, taking seriously the kids' knowledge and sometimes, but not always, changing their own opinions on a topic.

In the movement of working children, adults value the NATs' ways of seeing the world, even when their expressions of their knowledge are awkward, unclear, or incomplete from an adult frame of reference. Many adults, in different contexts in Peru and elsewhere, accept the position that kids have their own ideas about the world, and that they have some insights to offer. What is distinctive here is the claim that these ideas are *equally* valid and should therefore be fully incorporated into movement theory and practice. Instead of listening to children's ideas and then setting them aside as unrealistic, uninformed, insufficiently developed, or overly simplistic, movement participants take these ideas seriously. They engage with them as legitimate forms of knowledge. Of course, sometimes kids' ideas of the world can be incorrect, with factual errors or misunderstandings of how some system or process operates. But this can also be true of adults' ideas. Similarly, children's ideas, especially their political ideas, are often dismissed as being merely reflections or a mimicry of what they have heard from adults (parents, teachers, the *colaboradores*, and others). This method of dismissing children's knowledge simultaneously underestimates children's capacity for critical and reflective political thought and ignores the ways that adults' ideas are also the result of their social relationships and the discursive contexts in which they are located. Intergenerational equality of insight suggests that older individuals should not be assumed to have better or more thoroughly considered ideas simply because they are older. In both its discourse and its daily practice, the movement's approach actively destabilizes the linked binary pairs of adult/child, knowing/unknowing, and critical/passive.

Intergenerational Horizontal Collaboration: Thinking about Power

Each of the three movement beliefs that I've outlined above makes claims about children's fundamental equality with adults. Each re-values children and childhood and disrupts more common assumptions about the greater intrinsic worth, capability, or knowledge of adults. Each one challenges implicit ideas about adult superiority and authority and questions the relevance of age as a criterion for value, encouraging both adults and children to reconsider their assumptions about what children can and cannot do. The movement's aspirational vision of creating horizontal intergenerational relationships emerges from and is supported by these three interlocking beliefs on equality. Horizontalism is understood as an ideal that the movement is pursuing, rather than a fundamental state—it describes a vision for new forms of intergenerational social relations. The ideal of horizontalism is articulated as a direct challenge to age-based hierarchies and is primarily understood as embodied through relational practices where children and adults work together with mutual respect and responsibility, share decision-making authority, develop a critical age consciousness, and actively challenge instances of adultism both within and outside the movement.

Challenges to age-based power are often associated with a children's liberation framework. This approach, first explicitly articulated in the

1970s, argued that children were profoundly oppressed by adults and that they needed to be freed from an exploitative regime of age-based domination.[18] Such works were then heavily criticized for not taking into account children's specificity as a social group and the ways that they are necessarily more dependent on adults.[19] The liberationist model, according to many, oversimplified the complex social location of childhood in relation to power, but it was also an important intervention in that it represented a radical attempt to "recodify children's lives in relation to adults with regard to their authority in authorizing their actions and lives."[20] The liberationist emphasis on freeing children from adults and giving children autonomy, however, is not the only possible approach to challenging adultism and the ongoing marginalization of children.

According to Anthony Swift's history of the working children's movement in Peru,

> At the beginning, adults proposed that they would not participate in the movement but support it from outside, so this way it would be authentically a movement of children and adolescents. But after numerous discussions, the kids made clear that they wanted the adults to be part of the movement, committed to the process, but not directing it. If they stayed outside, how would the kids be sure of their commitment?[21]

The movement of working children considered taking a liberationist approach to the question of equality of power, giving children a space that was entirely their own, free of adult influence. However, kids themselves rejected this model and argued for creating an intergenerational movement where kids are not freed from adults, but where kids and adults would work together in an interdependent and horizontal community. Increasing children's social and political power and challenging adult domination, according to the movement, do not have to mean children's autonomy or liberation, but can instead be instantiated in relations of egalitarian collaboration.

Kids and adults in the movement regularly argue that kids need adults and that adults play an important role in the movement. In my interviews, I would ask both groups what they thought the movement would be like without adults. Carmen, a thirteen-year-old girl involved primarily in the activities at the Yerbateros house, said that without adults "it would be more chaotic, more noisy. And without the adults, who would cook for us? Who would teach us and help us with our homework, or with the workshops? Without the adults, I don't think we could do it all ourselves." Adults provide vital logistical, educational, and organizational support. Kids, in Carmen's view, shouldn't just be doing things on their own—they need adults. Later, she went on to say that this need for adults doesn't mean that kids are powerless, but that "we are here supporting each other and working with adults to exercise our rights. . . . And to make our own decisions." Graciela explained that it is a "complementary" relationship because the adults help provide the spaces and the structure, as well as the encouragement for youth to organize: "They call the meetings, reach out to us, let us know when and where to meet." Other NATs talked about how the adults are needed for their knowledge: they both think about the future and know about the past, while kids are, in fifteen-year-old Patricia's words, "only thinking about what is happening right now." In each of these examples, the NATs talk about the importance of adult support, adult knowledge, adult guidance, and adult resources. Kids, they suggest, cannot very easily organize on their own—they need adults and so do not want to be fully "liberated" from them. This position, of course, contrasts with the ideas of sameness that appear in many participants' visions of equality. It is a reminder that, while they see kids and adults as equals in some ways, both NATs and *colaboradores* understand that on the ground, in practice, children are not the same as adults and that they have some distinctive needs and interdependencies.

Horizontal collaboration, as it is understood in the movement, is not just adults and kids working together in a complementary fashion, but also requires the development and practice of what I would name critical age consciousness. Without a critical perspective on age, adults and kids would be much more likely to replicate hierarchical patterns of interaction, underestimating kids' capacities and limiting their authority and power. As Luis, a *colaborador* with many years of experience, explained, "A *colaborador* has to show them that they are totally convinced that children and adolescents are social subjects. The *colaborador* has to get rid of their own adultist perspectives and take on the challenge of changing the adult-centrism of the society." Learning to be self-critical and letting go of assumptions about children is understood as a key part of the process of becoming a good *colaborador*. Similarly, children also need to learn to rethink childhood, adulthood, and the responsibilities and capabilities of each group. Andrés described how before participating in the movement, "we thought adults were better than us, and that they had more voice than us, and then bit by bit we realized that they were not the only ones who could have voice and vote, but that we can also speak, and give our opinions on topics that affect us. And so our ideas about adults change." While Andrés focuses on adults here, it is also clear that the movement has changed how he thinks about children and his own abilities as a child. Learning to act as partners in an equal collaboration, according to movement participants, requires developing a new consciousness about age and age categories. In this way, the three core beliefs about intergenerational equality discussed above play a vital role in enabling the creation of horizontal partnerships. Adults can't work in horizontal collaboration with kids unless they truly value children's capacities and insights, and children can't work in horizontal collaboration with adults unless they have confidence in their own contributions.

According to movement participants, horizontalism requires a commitment to intergenerational democratic decision making. Horizontal collaboration is not just working together in respectful partnership but working together in such a way that both children and adults have a meaningful and powerful voice in all decisions. One of the movement's major goals, both internally and externally, is to increase children's decision-making power, giving them a much greater say in the many decisions that impact their lives, whether that be small things like what they will do in their free time or large things like national educational policies. Achieving this goal requires that adults cede some of their directive power to children, and requires that children take on more responsibilities. Elena described to me how this vision of sharing power emerged in the 1970s as the JOC youth began changing their language to one of collaboration. Shifting from talking about adults as *asesores* or advisors to talking about them as *colaboradores* was "how we began to work with a category that had this kind of meaning of equality." She continued, "The relation of co-*protagonismo* was understood as including all people in society. . . . We imagined a relation where we could all relate to one another as equal social and political actors." Or, as eleven-year-old Guillermo put it, the movement creates a space where "kids and adults all have the same rights to vote, to give their opinions, and to do what they can do." And, in Graciela's view, "In the movement we have equality in terms of being heard and in terms of making decisions. . . . When kids and adults enter MANTHOC they learn that we are trying to create horizontal relationships between us." Sharing power and decision-making authority is understood to be a vital part of the movement's framework for intergenerational relationships.

Movement participants are very clear that this kind of shared decision-making power is not commonplace, but is distinctive to the movement. Enrique, for example, noted that in the larger society, the belief is that

> because you are a kid you don't know anything, and you don't get to give your opinion, your ideas don't matter, you don't have a voice or a vote. But in the movement, we have the opposite, we have a will to listen to [the kids], to follow their lead, to raise up and support them. What they think, what they propose, what they imagine—we work together to make it happen.

NATs also often talk about how the majority of adults in their lives don't see them as social subjects, how laws discriminate against them, how their opinions and ideas are dismissed and not taken into account, and how they are seen as ignorant, incapable, and needing to be protected, guided, and controlled. They identify all of this as evidence of widespread adultism. As Yolanda put it, "We are aware and critical of adult-centrism, and our *colaboradores* are, but unfortunately many of the adults we encounter in other places, like the authorities, or in our families, or in school, they are not aware like this. They very much still see things in an adult-centric way." Legal structures and requirements can also limit children's full and equal participation. For example, children under eighteen need an adult with them to enter Congress, and the official directors of any formal legal entity or organization that can receive grants or donations must be over eighteen. The movement's desires for horizontalism are constrained by the larger social and political contexts of adultism.

For the most part, movement participants argue that adultism is largely external to the movement. But a small number acknowledge that creating intergenerational horizontalism is incredibly difficult in part because of the ways that the structures and beliefs of adultism continue to influence people in the movement. Learning to work together without hierarchy and domination is not easy for children or adults. Alejandro writes, "No one learns the concrete meaning of democratic relationships and the spirit and practice of being equal in just one day. . . . For this reason, lots of mistakes happen."[22] Indeed, taking on shared responsibility for an organization and its operation can be hard for adults who have to cede some of their normal power, but it is also hard for kids. As Alejandro describes it, kids are "accustomed to the dominant society in which adults make all the decisions . . . And so this is a gradual cultural change . . . and some, unfortunately, prefer to stay dependent, because in that dependence is safety." Moving toward horizontalism is not automatic or easy but requires significant reflection on the often subtle ways that both kids and adults perpetuate and sustain age-based hierarchies. And, while both NATs and *colaboradores* regularly reference the importance of being self-reflective and critical of their internal group practices, this remains an underdeveloped aspect of the movement's discourse and practices. Indeed, what horizontalism really means, as a model for intergenerational relationships, is not fully fleshed out in many movement spaces. It is put forward as the alternative to adultism, hierarchy, and children's oppression, but its more specific contours and qualities remain somewhat ambiguous.

Children's rights theorist Mehmoona Moosa-Mitha suggests one way to further specify this concept when she writes that children's rights in the context of democracy should be assessed by

> examining if children are able to have a presence in the many relationships in which they participate. By presence, I mean the degree to which the voice, contribution and agency of the child is acknowledged in their many relationships. Presence, more than autonomy, acknowledges the self as relational and dialogical, thereby suggesting that it is not enough to have a voice; it is equally important to also be heard in order for one to have a presence in society.[23]

Children's full and equal presence in relationships, political life, and social movements, rather than children's autonomy or liberation, provides an alternative metric for evaluating children's political power that does not erase children's need for adults, but instead draws our attention to the dynamics of intergenerational relationships and the ways children are included and heard in different spaces and institutions.[24] Striving for horizontalism, the sharing of decision making, and children's presence, rather than children's liberation, allows for an engagement with children's particularities, adult responsibilities, and the messy complexity of age-based power.

Children's Equality, Children's Difference, and Children's Power

Challenging Assumptions about Childhood

In arguing for children's equality, the movement of working children questions widespread assumptions about childhood and adulthood as fundamentally different states of being—what I have described as the assumption of binary difference. Many in the movement, like Joaquín, claim that children and adults are very much the same. Movement participants note that it is not only kids who are learning, developing, and in process, but also adults. They diminish or downplay children's differences by noting that children, when given the chance to learn, can do many of the things that adults do. Children's differences, in this view, are not as significant as many adults assume, and they are mutable, changing based on social and cultural learning opportunities. Children can possess traits commonly associated with adulthood (knowledge, experience, rationality, autonomy, critical agency), while adults also have many of the traits usually associated with childhood (ignorance, inexperience, emotionality, dependence, social compliance, and passivity). While the logic of the binary tries to expunge some of these less desirable traits from the category of adulthood, this expulsion is more fiction than fact.[25]

The movement also directly challenges the passivity assumption, or the idea that what children think is simply mimicry of adults, through an explicit appreciation for children's knowledge and insights. By reminding kids that they are experts and giving them lots of space to articulate their own positions, to define what they think is good, just, or dignified, and to disagree with adult *colaboradores*, the movement signals its commitment to taking kids' perspectives seriously and disrupts the all-too-common assertion by opponents that the kids in the movement are just unthinkingly repeating the ideas they hear from the movement adults. While the movement doesn't talk explicitly about the social production of knowledge or engage in debates about critical epistemology, its belief in children's equality of insight certainly implies that children's ideas about the world are not necessarily less "real" or "authentic" than the positions articulated by adults.

Finally, the movement's discourse of intergenerational horizontalism directly questions the assumption of age-based hierarchies and adult authority and power over children. While acknowledging children's general lack of social power, the movement seeks to flatten or reduce age-based hierarchies by striving for *more* horizontal and *more* egalitarian intergenerational relationships. Instead of assuming that adult authority is inescapable or always desirable, they argue for horizontal relations of collaboration and respect, actively increase the spaces for children's decision-making power, and encourage the development of a critical age consciousness. As I've discussed elsewhere in relation to girls' activism and youth movements, horizontalism is "something that is always being aimed for, but is never entirely achieved. It is always in process, existing as a utopian principle that is held out as something to move toward."[26] The ideal of horizontal collaboration, therefore, does not necessarily mean that movement participants think that adult power and authority can be entirely removed from social life; rather, it is an invitation to think carefully about when, how, and why power remains unequal and to develop strategies for increasing, fostering, and facilitating children's social and political power.

The Persistence of Age-Based Power

The practical challenges of implementing intergenerational horizontalism will be discussed in the following chapters, but the movement's vision for children's equality also draws our attention to the particularity of age-based power and its sticky relationship to time. Movement participants clearly articulate a belief in children's and adults' equal capacity for political participation, and emphasize that learning to participate is a process for everyone, regardless of age. Their discourse tries to de-link chronological age from political knowledge and skills. However, there is a very real and profound challenge to this vision of intergenerational equality: gaining experience and moving through the process of learning to participate takes time, and time has a direct impact on age. They are not wrong to argue that a ten-year-old can have more experience with something than a fifty-year-old, but that fifty-year-old will also probably possess some other potentially relevant knowledge and skills simply by having had more time on the planet. And, more significantly, the very youngest children are especially unlikely to have this important asset of experience, which is always something accrued over time. The turn to experience rather than chronological age as a marker for skills and knowledge opens up important possibilities for recognizing children as experts, but it also cannot fully escape the temporal logics and realities that are fundamental to the operation and legitimation of age-based power. As ethicist John Wall notes, one of the most significant differences between children and adults, which needs to be accounted for in any attempt to increase children's democratic inclusion, is "children's likelihood of having had less experience precisely in struggling for power. If nothing else, children have by definition taken part in political life for fewer years than adults and with less time, therefore, to accumulate educational, economic, and social capital. Age, in other words, makes a genuine difference in one's overall power to struggle on behalf of one's differences."[27] Because of their overall lack of time, which translates into a lack of capital, even children with some activist experience and education are unlikely to enter the political field on equal footing with adults.

The Movement as a Model for Intergenerational Politics

Organizations that pursue intergenerational equality, horizontalism, and children's meaningful presence in democracy are a marked departure from most contemporary social and political institutions. Many studies have identified the ways that children are marginalized and excluded from decision making in their schools and communities.[28] Children and youth regularly report feeling like authority figures don't take them seriously.[29] Dismissing children, telling them that they "don't understand," or simply assuming that adults are more knowledgeable and capable than kids are all common adult practices. Participants in Peru's movement of working children, however, suggest that such practices are unjust and that intergenerational relationships can and should be organized differently. They argue that organizations and institutions, including political groups and social movements, both can and should become more horizontal, egalitarian, and child-friendly spaces where children's capacities are not underestimated, where their knowledge is recognized and incorporated, and where their decision-making authority and collective power are fostered. This may be challenging, but to not even attempt it perpetuates and excuses the injustice of children's ongoing marginalization.

The movement's vision of equality and horizontalism offers a powerful and highly generative model for intergenerational politics. As a way of envisioning social justice for children, intergenerational horizontalism rejects both the liberal individualism of children's rights and the romantic idealism of children's liberation from adult influence. More than either of these other frameworks, the pursuit of horizontalism emphasizes interactional dynamics and engages with the diffuse and relational nature of power. It invites us to pay attention to the operation of age-based power in *all* of our relationships and institutions. While many children's organizations and municipal governments have embraced the broad concept of children's participation as an ideal, and schools around the world have tried to develop programs to increase student voice, horizontalism offers us a far more ambitious and radical goal. Instead of simply granting young people the right to speak and be heard and considering our obligation met, horizontalism requires a deep ongoing critical engagement with adult authority, power dynamics, and the meaning and practice of social justice as it relates to children and childhood.

The movement's emphasis on children's equal capacities also encourages a pedagogical approach to children's inclusion. Rather than simply accepting that children *can't* do something, acting from a belief in capacity pushes adults to create opportunities for children to actually learn new things. If more adults embraced the idea of children as capable political actors and created spaces for children to learn and grow as activists, how might the world be different? If schools, children's organizations, and even adult social movements took up the idea of equality of capacity, this could lead to a flourishing of programs and projects where children develop their political skills. The movement of working children is not the only example for how to do this work; models also can be found in other time periods and political contexts, including contemporary groups like the Radical Monarchs in Oakland, California, and the Zapatista children's organizations in Chiapas, Mexico.[30] But there are also many more adults who have yet to engage in this work either because they have assumed children to be incapable, have not thought about the possibilities for children's political inclusion, or simply need more concrete examples in order to know how to begin. Responding to this need, the next chapter delineates how these intergenerational political and pedagogical relationships are developed and enacted in the movement of working children.

PART II

The Practice of Intergenerational Activism

4

Teachers, Mothers, or *Compañeros*

Adult Roles in a Children's Movement

Joaquín, Jhasmila, and Yolanda all wished Elena "Happy Teacher's Day" and greeted her warmly with an embrace and a kiss on the cheek. The three teens, national leaders of MNNATSOP, had come to the IFEJANT office, where Elena works, in order to take her out to lunch at a nearby Chinese restaurant on this day that celebrates teachers. Elena, the elected *colaboradora* for the three teens who operate the MNNATSOP headquarters, is recognized by them as a teacher in that she offers them significant political education, but she is also much more than just their teacher: she takes on a wide range of roles, and the teens talk about her as also being a mentor, a friend, and a mother. Joaquín described how Elena is "like a mother because we are far from our families. There is a lot of trust between us. And the relationship, it is a working relationship in terms of the organization, and it is a friendship, with the trust of friends." And as Jhasmila stated, the relationship between *colaboradores* and NATs should be a relationship of "tenderness, understanding, affection, caring, and friendship." She continued, "If we are sick, she takes us to the doctor. Or if we feel bad, there is a lot of trust between us, so we can tell her whatever has happened to us, and she gives us advice."

Reflecting on her multiplicity of roles with the teens in the headquarters, Elena described how, on the one hand, she has to

> take into account the more personal issues, the relationships between them, the relationships they have in the schools where they study. And, on the other hand accompany them in the process of reflection and analysis of national issues. . . . You are also there to accompany them in implementing the strategic plan that was created at the national assembly. . . . In all of this, you have to be open-minded and not fall into either being too permissive or into indifference, but to really accomplish your role as an educator.

Elena's relationship with these teens is somewhat different than that of a typical *colaborador* because they are away from their families. But the differences are differences of intensity, more than differences in roles. Across multiple movement spaces, *colaboradores* and NATs describe their relationships as simultaneously personal, pedagogical, and political.

Article 18 of the MNNATSOP Declaration of Principles states that

> adults are part of MNNATSOP as *Colaboradores*. They are not represen-
> tatives of the movement; they are not directors of the movement; they
> are not teachers or managers. To collaborate means to co-accept re-
> sponsibility, to co-promote, to co-accompany, to co-act, to co-decide, to
> co-participate without substituting for or supplanting the NATs. To col-
> laborate is to exercise and develop one's own *protagonismo* alongside the
> permanent development of the *protagonismo* of the NATs.

Colaboradores, according to a MANTHOC training manual, are "educators, companions, promoters, friends, parents, mentors, cheerleaders,
and facilitators." Their tasks include "guiding, providing emotional
support, motivating the group, creating opportunities and spaces for
proposals, promoting critical consciousness, contributing to the development of *protagonismo*, listening, and watching." This incredible
multiplicity of roles and responsibilities sits alongside the political goal
of horizontalism articulated in the previous chapter; *colaboradores* are
meant to take on all these different roles in a way that does not place
them "above" children, and that fosters non-hierarchical interactions.
The relationship between *colaboradores* and NATs is an essential com-
ponent of the movement's prefigurative politics.

Francesca Polletta, in her thorough discussion of participatory democracy in US social movements, has persuasively argued that attempts
to build new forms of interaction are rooted in and modeled upon other
relationships and relational examples, including relations of friendship,
of tutelage, and of religious fellowship.[1] Each of these relational metaphors has its own strengths and liabilities and generates particular kinds
of dynamics within movements. A key insight here is that when movements and organizations are seeking to build new forms of relationship,
they necessarily incorporate and bring with them ideas and examples

from the larger society. In the case of the movement of working children, the concept of the *colaborador* is meant to mark a difference from the other adult roles in children's lives. However, both *colaboradores* and NATs continue to reference these other adults in order to make sense of their relationships, as when Joaquín says that Elena is like a mother but also a teacher, a coworker, and a friend.

Colaboración is intended to support the individual well-being of the NATs, foster their education and development as political and social subjects, and transform how children and adults interact by modeling horizontalism. In this chapter, I explore several different relational approaches *colaboradores* use as they try to achieve these three sometimes competing goals. In doing so, I show how the movement successfully challenges the assumption of children's exclusion from politics: the practices outlined here provide a concrete model for how to develop children's political skills, knowledge, and confidence. Further, these pedagogies and the NATs' responses to them undermine the passivity assumption; the NATs are not just absorbing adult opinions, but are active participants in the process of developing movement ideas. However, while the movement's pedagogies generally aim to minimize hierarchy, *colaboradores* confront a persistent tension between being educators and practicing horizontalism. How do they, with their years of experience and their particular forms of knowledge and expertise, support a process of political education for children and youth while resisting becoming authority figures or placing themselves "above" children? *Colaboradores* don't have a uniform response to this question; their relational practices for addressing this challenge are shaped in complex ways by their own identities, including age, gender, class background, movement history, and professional experiences. In the following sections, I therefore analyze three primary approaches to *colaboración* by sharing the stories of four *colaboradores* and some of the NATs who have worked closely with them. These *colaboradores*, while distinctive, are highlighted here because they effectively represent the most common methods of navigating the tensions embedded in the role.

By emphasizing the *colaboradores'* relational and pedagogical practices in this chapter, I do not mean to suggest that children don't have an active role in forging these relationships. Children certainly respond to *colaboradores'* actions and engage in relationship building on their own terms. But given the power differences between children and adults, the pervasive relational norms of hierarchy and respect for elders, and the fact that *colaboradores* are the main source of stability and continuity in the movement, their intentional relational practices are especially influential in the construction of movement culture and therefore deserving of significant attention and analysis.

Alejandro Cussianovich: El Gran Maestro

Alejandro's role in the movement is unique, and his visibility is far greater than that of any other single *colaborador* or movement adult. Current and former participants all know and value him as a founding figure, intellectual leader, and educator. When I asked then twelve-year-old Anabella for any concluding thoughts in our interview, she suggested that I read Alejandro's most recent book on *la pedagogía de la ternura*, or the pedagogy of tenderness. And every time someone posts a picture of Alejandro on one of the movement's many Facebook pages, the comments and well wishes start pouring in: "saludos a Chito, el gran maestro!" and "querido Chito!" and "Chito, mi amauta!"[2] These comments highlight how beloved Alejandro is within the movement and the fact that movement participants primarily see him as a teacher (*maestro* in Spanish, and *amauta* in Quechua). And, as *el gran maestro*, he is also often the model that other *colaboradores* look to when developing their own pedagogical practices.

Developed over the past fifty years, Alejandro's pedagogical writings and practices are clearly rooted in the radical tradition of Freirian *concientización*.[3] The Freirian method relies upon asking kids to share their thoughts and feelings on something and then generating an analysis based on the collective's thoughts and feelings. It values everyone as a "producer of knowledge," and fits well with the movement's beliefs in equality of insight. In most of its uses in the movement, after children present their ideas, Alejandro and other *colaboradores* re-present children's knowledge back to them, with more conceptual and theoretical frameworks, using some of the movement's key language. In this way, children's knowledge is not simply left in children's terms, but is integrated into the movement's long-standing vocabularies and conceptual paradigms by the adult *colaboradores*. Children's knowledge and ideas can transform and add to movement theories over time, and Alejandro has written about countless instances when children's comments have influenced the movement's theories over the past four decades, but it is notable that adults are usually the ones who do the intellectual task of situating children's ideas in these larger contexts. Freirian education is not exactly horizontal in that the teacher takes on a powerful role in the facilitation process and in the synthesis of knowledge, but it is certainly *more* horizontal than traditional education,[4] or what Freire referred to as a "banking model," in which "knowledge is a gift bestowed by those who consider themselves knowledgeable upon those whom they consider to know nothing."[5]

As a teacher and writer, Alejandro has increasingly emphasized the vital role of emotion, feeling, and love in pedagogy.[6] He has done this primarily through the articulation of the concept of a pedagogy of tenderness. He writes, "We recuperate from Freire the call to cultivate an affectionate and profoundly respectful attitude and perspective. . . . The pedagogy of tenderness could be called a pedagogy of happiness, enthusiasm, and re-enchantment as the results of a critical pedagogy."[7] The pedagogy of tenderness, with its explicit emphasis on the educational relationship as an affective and loving relationship,[8] and the idea of collaboration as "a pedagogical tactic based on trust and mutual respect"[9] both highlight the personal and emotional dimensions of *colaboración*. And Alejandro, like other adults in the movement, has his own strategies for connecting personally with kids, showing them his love, and diminishing social distance and hierarchy in their relationships. In his case, the primary strategies I observed were humor and physical affection.

When Alejandro is teaching, whether he is using the Freirian practices of questions, discussion, and synthesis, or a more traditional lecture format, his style is lighthearted and very funny, and he seems to be gifted with a comedian's excellent sense of timing. For example, during an extended presentation on the International Labor Organization conventions on child labor to MOLACNATs delegates, I noted a whole series of little jokes. He made big, over-the-top, slapstick facial expressions to show his skepticism, surprise, disbelief, or disappointment with various elements of the conventions. When talking about the desire to control young people, he squeezed his hand closed into a fist, timed precisely with the word "control," and made a croaking noise, as if his breathing were being cut off. Later in the session, one of the *colaboradores* was taking photos and he noticed the camera, paused, looked directly at it, and raised his eyebrows and made a silly face. When he thought the kids might be getting a bit bored and distracted, he suddenly smacked the white board for emphasis on a point, with so much force that many people jumped out of their seats, but he then began tapping out a catchy rhythm and whistling. Writing a line on the board to divide two sets of ideas, he made a whirring sound, and the kids all giggled. He continued to make funny noises as he drew faces on the board to distinguish between different kinds of children's work (happy face, okay face, sad face, and so on). At one point, he added a mohawk on one of the faces and was met with another round of giggles. Presenting one of the ILO's positions, he snorted in disbelief. This was too much: the kids could no longer contain their giggles and they all burst out laughing. At the end of his session, he put on his cap, gave the kids a jaunty little salute, and walked out. The whole room was smiling broadly, despite the fact that they had just sat through what was, in essence, a nearly two-hour lecture about international legal conventions.

Humor, joking, and playfulness are not unique to Alejandro's pedagogical practices, and they don't just serve to make learning more fun; they also have an important place in the intergenerational collaborative culture of affection being created in movement spaces. Kids and adults in the movement are not afraid to tease one another, as when Laura jokingly asked how could it be that the girls from one base were so attractive while their boys were not, or when Guillermo laughingly told the elderly and frail-looking Rosa that she needed to remember her bikini for the upcoming field trip to a recreation center. The teasing was always friendly, not mean-spirited, and shows kids' comfort and more egalitarian relationship with the *colaboradores*. Indeed, such explicit teasing would be unlikely in the more hierarchical contexts of their schools as well as in some of their families. The friendly joking and mutual teasing are quite different from an educational culture of quiet or dutiful respect.

In addition to humor, Alejandro connects with kids through genuine expressions of affection, including physical affection. For example, when the mayor of Lima gave Alejandro an award for people who have made extraordinary contributions to teaching, many kids in the move-

Figure 4.1. Alejandro Cussianovich, *right*, teaching at a national gathering for youth involved in PROMINATs, the movement's micro-finance program for working children's businesses. Photo courtesy of Instituto de Formación para Educadores de Jóvenes, Adolescentes y Niños Trabajadores.

ment decided to attend the ceremony honoring him and several other educators. In the elegant Hall of Mirrors, with gilded mirrors and heavy velvet curtains, NATs and *colaboradores* sat patiently until the end of the hours-long event waiting to give their congratulations. Each child wanted a picture with Alejandro and his medal, and each one got this picture, but only after Alejandro greeted him or her with a huge smile and a hug that communicated his surprise and genuine pleasure that they had taken the time to attend this "boring" event for him. He knelt down to give an eight-year-old boy a high-five, and everyone received a warm, affectionate, and personalized greeting. Alejandro's manner in these moments showed each person how much he valued their individual presence.

Physical affection is very common in the movement and is a way for *colaboradores* and kids to connect with one another. In addition to the normal polite greeting of a kiss on the cheek, many NATs greet *colaboradores* (and researchers!) they have not seen in a few weeks or months with huge, long-lasting hugs. But there are also some significant gender and age differences in how adults use physicality to communicate their love and affection for the NATs. Most men's displays of physical affection are more playful: they ruffle children's hair and give gentle squeezes of children's hands. They also hug some children, but these hugs tend to be shorter and more cursory than those offered by most of the women. This, of course, is not surprising given the ways that men's physical affection with children is regularly positioned as a threat. Homophobia, hegemonic masculinity, and misogyny all intertwine in the ways that "teaching, especially in the early years, is associated with caring, and with the presumption that caring is women's work, thereby implying that men who want to be primary teachers are rejecting traditional masculine behaviors and as such must be gay."[10] Men who work with young children are "suspect" and therefore must limit their displays of physical affection and tenderness and engage in overt performances of heterosexuality and hegemonic masculinity. The male *colaboradores* in the movement may be significantly more physically affectionate with children than many other Peruvian adult men, but their ability to enact tenderness in this way is generally more circumscribed than that of women in the movement. Alejandro is an exception to this, as his age (nearly eighty) enables him to be "grandfatherly," a role that can be more physically "soft."

In a context that is highly feminized both because it is a child-centered space and as a result of the movement's discursive emphasis on tenderness and emotion, Alejandro provides an important example of a man engaging deeply in this work. But while Alejandro's age allows him to blend serious political education with tenderness and affection in a very particular way, younger men have a harder time navigating these dual dimensions of the role while still enacting the expectations of appropriate masculinity. Other men's collaboration, while certainly compassionate and emotional, and involving personal connections, also tends to emphasize intellect, ideas, and political education over dynamics of affection, love, and tenderness. Modeling themselves after Alejandro, many of the men in the movement primarily understand the *colaborador* as an educator or teacher. While Alejandro is *el gran maestro*, some other men are also seen as teachers and are pleased to be called "Profe" by the NATs in their base groups.

The NATs who work closely with Alejandro tend to be national and international delegates from MANTHOC, MNNATSOP, or the RedNNA. They spend time with him in workshops designed to deepen their critical political analysis, in meetings writing proclamations, or in planning sessions preparing to meet with government officials or the ILO. Joaquín, for example, spent significant time with Alejandro as a MNNATSOP national delegate. Their many formal and informal discussions had supported the development of his critical vocabulary and political perspective: "Talking with Chito, and with Elena, and other *colaboradores*, I've learned more about different policies, about the ILO, about paradigms of childhood, and I have had a chance to think more about the world, and how it works right now, and how I want it to be." He was an eloquent and passionate speaker on child labor politics:

> We [NATs] are all capable. We are the future, and we are the present. . . . It is painful that there are negative ideas about working children: that we are a problem, or that we are the cause of poverty in the country. This is all totally a lie, and it hurts us, but it also gives us strength to continue struggling, to continue in this process, and to try to get the authorities and the society to see us as something positive.

He regularly took the lead in the discussions about organizing campaigns against ILO Conventions 182 and 138, and in the analysis of the changes to the Peruvian laws, laying out the details and implications of policies with startling clarity for a fifteen-year-old. Critical political education in the Freirian tradition and extended political discussions with *colaboradores* encourage NATs like Joaquín to reflect on their own experiences and offer them theoretical vocabularies to better describe and analyze those experiences. Through relationships with *colaboradores*, they learn to place their own experiences in the larger social and economic context and directly compare their experiences to international discourses and to international and national policies.

The Freirian educational relationship, infused with additional humor, playfulness, and frequent expressions of affection, is one model for how adults and kids can interact with one another in the context of social movements. But the *colaborador*'s role as a teacher in this process positions the *colaborador* in a more vertical relationship with the NATs, even when that teacher sees children as producers of knowledge and is funny, caring, and full of deep respect for children and their ideas. The facilitator of a Freirian process of *conscientización* is never just a facilitator, but also a guide whose questions and analysis shape the conversation. And Alejandro's lectures, while accessible, child-friendly, and open to NATs' interventions and commentary, also identify him as the expert on the topic at hand. When thinking about *colaboradores* as educators, therefore, we can't help but see some of the unevenness of the intergenerational relationship. Adults have information and ideas that NATs may not have, and while there are times when NATs facilitate these learning processes or offer lectures for their peers, the role of educator is far more frequently taken on by adults. And as I'll discuss more in the following chapter, this kind of relationship gives adults a particular kind of power.

The Freirian political educational relationship helps NATs put their experiences in larger contextual perspective, develop their vocabularies for political analysis, and think critically about a variety of social and political issues. And while this educational relationship is not exactly horizontal, kids are not passive in this process; they are actively developing their own political ideas in dialogue with both adults and peers. Further, adults diminish the more vertical tendencies of the educator role by explicitly encouraging and valuing kids' knowledge contributions, downplaying their own status and authority through humor, and reducing social distance through their articulations of care, love, affection, and respect. Offering kids a political education that takes them seriously as critical thinkers is one way that adults support children's activism and social movement participation, undermining the assumptions of children's passivity and children's exclusion from politics.

Mónica and Juliana: Teaching, Caring, and Mothering in the Base Groups

Mónica, one of the *colaboradoras* for the Yerbateros base group, is particularly skilled at finding ways for even the youngest NATs to contribute their ideas to a political conversation. Using games, drawing, songs, and theatre, she engages the NATs in the practice of building and synthesizing knowledge, while also building relationships of pleasure, fun, and trust between kids and adults. The kids write skits about *trabajo digno*, draw pictures of what constitutes respectful treatment of each other, and sing songs about children's rights. In these instances, creative activities are used to generate ideas and to spark conversation, but they also produce a relational dynamic that isn't just rational. Kids and adults don't just share their perspectives, but they also laugh together at silly skits, sing passionately, stomp their feet in time to a shared rhythm, and play with one another. Through these practices, kids and *colaboradores* produce collective knowledge *and* build emotional connections that strengthen their relationships to one another. Mónica actively guides these processes in the Yerbateros house, playing a central role in determining the questions for the discussion, inviting the kids to comment on each others' ideas, and synthesizing the central lessons. Like Alejandro and other *colaboradores*-as-teachers, she takes responsibility for setting up an educational experience and facilitating that experience. Mónica, however, uses a different strategy for responding to the tension between her implicit authority as an educator and the prefigurative political goal of horizontal intergenerational relationships: offering extensive emotional support through caring relationships with individual NATs.

As a *colaboradora* in a base group that provides social services, Mónica sees the same group of NATs nearly every day. She engages with the entirety of their lives, not just their participation in the movement. She knows who is struggling in school and needs extra support with math, and she knows who is dealing with family stresses. My field notes are full of examples of Mónica and other *colaboradores* engaging in deep and active listening with kids. They maintain eye contact, ask thoughtful follow-up questions, and are fully present in the conversations, whether kids are talking about a conflict with their parents, a problem at school, or a movie they just saw. And in interviews with both kids and adults, listening was regularly referenced as one of the most important characteristics of a good *colaborador*. Juliana, also a *colaboradora* with lots of experience in the base groups, said that listening to kids and being there to listen to them is part of what she loves about being a *colaboradora*: "For me, the most satisfying thing about it is that I have worked with kids . . . who tell me things that are very personal, very internal, that they haven't talked about with their mother or father, or that they felt were not heard." Listening to kids and taking their perspectives seriously

Figure 4.2. Working alongside the NATs on various collective tasks gives *colaboradores* a chance to talk informally and connect with individual NATs. Photo courtesy of Movimiento de Adolescentes y Niños Trabajadores Hijos de Obreros Cristianos—Nacional.

constitute a radical challenge to the still-common tendency to dismiss children's feelings and desires as silly, juvenile, and temporary.[11]

Mónica and Juliana don't just listen; they provide active support. They give advice and even intervene on kids' behalf or alongside the kids when the kids are facing particularly powerful challenges, going with kids to meet with teachers, or mediating family dynamics. I often would arrive at the Yerbateros house to find Mónica talking with Patricia about her parents, discussing with her why they acted in the ways that they did and how to respond. She, like other *colaboradores*, also builds relationships with the NATs' parents so that they can help moderate family conflicts or facilitate communication within families. As Mónica reminded the kids in her base group at one meeting, "Our work as *colaboradores* is to talk to your parents, to address the problems you are having, and talk with them about how to better help and support you." Parents I met usually knew the *colaboradores* who work with their kids because the *colaboradores* had come to the house at least a few times to talk with them about the movement, ask their permission for children's involvement in movement events or activities, better understand the children's contexts and life experiences, and discuss with them some of the challenges that their children are facing in order to figure out solutions and strategies to support the kids.

Colaboradores and NATs sometimes describe the deeply caring relationships they have found in the movement through metaphors of family and familial love. Kids talk about the organization as a "second home," or the movement as being "like a family." And, given the age dynamics of the movement, this means sometimes referring to the middle-aged *colaboradores* as being "like parents." As Jhasmila put it, "More than anything, *colaboradores* support us like parents. It is like a family in this movement." At a workshop for *colaboradores*, Juliana described to the group how she had once had a long conversation with a boy about why he was fighting with other boys. She told the group that "at the end of this, he gave me a hug and said he wanted me to be his mama because his mama didn't talk with him like this." In her reflection on this, Juliana emphasized that adults in the movement can provide things to the kids that parents, in her view, should be providing but cannot for various reasons. She was quite comfortable taking on the identity of "another mother."

There were only a few isolated cases in which NATs or *colaboradores* talked about men in the movement as being "like fathers," but it was quite common for kids to describe women *colaboradores* as being "like mothers." The substantial emotional labor of women *colaboradores*, especially women in their thirties or older, was often made legible to children by linking it to the maternal. Kids see similarities between the care offered to them by adult women and the role of mothers, even when *colaboradores* would prefer that kids not make this comparison. Male *colaboradores* engage in some of the same caring practices as women, like listening deeply and providing individual support, but there are also some expressions of care that they are less likely to enact. Women *colaboradores* make coffee, tea, or hot chocolate for meetings, bring out bags of fruit and pass the tangerines and bananas among the kids, or carry plates of home-cooked meals out from the MANTHOC kitchen at Yerbateros. Men do not usually engage in any of these tasks, and do not seem to be particularly aware of this gendered division of labor. My attempts to get both men and women to talk about this often fell quite flat, with many people reiterating that the movement practiced gender equality and that there were no real differences between the work men and women did in the movement. The fact that women do this work, however, offers yet another reason that kids may describe them as being "like mothers."

Mónica and Juliana both sought to move beyond the traditionally hierarchical and more emotionally distant "teacher" role by building individualized and personal relationships with kids and providing them with significant care, affection, and support, but without punishment. And, as women in their thirties, they were sometimes talked about by NATs as being "like mothers." But "being like a mother" can place substantial additional burdens and expectations on *colaboradores* that they do not necessarily want to take on, or that they may be unable to fulfill. Further, while there are many different models for the mothering relationship and the meaning of motherhood is far from universal, it often implies not just love but also at least some level of guidance and responsibility. Invoking the relational framework of family and parent-child relationships signals the love and care between NATs and *colaboradores*, but feminist theorists have long argued that family structures are also deeply unequal. When describing some *colaboradores* as being as "like mothers" rather than aunts, older sisters, or friends, movement participants imagine a relationship that is extremely close but also potentially more directive and vertical.[12] Elena was distinctly uncomfortable with the fact that Joaquín described her this way for exactly this reason: "We are trying to create new kinds of relationships, not replicate old ones, with their inequalities." Juliana and many other *colaboradores*, however, did not share her concerns about how the language of parenting could undermine the goal of horizontalism.

Personal and supportive relationships with *colaboradores* were deeply appreciated by the NATs. Graciela came out of the base group at Yerbateros, with Mónica as her first *colaboradora*. Then, when she was elected as a national delegate for MANTHOC and was given additional responsibilities, Juliana became her primary *colaboradora*, helping her develop her leadership skills and navigate national politics. While she would happily chat with other *colaboradores* about what was going on in her life, her primary sources of support were always Mónica and Juliana. In an interview in 2013 she told me, "They are more than *colab-*

oradores, they are our friends. We can tell them everything, including the most personal things. And you know, at this age, being sixteen, we are falling in love and so many things." She continued, "I really rely on them for advice." And when I saw Graciela in 2015, after she had turned eighteen and left the movement, she told me that she still calls on both *colaboradores*, and that these relationships "give me the confidence to face anything." Like Graciela, many NATs described how the relationship with *colaboradores* helps them deal with their personal lives and increases their self-confidence. As Yovanna put it, "The trust they have in us, and our trust in them, and the advice they give us, all of it helps me to have more confidence in myself." Listening deeply to kids and caring about their lives not only helps individual NATs feel supported, but also serves as one of many reminders that *colaboradores* care about children's voices, ideas, and feelings. Having *colaboradores* who listen to them talk about their friends, families, and schools also can help kids feel like their voices matter on a variety of other topics, including political ones.

Close, supportive, and affectionate relationships with caring adults have consistently been found to be beneficial for marginalized young people's individual well-being, their success in school, and their overall life trajectories.[13] In this aspect of its approach, the movement of working children is not necessarily different from many other youth programs found around the world. However, the distinctive context as a social movement means that the relationships being built do not exist simply for their own sake or the sake of the individual participants, but make up the fabric of a community that also has an explicit social change agenda. Kids and adults rely upon these personal relationships as they prepare to speak to Congress, march in the streets, and write proclamations. Their emotional connections and relationships are the affective base from which they take political action. The relational work and kids' deep sense of being supported and valued provide a strong foundation that explicitly enables the expansion and enactment of their political agency in other spaces.

Enrique: *Compañeros* and Friends Organizing Together

Colaboradores are not just teachers or caregivers; they are co-participants in an intergenerational social movement. This particular understanding of the role was absolutely central to Enrique's approach to being a *colaborador*. In his early thirties when I met him, Enrique had been part of working children's organizations since he was about seven years old. After being a national delegate in MANTHOC, he left his small rural hometown outside Puno to study and work in Arequipa. While there, he and several friends, also ex-delegates, formed a new base group of working children and became *colaboradores* for that group. He participated in trainings and courses with IFEJANT, continued to be involved in the movement, and was one of the *colaboradores* supporting the MANTHOC national delegates in Lima during two years of my fieldwork. Enrique described *colaboradores* as "the people who are always there, ready, with the group, motivating them when they aren't motivated, giving our opinions when it is needed, helping them think through options and ideas, being there with them, deciding things together, . . . working with them in whatever activity, but always behind them, behind the kids." As a national *colaborador*, Enrique was especially involved in making decisions about the political direction of the movement alongside the NATs and, in the process, helping the NATs develop their political organizing skills.

In addition to meeting regularly with Marco, Graciela, and Lili individually as they each developed their skills as national and regional delegates, Enrique was a regular presence at the small-group meetings of the regional and national coordinating bodies of MANTHOC and MNNATSOP, as well as the Lima-RedNNA. These meetings usually involved between five and fifteen people, with about one quarter to one third of the participants being adult *colaboradores*. Adults and kids work together in these spaces to move forward on their organizational and political agendas. And, in this process, kids learn how to plan marches, write press releases and proclamations, mobilize other organizations to turn out for events, develop biannual strategic plans and annual work plans, identify movement strengths and weaknesses, look for opportunities for influence, prepare to meet with government officials and other decision makers, and develop other political advocacy skills. *Colaboradores* do not just sit back in these meetings and let kids flounder through their discussions. Instead, by working alongside the kids in the entire process, they show them how to do each of the various tasks of a social movement. This model of educating through working on a project together, with kids taking on increasing responsibility over time, creates a strong sense of community and connection. In these meetings, kids and adults are a unified team, striving to achieve the same larger goals.

Over the course of their time in the movement, kids increase their comfort and ability to direct these meetings as well as their ability to contribute to the discussions. The quality of their participation in these collective endeavors changes as they develop their skills and increase their confidence in those skills. When I met Anabella in 2012, she never wanted to facilitate a meeting. When asked, she would usually instead offer to take notes—to be the secretary. In 2013 I attended at least one meeting where she did indeed facilitate, and in which her *colaboradora*, like many *colaboradores* supporting new facilitators, would remind her of what to do in this role. *Colaboradores* working with new facilitators will often notice when the discussion is winding down on a topic, and turn to the developing facilitator and ask, "What next?" or "Where are we with the agenda?" or "Do you think we are ready to move on?" When I came back to Lima in 2015, Anabella was a competent meeting facilita- tor who, when asked to facilitate a meeting of MNNATSOP-Lima, im- mediately agreed, asked the group for agenda items, and, after creating the agenda, began the discussion of the first point. By participating in many meetings, and then having someone support her with questions and bits and pieces of guidance when needed, Anabella developed the skills she needed to take on greater leadership in the movement.

This pedagogical relationship resonates with what developmental psychologist Barbara Rogoff has variously described as apprenticeship learning, learning through guided participation, and learning through intent participation.[14] According to Rogoff, a key way that people learn is through observation, interaction, and participation in social and cultural activities alongside more experienced participants in those activities. In this pedagogical model, "the collaborative arrangement of children's learning includes transfer of responsibility to children as they become more capable of handling problems."[15] Rogoff finds that many indigenous communities across the Americas have this approach to learning,[16] and educational scholar Ben Kirshner has also identified these practices in youth activist organizations in the United States.[17] This pedagogical approach helps manage implicit tensions between the fact that "some adult support may be necessary for youth to achieve political goals" and yet "too much involvement might undermine [youth] initiative or lead to a slippery slope where adults end up co-opting youths' roles."[18] Apprenticeship is a way for adults to work alongside youth while also enacting strategies that will continually increase young people's participation and leadership while diminishing the role of the adult.

Enrique was especially skilled at this kind of collaboration. In all of my observations of his participation style in meetings, I was struck by his careful attention to the implications of his actions. He tended to sit back in meetings, not take on any kind of leadership or directive responsibilities, and to focus instead on thoroughly answering any questions that kids asked him, providing individualized guidance, or offering very specific suggestions regarding particular tasks and outlining different options for how those tasks might be accomplished. Enrique was willing to "orient" the NATs on a given issue, and do some of the different tasks of the group, but, in his words, he usually tried to position himself as a *compañero* rather than a leader, facilitator, or teacher. While often translated as "companion," "friend," or "associate," *compañero* also has a political connotation: a comrade in the struggle. In addition to this politicized sense of togetherness, *compañero*, as a relational concept, does not imply any particular hierarchy or difference: it signals an equal relationship in which both participants play more or less the same role, rather than one in which the roles on either side of the connection are clearly differentiated (as in teacher/student or mother/child). Enrique and a few others would talk about their *compañeros* in the movement in a way that included both *colaboradores* and NATs, but this was quite unusual. Instead, many of the NATs talked about their fellow organized children and adolescents, or the other members of their base groups as their *compañeros*, but they didn't apply the term to the *colaboradores*. Similarly, most *colaboradores* talked about their fellow *colaboradores* as their *compañeros*. Despite the movement's explicit discourses of horizontalism and mutuality, the *colaborador*-NAT relationship was not generally imagined in these terms, suggesting that there remains, for both kids and adults, an implicit and enduring assumption of their difference from one another.

Being *compañeros*, for Enrique, was a way to signal a relationship that included friendship, but also went beyond it: "We talk like friends, and there are spaces and moments of fun, where we are with them. But there are also times in meetings that are very serious, highly contentious, with lots of debate." Friendship, for him, can't quite capture the kinds of relations being built in the movement—NATs and *colaboradores* may be friends, but they are also working together on a political project. But, while Enrique preferred the language of being a *compañero*, many more people invoked the model of friendship as a way to describe these intergenerational relationships, particularly when referencing the emotional labor of young men in the movement. Younger men's emotional connections with kids and deep engagement with kids' personal thoughts, feelings, and struggles were often described by NATs as the behavior of an especially supportive and more experienced friend. This was also true of the young women who, in the eyes of the kids, were not yet old enough to be motherly. Like that of family, the relational model of friendship references emotional care and personal connection, but also suggests a more horizontal mode of interaction. As Raúl put it, "They know I am their *colaborador*, but they treat me as one of them. I try to maintain a friendship with them. . . . They tell me things, and I am another friend. Sometimes they tease me, and I tease them. . . . Even though I am an adult, I feel like I am one of them." Friendship, like being a *compañero*, emphasizes the similarities between the adults and the kids, rather than the differences, and sets up different relational expectations than the idea of *colaboradores* as either teachers or parents. Friendship includes relations of care and concern, but far less guidance and responsibility than either the teacher or parent role.

Not all adults are seen as equally likely to be a potential friend. This was an important topic of conversation during breakfast the day that the youth in MNNATSOP-Ica were going to vote to select their next regional *colaborador*. Two teens were talking about the candidates, sharing information about the options. Diana described one woman, Karla, who had taken her and some other NATs to an event, but on the way to the event they stopped for some food, ate a meal together, and had a really good time. She told Ronaldo, the other teen, that Karla is "pretty young and can be like a friend, not just a *colaborador*." Ronaldo nodded, and said that was good, and that it isn't always the case with the older *colaboradores*. Then he paused, and said, "Well, maybe Eva can be like a friend, but not Sarita." Diana agreed, "Definitely not Sarita." She then asked Ronaldo, "What about Victoria?" Ronaldo replied, "I like her, but she's a little crazy!" Diana's first assertion was that age was what made a *colaborador* more "like a friend," but then she and Ronaldo reflected on this a bit and decided that it wasn't *just* age that mattered. Instead, while being younger certainly helps to make the relationship more like a friendship, there are older adults whose actions and style can make them more friend-like. In my days with this group, I certainly saw significant differences between Eva, Victoria, and Sarita. Eva tended to hang back in most meetings and events, letting the kids take the lead and occasionally offering various statements of support and encouragement when it seemed like these would be needed. Victoria was more present in the space, but primarily in individualized interactions with kids, and was quite silly and playful. Sarita, on the other hand, often lectured the group on what she thought would be best in a given situation. Her behavior was thus much more traditionally and typically adult—it was more hierarchical, making her a much less likely candidate for being considered a friend.

"Being like a friend" was often a way for kids to talk about the *colaboradores* whose practices were least like those of other adults in their lives—the *colaboradores* who didn't enforce rules, lecture them, quiz them, or talk down to them. It was a way to name those *colaboradores* who were more skilled at diminishing social distance and hierarchy, but it doesn't capture the work being done, or the political nature of this intergenerational community.

I saw some of this ambiguity about the idea of "being friends" reflected when Victoria, one of the Ica *colaboradores*, came up to Daniel, a regional delegate, and greeted him with "Hola, amigo" (Hello, friend). Luis, another teen, corrected her: "Daniel isn't your friend, he is your coworker" (*compañero de trabajo*). Luis rejected the idea of a friendship with Victoria not because he wanted to imagine a more hierarchical or more distant relationship, but in order to redefine the movement primarily as a space of work rather than play.

Enrique, then, serves as a very important example of a *colaborador* whose practices and language instantiate a relationship that supports kids' continued learning and growth, recognizes the distinctiveness of the intergenerational social movement space, and yet is always clearly oriented toward reducing hierarchy. In contrast to both *colaboradores-*

as-educators and *colaboradores*-as-mothers, trying to be a *colaborador*-as-*compañero* pushes adults toward a more mutual relationship. This conceptual framework also clearly pairs well with the practices of learning through apprenticeship. Rogoff and her colleagues write that in this pedagogy, also called guided participation, "both mature members and less mature members are conceived as active"[19] and that the model encourages a "collaborative, horizontal participation structure with fluid responsibilities."[20] In the context of the movement of working children, apprenticeship learning encourages *colaboradores* to be actively engaged with kids on joint projects, building a strong sense of alliance and community. It encourages kids to see themselves as capable of increasing responsibility and leadership, but how much initiative and power they take on in any interaction is left largely up to them. Guided participation gives kids a chance to slowly develop new skills, becoming increasingly engaged and active participants in movement spaces, and honors their initiative in this process, but it also, as I'll discuss in the next chapter, sometimes means that *colaboradores* end up dominating these spaces and that such domination can be justified on the grounds that the kids are still developing and not yet ready to take the lead. Working together with kids on a shared political agenda creates a flexible relationship that lets adults and kids each take leadership and control in different moments, but that very same flexibility can sometimes allow for a return to habituated hierarchical practices. Despite these challenges, however, the model of *colaborador*-as-*compañero* is a powerful and generative example of one way to effectively and meaningfully incorporate kids into social movement spaces.

Difference, Conflict, and Ambiguity in the Role of the *Colaborador*

Individual *colaboradores* engage with the multiplicity of the *colaborador* role in different ways, with each person emphasizing some parts of the role more than others. Some emphasize being teachers while others see themselves as more like family members or as *compañeros* and friends. Graciela noted that "each *colaborador* has their own personality: there are some with a lot of humility, others with only a little humility, others who are grumpy." Marco said, "Each *colaborador* has their own way of working. Some have a particular methodology, others just have the experience of being organized themselves." As these NATs and the examples above make clear, *colaboradores* are not all the same in their interpretation and implementation of the role, and the roles available to a given *colaborador* are shaped by their own identities, most especially gender and age.[21]

In addition to these differences, *colaboradores* also make distinctions between those who were former NATs and child participants in the movement and those who were not. The ex-NATs have a distinctive sense of obligation to the movement, and they talk frequently about wanting to give back to the organizations that meant so much to them as children. They also talk about themselves as being role models for the current NATs in a way that the other *colaboradores* do not. Juan discussed with me how he feels that he and the other ex-NAT *colaboradores*, many of whom have gone on to university and professional careers, can be examples and can show the kids what is possible. Enrique also described how he thinks his years of experience as a delegate in the movement give him a deeper and more personal sense of what the NATs are going through. He was quick to point out that he didn't think that the other *colaboradores* don't understand the kids, or that they were not important and valuable participants in the movement, but simply that his own experiences give him a different kind of understanding and personal connection to the NATs. The transition from delegate to *colaborador* can be a difficult one, but ex-NATs who become *colaboradores* feel a powerful emotional affinity with the current NATs and regularly articulate their feelings of gratitude for what the movement has done for them. The movement also continues to be a central and defining space in their lives.

Of the *colaboradores* who are not ex-NATs, several have been involved in the movement since its founding years. Some of these individuals were among the youth in the JOC who helped to create MANTHOC; others were adults who were already supporting the JOC youth during this period or got involved in the movement in its early years. These elders are highly respected by both the younger *colaboradores* and the current NATs for their deep historical knowledge and enduring commitment to the movement. Their place in the movement is somewhat distinct. Younger *colaboradores* look to them for advice and guidance as they take on their new role, and these more experienced *colaboradores* regularly lead the workshops discussing and reflecting on the place of adults in the movement. The movement has, for a few of these foundational individuals, become their source of financial support: being a *colaborador* is not just their vocation, but also their profession. Thanks largely to international NGOs, they've been able to piece together sufficient funds to devote themselves to the movement full-time. These individuals have spent decades thinking about and practicing being a *colaborador* and are incredibly reflective about this role.

A third group of *colaboradores* are young adults who entered the movement initially as long-term volunteers, but have stayed involved and become sufficiently enmeshed in and committed to the movement for both kids and other adults to see them now as *colaboradores*, rather than just the more temporary designation of "volunteer." There are also a couple of *colaboradores* whose entry to the movement came via their educational experiences: courses with Alejandro that were transformational and that led them to participate in the movement, mostly through working at IFEJANT. These individuals tend to be from slightly more middle-class backgrounds than the NATs, but this class difference was not something I ever heard discussed in the movement, and these individuals did not appear, as a group, to interact with the NATs in a manner that was particularly different from the other *colaboradores*. Instead, the primary difference seems to be in how they relate emotionally to the movement. While they are obviously very committed to the movement, it is not a defining part of their lives in the way that it is for both the ex-NATs and the professional movement elders.

I never encountered *colaboradores* referencing their individual histories (as ex-NATs or not) as a way to impose their version of collaboration on others, but there were certainly conflicts between *colaboradores* who understood their roles differently and whose pedagogical and personal approaches were in direct opposition to one another. The most ongoing example of this was the fraught relationship between Laura and Enrique. The two worked together frequently as *colaboradores* supporting the organizing activities of the RedNNA (National Network of Children and Adolescents), but they had very different styles. Enrique's model of *colaborador*-as-*compañero* was in direct contrast to Laura's "teacher" practices, which often replicated more traditional and hierarchical pedagogies. For example, she would quiz NATs about various subjects as a way to review material. In one instance, she asked the RedNNA kids a series of questions to review the visit of a staff member from Save the Children. Rather than ask for their assessment of the visit or letting the conversation be guided by their concerns, she turned to one of the younger girls in the group, Daniela, and asked her to restate factual information presented by the visitor: "What is the third protocol on the CRC?" Daniela took a deep breath, as if preparing her response, and then responded that the third protocol would create ways for kids to complain about violations of their rights so that they can be addressed. Each time someone answered one of her questions correctly, Laura would smile and offer praise. She did not criticize wrong answers, but would ask someone else. These questions certainly helped to strengthen the understanding of the kids, solidifying some of their knowledge by repeating it, but this model of collaboration clearly set Laura in a position of power, with her as the source of correct information. While in other moments Laura did not behave like a teacher, and she often had close personal relationships with some of the younger NATs, in these instances her pedagogy was enough like that of "typical" teachers that it was quite easy for both she and the kids in the relationship to slide into this far more widespread and hierarchical way of relating to one another, with Laura leading the way and the kids simply following behind, seeking to give the right answers.

In that meeting and several others, Enrique would sometimes try to intervene in the direction and flow of the conversation, suggesting that Laura move on to the organizing work of the meeting, rather than spending time reviewing information. But, because his own style was to sit back and let the kids lead, in contrast to Laura's much more active version of collaboration, he was often visibly uncomfortable long before he would step in and suggest shifting the meeting toward specific tasks and projects. His subtle interventions, however, were not having the impact he wanted, and his frustration grew over the course of months. At one very tense and emotional meeting, those frustrations boiled over and he expressed his critiques much more directly. After a small disagreement over who was collecting petition signatures from which base groups became heated due to the simmering dissatisfaction, Enrique told Laura, "You are far too active and present in the group's meetings and conversations. The group would not function without you and this is a problem. You are not letting the kids develop their own leadership." Laura, though, disagreed with him in his analysis of the implications of her style. "No, I am supporting the younger ones, the ones who don't have all of Graciela's experience, and they need more guidance." Laura implied that Enrique, Graciela's *colaborador*, could sit back and be more of a *compañero* because he was thinking primarily about the more experienced NATs, but that the younger kids need her to be a teacher and to be more directive. Enrique responded, "They won't develop if you keep doing everything for them." Laura clarified, "I don't do everything—I ask them what they want on the Facebook page, what they want in the emails." Enrique continued to shake his head, and said, "Asking them what they want isn't letting them do things." In Laura's eyes, she was just providing the necessary guidance, education, and encouragement for a less experienced group of kids. But in Enrique's view, she was acting too much like a teacher and an authority figure, enabling them to continue to be passive within the movement, rather than guiding them to become more active protagonists and leaders. Overt conflicts between *colaboradores* were rare, but the tension between Enrique and Laura signaled a substantial disagreement over what it means to be a "good" *colaborador*, and how *colaboradores* should support the development and learning of the NATs.

These disagreements about how to be an effective *colaborador* are rooted in the role's ambiguities and an enduring tension between horizontalism and being an educator. Or, as Carlos, an ex-NAT and *colaborador* in his thirties, articulated this challenge,

> At first, in the early years of the movement, the *colaborador* had a role that was more intense—they were involved in the formation of the group, the formation and education of the members. But more recently the kids have questioned the role of the adult more. . . . So there are some *colaboradores* who got rid of the character of being educators—they accompany, but don't try to shape the movement. Others don't differentiate themselves from the kids. Others have reclaimed the role and are saying that you can't just say, "Yes, chicos" to everything. They are thinking about what is the responsibility of adults in an organization of kids. There is an authority, but what kind of authority? How can we be educators without

disrupting the autonomy of the kids? And for a six-year-old, what is the significance of being a protagonist? If they want to stay up all night, to go to the beach? There are differences between ten-year-olds and fourteen-year-olds also. What is the role of the adult when we think about these differences and the participation of different kids?

Carlos's comments here suggest that *colaboradores* in the movement are aware of the challenges of integrating their commitment to horizontalism with being an educator, and that the question of adults' responsibilities and place in the movement is an ongoing subject of discussion. But his analysis also sets up a false binary: *colaboradores* are either stepping back too much, abdicating their appropriate roles as adults in favor of too much horizontalism, or they are willing to take up a position of authority and be a teacher. This framing does not acknowledge the practices of *colaboradores* like Enrique who neither sit back and do nothing nor become teachers who are fully willing to "shape the movement." While the challenges of the role are very real, and Enrique would not necessarily be able to use the approach he does without the presence of *colaboradores* who take up its other dimensions (including more directed political education), some *colaboradores* have found ways to minimize the tensions between horizontalism and an active pedagogical relationship with the NATs.

Colaboradores come to the movement with different experiences, histories, skill sets, and identities. The role of the *colaborador* is also complex, multiple, and full of potential challenges. *Colaboradores* articulate a shared vision for horizontal, affective intergenerational relationships, but each constructs those relationships in their own distinctive way, shaped by larger contexts of gender and age expectations. While trying to create an entirely new mode of intergenerational interaction, *colaboración*, they reference and draw upon already meaningful models for intergenerational relationships. Kids too use these already existing relational frameworks as a way to make sense of the *colaboradores*, saying that they are "like teachers but not" or "like mothers but not" and so on. The comparison to other adults in their lives enables the kids not only to put their relationships with *colaboradores* into familiar terms, but also to identify how their relationships with the *colaboradores* are different from their relationships with other adults, identifying what is transformed in these interactions: *colaboradores* listen more, respect their rights, care more about their opinions, and don't punish them, for example. The *colaboradores* are a diverse group of adults who each relate to kids in their own manner, but the common discursive and political context of the movement also shapes all of their relationships, encouraging critical reflection on interactions and the development of affectionate, educational, and less hierarchical relationships with kids.

Colaboración and Transformative Intergenerational Relationships
Challenging Assumptions about Childhood

The pedagogy of the movement of working children consistently engages children as active subjects who are capable of critical thinking and analysis, challenging both the assumption that children are merely passive objects of socialization *and* the assumption that children should be excluded from complex political discussion and action. Although it is not entirely horizontal, the relationship between *colaboradores* and NATs certainly empowers the kids to develop and articulate their ideas about the world around them. The daily practices of the movement are full of opportunities for kids to increase their knowledge of their rights, discuss what kinds of work are dignified and what kinds of work are exploitative, think together about their own experiences and how those experiences relate to those of others, and consider how the larger political and social contexts currently operate and how they should be transformed in order to support working children's dignity and well-being. Kids in the movement don't just listen to and repeat what adults tell them, but engage in meaningful political dialogue with adults who they know will listen to them, respect them, and take their ideas seriously, even when they disagree.

One of the common criticisms of the movement of working children and other spaces that engage kids in political discourse is that they are "brainwashing" children. The pedagogical and relational practices I've described above, however, suggest a very different kind of educational relationship. While adults in the movement certainly have influence, the practices of *colaboración* create a context where children can and do articulate their own points of view, raise critical questions, and express disagreement with the adults. The education that happens in the movement is no more "brainwashing" than any interaction where children learn something alongside adults, and, in fact, gives kids far more encouragement to challenge and question the adults' perspectives than occurs in most schooling contexts. Any claim that the NATs are just mimicking or parroting adults is willfully ignoring the movement's critical and dialogic pedagogy and underestimating children's abilities to express their desires, visions, and perspectives. The practices I've outlined in this chapter highlight how meaningful and caring personal relationships, Freirian dialogue, and apprenticeship learning can combine to create social movements where kids are included not as pawns, but as engaged, questioning, thinking participants. The pedagogical, political, and personal relationship of *colaboración* therefore fundamentally challenges the common justifications for excluding children from political power.

The Persistence of Age-Based Power

Becoming an activist and learning to participate in social movements always requires some kind of process of political education.[22] Adults' relationships with children in these kinds of political contexts are therefore inevitably pedagogical, and pedagogical relationships, even in the radical Freirian vision, are never entirely horizontal. As Lesley Bartlett notes, Freire's early works positing a truly horizontal relationship between student and teacher "generated a staggering amount of debate over the teacher's role in a democratic classroom." This led Freire to refine his position and note that "dialogue between teachers and students does not place them on the same footing" and to argue, in Bartlett's terms, that teachers should be "egalitarian without attempting to be equal."[23] The inequality between teacher and student exists in all educational spaces and interactions, but has a distinctive set of implications in the context of intergenerational relationships. In contrast to the political education that might take place among peers with a shared set of social identities, the adult facilitator of the Freirian process in a children's movement is not located within the oppressed constituency that is the focus of critical analysis and discussion. Further, one of the structural aspects of age-based power is that adults are primarily responsible for children's learning and development. Therefore, the power of the adult educator is heightened in relationships with children. Children's learning—including their political learning—can certainly sometimes come from peers, but adults, across cultural and historical contexts, consistently play a central role in children's education. In a sense, a totally horizontal intergenerational relationship is always going to be undercut by this enduring dynamic of age-based power.

In the movement of working children, personalized and caring relationships are meant to reduce the inequality that is always present in the pedagogical relationship between children and adults. However, in enacting these dynamics of care, *colaboradores* are also drawing on hegemonic models of childhood that expect children to be vulnerable. These expectations often imply that children are the group that needs care while adults are the ones who provide care. And, in the affective politics of the movement of working children, I note a tendency to slide back into this dominant relational model, with movement participants unwittingly repositioning children in a passive position as recipients of adults' care and tenderness, rather than as partners in a multidirectional relationship of mutual care and concern. I do not want to suggest here that the movement (or other intergenerational movements) should reject an affective or emotional approach or that adults should stop providing care and affection to kids. Rather, my intention is to caution that, in the context of intergenerational relationships, there is a tendency for discourses and practices of care, affect, and tenderness to be articulated and enacted as a one-sided rather than mutual relationship between children and adults. Adults are rarely discussed as needing to be treated with tenderness, and there is little sense that kids can provide care and support for the *colaboradores*. When these relations are primarily articulated in this way, with adults seeing themselves as caring *for* children, this can also replicate age-based hierarchies and potentially produce a paternalistic attitude toward children. While we should certainly be wary of pushing children to take on unwanted responsibilities as caregivers, I would like to suggest that there is some room for rethinking and reframing caring as a multidirectional dynamic within intergenerational relationships.

The pedagogical and personal relationships between adults and children raise important questions about adults' structured social responsibility for children's education and well-being, and the extent to which this responsibility can be reconciled with the ideal of intergenerational horizontalism. I've indicated previously that horizontalism does not have to mean that children and adults have identical roles in a relationship, or that children and adults are the same kind of social beings. Therefore, rather than ignoring this unequal dynamic of responsibility, we need to consider how adults' differential responsibility functions. For example, in some instances, adults' enactments of their pedagogical and caring responsibilities foster an increase in children's capabilities, as adults strive to transfer more autonomy and power to children over time. In other scenarios, the social prevalence of adults' responsibility for children can become a cover that is used to justify arbitrary acts of power and authority. While adults in the movement of working children consistently strive toward the former approach and attempt to mitigate and reduce the inequality inherent in their pedagogical relationships with the NATs, this remains an uneasy and unsettled tension.

The Movement as a Model for Intergenerational Politics

The intergenerational relationships created in the movement of working children are profoundly transformative for the NATs. Through the relationships with *colaboradores* as teachers, they develop new political vocabularies, learn to put their own lives in political and social context, and become confident in their ability to articulate their visions and desires for their communities and the world. Through their relationships with *colaboradores* as caregivers, they feel empowered, supported, loved, and listened to. This helps them to not only confront personal problems and challenges, but also to value their own voices and take action in their schools and communities. Through their relationships with *colaboradores* as friends and *compañeros*, and the processes of apprenticeship, they learn how to organize themselves and their peers, developing their skills for activism and collective political engagement. Further, in all of these relationships, they encounter adults who are pursuing, even if not always achieving, a more horizontal connection with kids, or a connection in which the adult seeks to reduce both social distance and arbitrary age-based authority. Having meaningful personal relationships, opportunities to learn new ideas and skills, and a context in which kids know that the adults believe in their capability and equality are three necessary ingredients for kids to feel like they can speak up, disagree with adults, ask tough questions, and actively engage in the political debate. Collaborative intergenerational relationships are clearly essential to kids' political empowerment and engagement.

The pedagogical and relational practices of *colaboración* give children the opportunity to develop political knowledge and skills that they actually use to amplify their power in the present. In this sense, it is very different from the many civic engagement programs that treat children as "citizens-in-the-making," where their political engagement is without real authority and is only practice for their adult future.[24] Working alongside adults, kids are able to plan events, organize press conferences, release proclamations, and lobby politicians. This is not unlike many examples of youth organizing in the United States, but it occurs here with younger children as well as teenagers. Instead of assuming that such programs and opportunities for engagement should be available only to teenagers, this movement highlights the possibilities for creating activist communities that also include children.

The pedagogical relationship between the NATs and *colaboradores* also models how to support children's development as political thinkers. First, this requires making significant time and space for kids to articulate their own experiences and to link those experiences to larger themes, concepts, and policies. Second, by using Freirian strategies and regularly articulating a belief in children's equality of insight, the movement has generated a context in which kids are able to ask questions, raise concerns, and consider their own viewpoints. The movement's pedagogy, along with the relationships of trust that undergird it, demonstrates a method for moving beyond tokenism and thin forms of participation. Children's councils, opportunities for "student voice," and other mechanisms of participation could be bolstered and strengthened by having both deeper relationships and more time for kids to learn, talk, and think together about a subject before being asked to speak publicly on that topic.

The practices of *colaboración* create a vibrant intergenerational culture where NATs are supported in the development of their political subjectivities, in their skill building, and in their personal lives. This affectionate and educational culture, combined with the discourses of *protagonismo* and intergenerational equality, encourages kids to become vocal, empowered, confident participants in the movement and in the wider political and social landscape. The movement generates incredibly positive and supportive relationships between kids and adults and creates a community where kids feel like they really matter. In this way, *colaboración* supports kids' outward-facing political action and social movement activity and prefigures a world in which kids are respected, valued, and treated as capable political subjects. As such, it provides a promising model for organizations, schools, or individual adults who want to facilitate and amplify children's political learning and political power.

"The Kids Are in Charge" but "Adults Talk Too Much"

The Everyday Dynamics of Age-Based Power

Riding on the bus through the dry and dusty coastal countryside, I was excited to be on my way to Ica, a medium-sized agricultural city about two hundred miles south of Lima, where I would attend a MNNAT-SOP regional assembly. Jhasmila, a member of the national secretariat for MNNATSOP, had been telling me for weeks about how she thought Ica was a place where the kids really lead the organization. She often referenced MNNATSOP-Ica as a model for how power should operate in the movement: the adults, she would say, "really know their role in Ica." For Jhasmila, this meant that the adults mostly stay out of the way, remaining in the background of the movement's political activities and discussions. Over the next three days, I came to generally agree with Jhasmila's assessment. The *colaboradores* provided a lot of logistical support, but only rarely spoke in front of the entire assembly. The gathering was organized, coordinated, and facilitated by a small group of teenagers who made up the regional coordinating body. These regional delegates, aged thirteen to seventeen, shepherded the group of fifty NATs from activity to activity, reminded them of the rules and expectations for behavior, and facilitated most of the discussions. They organized the teams for chores, including setting the tables, serving the food, doing the dishes, and cleaning the meeting space. They encouraged participation from the youngest children and took time to sit and talk individually with kids who seemed shy or less connected. Overall, the assembly highlighted the ways that more experienced NATs can take on significant power and authority in defining the movement's politics and culture, allowing *colaboradores* to step back and limit their influence.

Many experienced NATs and national leaders, like Jhasmila, argued strongly that kids should be the primary and dominant force in the movement. Expressing this idea in another context, Graciela said, "The good thing about the organization is that we are always questioning, always clarifying that the importance of the organization is what is happening among the kids, and that the kids are the decision makers in the daily life of the organization." And Yolanda, another national leader, told me, "It is our movement. We are the ones in charge." These teenagers prioritize children's ideas and leadership over and above that of adults, drawing on the widespread discourse in the movement that it is "kid-led." Or, as Elena put it, "When addressing the issues of childhood, it is childhood that should speak." This position goes beyond the concept of equality of insight, discussed in chapter 3, in that it suggests that kids not only have important things to say, but that their voices and ideas matter *more*—especially on the subject of their own lives. In this way of thinking, if the movement is to be truly democratic and respect kids' rights to self-determination, kids should be the primary forces shaping the movement's direction. However, there is an ongoing and unresolved tension between the idea that the kids should have *more* power in shaping the movement's direction and the pervasive narratives of the movement as a space of horizontal intergenerational dialogue and collaboration, where kids and adults share power equally and are both valued for their different contributions. This discursive ambiguity, the larger social context of age-based inequality, and the multiple roles of *colaboradores* discussed in the previous chapter combine to produce a complex field of power relations between children and adults.

The leadership of teenagers at the Ica assembly also draws our attention to the ways that age-based power (in the movement and beyond) should not be seen just through a binary lens that focuses on the adult/child comparison. This chapter therefore traces the micro-relations of age-based power in the movement, directly examining the power dynamics of the relationships between *colaboradores* and NATs, but also power among the NATs, who range in age from eight to seventeen, and who have widely varying years of experience in the movement.[1] Following Foucault, I treat power as "a mode of action upon other actions" that is relational and productive, not simply coercive. "It incites; it induces; it seduces; it makes easier or more difficult; in the extreme it constrains or forbids absolutely."[2] While other chapters have focused on the productive power of subject making—of defining children and adults as particular kinds of people, with particular capabilities and skills—this chapter focuses on how adults, adolescents, and kids enforce behavioral and social norms, organize and plan movement activities, and listen to one another as they make collective decisions. I take a sociological approach that explores the visible but often subtle enactment of political power and democratic governance in the movement. In doing so, I map how different movement practices contest or reinforce the accumulation of various kinds of power and authority in the hands of older individuals. Further, since one of the major social change goals of the movement is to prefigure non-hierarchical intergenerational relationships, this chapter also serves as an assessment of the movement's collective progress in this direction.

One of the critiques that has been made of the movement is that children are being manipulated and used by adults—that they are just pawns in adults' political maneuvers.[3] In response to this narrative of manipulation, defenders of working children's movements and children's activism in general sometimes bend over backward to argue that these spaces are entirely child-led and express children's autonomous and authentic perspectives. Power, in both of these accounts, is understood as a singular force that belongs to either children or adults. Both the detractors and supporters want to argue that one group is "in charge." In contrast, my approach does not catalogue power as a singular quantity or assess who has more and who has less; instead, it looks at the distribution and operation of different modalities, or different forms, of power in the movement. This includes disciplinary power, the power of speech, the power of influence that comes with the identification of expertise, and the authority of planning associated with formal leadership responsibilities. By offering a textured accounting of some of the central modalities of power at play in this space, I aim to move beyond the simplistic binaries that frequently characterize discussions of children's politics and children's power.

The Rules of Participation: Disciplinary Power in the Movement of Working Children

Setting and enforcing expectations for behavior are responsibilities that are often assigned to adults in intergenerational spaces. The movement of working children, however, actively flips this normative power dynamic. In the context of the movement, the NATs not only set all the rules and regulations for each other, but also, through the process of voting on *colaboradores*, reward or punish specific adult behaviors and determine which adults get to participate in which movement spaces. In regional and national assemblies, NATs elect the delegates for regional, national, and international coordinating groups *and* discuss and choose the *colaboradores* who will accompany these coordinating groups. At each assembly, the gathered NATs identify a list of key traits they think are important in a *colaborador*: humble, a good listener, responsible, caring, and so forth. Then they discuss the various individuals who have agreed to be nominated for a position, commenting on what they like and don't like about that particular *colaborador*'s style and approach. Finally, they vote, choosing the adult who they think is best suited to support the coordinating group and its work for the upcoming two-year period. While I saw this process unfold only once, at the Ica assembly, and it was fairly painless in that instance, many NATs told me that it can be very tense and uncomfortable for the *colaboradores*. Kids, they noted, can be pretty direct when talking about the strengths and weaknesses of each candidate. Luis, a *colaborador* with many years of experience, explained, "The kids can ask you to leave the movement, or they can say, 'Thanks, what you are doing is really good.'" Or, in Yolanda's words, "If we don't like what the adults are doing, we get to replace them."

In this practice, we can see one way that the movement seeks to increase children's formal authority in the movement—it makes individual adults' participation in some of the movement's key political spaces entirely contingent upon the kids' approval and acclamation. Adults whose behaviors do not measure up to kids' standards for a "good *colaborador*" are either asked to leave or simply not given key roles in the movement. Kids have the official and institutionalized power to determine the desired characteristics of their adult supporters and to evaluate and select their adult *colaboradores* on the basis of these characteristics. The election of the *colaborador* is one site where the organizational authority of kids is formalized, and is one of the most visible and ritualized examples of kids' decision-making power in the movement. It should be obvious that this kind of power is not common in intergenerational spaces: youth don't hire the staff for most community-based organizations that cater to them, and children don't get to select the mentors or tutors in their after-school programs. In most programs, adults select the children for inclusion, not the other way around.

The NATs are also entirely responsible for the systems of discipline and punishment of other children in the movement. At meetings and assemblies, adults sometimes remind kids to pay attention, occasionally separate kids who are being disruptive by talking or having side conversations, and intervene to stop various small fights between kids, but they don't mete out any kind of punishments. There are no detentions, no time-outs, and no extra tasks given for misbehavior. Juliana noted that punishing kids is outside the role of a *colaborador*. When I asked her whether she had ever seen *colaboradores* do things that she thought were problems, or incorrect, she replied,

> I've seen a *colaborador* who didn't understand their role, and who didn't get along well with a particular kid, and who tried to punish him. So I said that MANTHOC doesn't do this, we don't penalize, we teach. If you punish, you are not inspiring and motivating, and we don't want that in MANTHOC. These have been some of the worst *colaboradores* I've seen: ones who try to punish and not to educate.

Kids also take on a lot of the tasks of managing each other's behaviors: they shush each other when someone is having a side conversation, criticize latecomers, and call out individuals who have been shirking their tasks. In the Yerbateros house, there have often been problems with kids not attending the weekly assemblies. Assemblies are the very heart of the movement—they are what makes the space not just a site for social programming and support services, but an organization and movement of children led by children. So when kids are not attending the assemblies, they are not really participating in the movement. At two different assemblies, in two different years, the NATs decided that in order to better motivate their peers to attend the assembly, they would impose punishments on those who had unexcused absences. They decided to charge them a fine of three *soles* (approximately one dollar) and to prohibit them from participation in the house activities for the following week. While it was never clear to me whether the kids actually implemented this punishment, these practices position kids themselves as the arbiters of acceptable and unacceptable behavior in the movement, displacing some of this kind of authority from the adults in the movement, and thereby enabling mechanisms for rule enforcement without placing this burden on the intergenerational relationship. This allows adults and kids in the movement to have a relationship that is not tied to dynamics of punishment, while encouraging kids to feel responsible for and to each other.

In the movement of working children, the NATs have significant disciplinary power, determining who is included or excluded from certain spaces and collectively enforcing behavioral norms. For adults, this happens through formalized structures of critique and regular election procedures. For kids, this occurs primarily via the enforcement of rules and regulations for participation. However, the NATs' election of their own leaders and delegates, which I'll return to shortly, also provides an arena for rewarding and punishing certain ways of being and acting in the movement. Through these practices, the movement of working children clearly upends the more common intergenerational dynamic in which adults are the primary agents of discipline.

Voice, Dialogue, and the Power of Speech

Social movements are not just locations for interpersonal relationships; they are also essentially deliberative spaces.[4] Activists must discuss their visions and goals and make decisions about their strategies and tactics. In this context, questions about the power of speech are essential. While *colaboradores* and NATs both speak up and have voice in the deliberations and decisions in the movement of working children, there are clear differences in how their voices emerge. Adults and kids talk about how the movement is a place where "we respect the voices of each other," but the power of speech is experienced and deployed very differently by children and adults. Children's voices in all movement discussions are highly valued, but often have to be drawn out; adult speech, on the other hand, requires no encouragement and, despite *colaboradores'* explicit commitments to children's leadership, sometimes dominates important conversations.

The concepts of *protagonismo* and the movement's ideas about children's equality of capacity and insight, as well as the position that the movement should be kid-led, all lead to the frequent encouragement of children's speech. Vocal and talkative children are highly valued in the movement, and *colaboradores* and older NATs frequently try to encourage newer and quieter members to "be less shy" and "speak up more." Kids and adults talk about how participating in the movement is "a process," and that many kids start out "very quiet." Jhasmila noted that "at the beginning it isn't easy for the kids. . . . For them to begin to speak, to act in their communities, it sometimes takes a process of almost two years. . . . They have to be convinced." In order to facilitate this process, *colaboradores* and adolescents often directly encourage children to talk, articulating the movement's position on the inherent value of speaking. For example, in one meeting in which many of the kids were fairly quiet, Laura said, "I feel like some of you are not really participating. I'd like to see you ask more, push back against what I say, or against what Graciela says. We have to discuss. This space can be really rich. You need to take on more *protagonismo*." Or, in another instance, debriefing an international visit, Emilia reminded the Yerbateros assembly, "I know that it can be hard to talk in front of a group of people, but these people were other NATs, and this is something to work on, something to practice, to learn, to develop." *Colaboradores* are very clear that they expect and desire NATs to become more confident and outspoken—being an effective social movement participant, from their point of view, requires speaking up.

In addition to reminding kids that their voices are valued and directly inviting them to speak, many *colaboradores* have developed practices that foster children's participation in movement discussions and decisions. They often encourage children to speak up by asking *a lot* of questions. They'll ask informational questions about what kids remember from previous meetings or about upcoming events ("What did your base group do this past Saturday?" and "Where is tomorrow's workshop?"), theoretical questions that encourage the kids to articulate their own interpretations of movement ideas ("What makes a job exploitative?"), analytic questions about the subject of discussion ("What differences do you see in these two different laws about child labor?"), and personal questions about their own lives and experiences ("What things do you like about your work?"). Learning to ask good questions, rather than questions after which kids stare blankly at each other, is part of the process of becoming a more effective adult *colaborador*. These questions are designed to simply "get kids talking," a vital first step in the movement's construction of democratic, kid-led organizations. This first step is no small feat, given that many children are used to listening and following directions in both their homes and schools.[5]

Some *colaboradores* are also intentional in their use of activities that will help all kids express their ideas. For example, in one meeting, after a statement encouraging kids to speak up fell flat, a *colaborador* suggested that each kid write down a few ideas, then they would go around in a circle and share. The time to process and think and the very clear expectation of everyone's contribution led to a useful brainstorm and discussion. Similarly, in a meeting where adults were generally dominating conversation, a *colaborador* asked the facilitator to try a new strategy and have all the kids write their ideas about the strengths, weaknesses, opportunities, and challenges for the movement on pieces of paper, then to tape these onto the wall. This generated a rich conversation as kids then explained their ideas to each other. These kinds of mechanisms are quite successful at amplifying kids' voices, including the voices of kids who are often quieter in general discussion, but surprisingly, they were only rarely used. *Colaboradores* turn to them only when they notice that the kids are not participating fully or when they are concerned that adult voices are overwhelming a conversation.

A few features of the movement's structure and approach help explain the infrequent use of these pedagogical strategies for eliciting kids' voices. First, most *colaboradores* are volunteers, and this voluntary status clearly limits the amount of time that they are able to put into planning and preparation for each meeting or event. Setting up and developing a specific educational plan for each meeting takes more time than many *colaboradores* have to give. Second, *colaboradores* often do not think that it is their role to plan the meetings or to set up these kinds of mechanisms for participation. Rather, movement traditions and organizational regulations emphasize that kids should be in charge of the planning and facilitation of events and meetings. When *colaboradores* work with a few kids right before each meeting to make an agenda and plan out a process, they don't often have time to think through these issues, or are hesitant to make strong suggestions. Third, *colaboradores* are rarely trained in these kinds of concrete teaching tools and facilitation methodologies. Much of the training of *colaboradores* focuses on theories and concepts, encouraging them to see children as protagonists and to develop commitments to intergenerational collaboration. Trainings and workshops focus on the educational/political philosophy of the movement far more than on tools and strategies to use in meetings and activities. This approach goes a long way in transforming how *colaboradores* think about children, childhood, and work, and it is a key part of building the movement's culture of respect and care, but the culture and discourses of egalitarianism are not necessarily enough to reshape age-based power dynamics. Without the concrete pedagogical tools and strategies to encourage kids' participation, many *colaboradores* rely on the few (usually older or more experienced) NATs who speak up more readily, give their own ideas to get a conversation started, or spend substantial energy exhorting the quiet kids to speak up more.

The voices of NATs, while highly valued in the movement, often have to be explicitly encouraged and fostered. In contrast, adults rarely need to be invited to speak. Instead, some *colaboradores*, as several NATs and adults stated, "talk too much." According to Joaquín, "A lot of the time—how can I put this—the adults talk, blah blah blah blah, and they don't stop, and sometimes the kids get bored, or don't feel comfortable, and they know that this is our space." He went on to say, "Some *colaboradores* . . . go on for a long time without taking into account the fact that there are kids who also want to participate and that they are the ones who really should be participating." Yolanda agreed: "I've seen *colaboradores* who declare and proclaim a lot, and sometimes I don't like this." I also observed *colaboradores* who wanted to give their opinions on every discussion point, with some meetings feeling more like a debate between *colaboradores* than a conversation among the kid delegates. For example, in a MNNATSOP national meeting, the movement had an important decision to make about national structure and whether to maintain a national headquarters in Lima. During the discussion of this decision, I wrote the following field notes: "A *colaborador* suggests that they not make a decision right now, but simply discuss the various structural options and proposals. 1 more *colaborador* adds his thoughts and another asks a clarifying question about one proposal. A teen answers the question. 4 *colaboradores* then give their opinions on the proposal and the issues it raises for them." Adults clearly dominated that day's large-group conversation.

Such conversational domination by adults was not uncommon and can be seen as the result of the intersection of a few distinct factors. Adults, living in a society that generally values them and their ideas, feel far greater confidence in their voices than kids do, and, like other social groups with various kinds of privilege, are relatively quick to speak up when given an opportunity. Further, because the movement also articulates a belief in the value of intergenerational dialogue, not just children's leadership, adults feel empowered to express themselves in these spaces, knowing that their voices are considered an important part of the conversation.[6] Adults care deeply about the movement and want it to succeed, and this commitment encourages them to participate in order to strengthen the movement. But the dynamic of adults talking too much is also relational—the result of the relationships between kids and adults—not merely the actions of adults. Kids, despite the movement's explicit celebration of their voices, are far less confident in their contributions, especially when they first enter the movement. As Lili stated, "We are afraid that what we say won't be something important, or that someone else will say it is wrong." Therefore, kids often cede the floor to adults and don't speak, even when asked to give their opinions or encouraged to participate more. Rather than sitting with silence, adults tend to step in, so kids have found that it is often easier and more comfortable to simply be quiet and wait for the adults to talk.

Adults in the movement will acknowledge that they are talking too much, and many try to mitigate their influence by prefacing their commentaries with phrases like "just to add a little bit . . . ," "I don't want to take up a lot of space, but . . . ," "I just have a small question . . . ," or "I know that the adults are speaking a lot, but . . ." They also sometimes end with statements of humility as well: "This is just my opinion" or "The decision is yours." In one sense, all of these statements are an attempt to reduce the force of adult voice, to diminish its power in some way. However, they also enable continued adult commentary. This patterned behavior highlights how good intentions are not enough to interrupt adults' habituated speaking practices.

A few *colaboradores* have developed methodologies for reducing the power of their own voices (and, occasionally, those of other adults). One effective strategy I observed was focusing entirely on group process rather than on content. Ofelia, a *colaborador* with many years of experience, frequently stated that her task was to help the group to move forward in its decision-making processes and discussions, but not to contribute ideas. For example, in one meeting, before raising a question about the criteria they want to use to select future campaign activities, she said, "I have another question about how we are making this decision. This is my role." By focusing on process and form rather than the substance of the debate, Ofelia was able to make important contributions without trying to move the NATs in a particular strategic or political direction. Ofelia had created a role for herself in the group that allowed her to contribute and to add value to the movement, but that also defined clear limits for her contributions.

Enrique, as I indicated in the previous chapter, was also skilled at minimizing his own voice. He frequently did this by adding his commentary only after nearly all of the kids had shared their own perspectives or when he was directly asked. Enrique almost never presented ideas until the end of a discussion, and even then always did so with caution and without being forceful in his presentation. While other *colaboradores* sometimes used both of these practices, what made Enrique and Ofelia distinctive is that they both nearly always behaved in the same way in all meetings. Their consistency amplified the value of what were generally already quite valuable practices. As education scholars have noted, routines allow kids to focus on ideas and content, rather than requiring them to try to figure out the process and procedures of a given space.[7] Because Enrique and Ofelia almost always acted in the same way, in nearly every meeting, kids knew what to expect of them and knew that these two adults would not step in and speak up in order to direct the meeting. This then meant that kids, when interacting with these two *colaboradores*, knew that they had to take more ownership over their meetings. In contrast, while other *colaboradores* sometimes used the same practices, their inconsistency meant that kids could, when they wanted, step back and wait for these adults to take charge of the meeting.

A controversial strategy for amplifying kids' voices and minimizing the speaking power of adults involves separating the two groups. In 2012 I attended one of the last meetings of a group of national delegates for MNNATSOP—delegates who were very near the end of their two-year term. Then, in 2013, I attended one of the first meetings of the newly elected delegates. At the 2012 meeting, most of the work was done with the *colaboradores* and NATs working separately. Jhasmila, one of the teenage coordinators of the first meeting, was a strong advocate for giving kids their own space. She told me multiple times that adults intervene too much, forget their roles, and interrupt kids' decision-making and discussion processes. The solution she and her peers proposed was to have separate working groups, then to bring the adults into conversation with the kids after the kids had already developed their own positions. At the second meeting, with the new delegation and new leadership, Jhasmila's model of working separately was explicitly critiqued and abandoned. One *colaboradora*, Selena, discussed this with her mixed-age small group as they were developing the movement's strategic plan. She said, "Last year it seemed like when the *colaboradores* were present, the kids didn't really talk, so they wanted the *colaboradores* to be separate, in their own space. This year, it seems like you, the kids, are talking more, and we are all welcome to participate. We are all together much more, and there is more openness to participate together, all of us." Several NATs nodded in agreement and a few stated that they liked the relationship this year. Selena then went on to say that she understands wanting separate space because "it is still an adult-centric country, and society doesn't give you your space." These comments indicate Selena's, and the movement's, ambiguous position on the role of adults. There is a real desire to give kids space, to let them lead, and an acknowledgment that sometimes adults make that more difficult, but *colaboradores* also believe strongly in the value of adult involvement in the process. Dividing the kids and adults disrupts the movement's idealized claim that it has mastered intergenerational democracy and dialogue, but it also significantly increases the expression of kids' voices.

Adult conversational domination is not malicious or even intentional, and adults have important things to offer to movement discussions. But the phenomenon of "adults talking too much" can get in the way of the development of kids' voices and kids' confidence in their voices. Indeed, when adults "talk too much," the NATs never have to figure out what they think about a subject and what they want to say. They can return to the far more socially comfortable (and easier) habits of listening and following adult guidance. However, kids' silences should not only be read as a return to habituated passivity or a marker of their social marginalization. Rather, such silences also, at times, may be enactments of kids' authority via the power of refusal. To sit quietly or to not participate in the way that adults want can be methods for rejecting the adults' proposals and ideas. NATs' refusals and stubborn silences can themselves be forms of "participation" in the sense that they are enacting their authority and political will. Rejecting the incitement to speech, choosing not to participate in different activities, and choosing not to respond to particular questions can be a way that kids in the movement indirectly express their desires. As Tanya commented one afternoon, "The kids show their power sometimes by not coming to meetings, or by not participating in the things that don't interest them." We were discussing Flor's absence at an earlier planning meeting, and Tanya noted that she tends to skip things that don't speak to her particular concerns, and that this is her choice, and a form of having power in the movement: "When lots of kids don't come to a workshop on participatory budgeting, then we know they aren't interested and we should stop holding these workshops, or we have to do something else to make clear why this is important, to help them understand what it might do for them, or for the movement." Absences, silences, and refusals can certainly be a kind of power and influence.

Silence, however, can only do so much in the context of social movement deliberations and decision making. Indeed, while people make many important contributions to the movement that don't involve speech, from taking notes to making flyers to providing food for meetings, vocalizing one's perspectives to a group is an especially valuable and valued form of democratic engagement across multiple political contexts. And it is a form of political engagement that is deeply shaped by age dynamics. Notably, the power of speech comes fairly readily to adults. They are confident in their voices and often find themselves working (with various levels of success) to minimize their contributions to discussions. On the other hand, the youngest and newest movement participants need to be explicitly invited to participate in this way, and to be given time and space to develop their thoughts in advance of speaking. With this time and space, these younger and newer members sometimes can and do participate meaningfully in movement discussions. Adolescents and more experienced NATs also acknowledge that it is easier for them to contribute. However, unlike adults who tend to identify a need to constrain their own participation, the more experienced (usually older) NATs continue to see their voices as central to the movement: they are, after all, the regional and national delegates. While both adults and adolescents are cognizant of their own potential dominance and want to facilitate a more egalitarian space, age clearly remains highly relevant to how individuals in the movement participate, as older individuals more easily access and deploy the power of speech. All of this suggests that intergenerational activism that includes children, adolescents, and adults requires substantial attention to the power dynamics of habituated patterns of speaking and silence.

The ideal of an egalitarian intergenerational dialogue between children and adults is a persuasive vision for many advocates of children's rights and youth empowerment.[8] However, it is also an ideal that is incredibly difficult to implement, given our dominant intergenerational habitus. And, as the adult attempts to explain their interventions above suggest, the ideal of dialogue can also sometimes function to enable and justify a recentering of adult power and voice. In this way, a call for intergenerational dialogue can paradoxically undermine the goal of challenging age-based hierarchies and creating more horizontal relationships.

Being Heard and Having Influence

Different voices, of course, are also heard differently. Simply expressing oneself does not automatically mean being listened to, and how someone is heard within the movement of working children remains at least somewhat tied to their age and movement experience. On the one hand, the narrative that the movement "belongs to the kids" encourages particular attention to children's voices and encourages adults to be better listeners. From this perspective, kids' voices are prioritized, with the youngest children often having significant authority in the eyes of adolescents and adults. However, at the same time, kids and adults often see adult voices as particularly "expert" or more knowledgeable, and are therefore inclined to listen more carefully to their ideas and arguments.

Adults and kids in the movement generally agree that adults need to learn how to listen to kids. Listening to kids is not necessarily part of adults' habituated behavior, and requires an adult to "control your impulses," in Elena's words. Further, as Alejandro Cussianovich elaborated at a national gathering of adults and kids involved in municipal CCONNAs, "We are learning how to listen to you. . . . We have to learn how to understand what you say . . . and what you say is often less than what you feel, right?" Here, Alejandro suggests that listening to kids and truly hearing what they say require adults to develop a new skill set, to hear beyond the kids' words to their deeper meanings. Juan also noted that "the important thing for a *colaborador* is to listen. . . . You may say, 'no, but this,' and then realize that this isn't your role anymore. You have to listen. It is hard, but . . . I keep working on it." Although it may not always be easy, listening to kids is seen as an important task for the *colaborador*.

Listening to kids is vitally important for *colaboradores* because they need to be able to truly hear kids' desires in order to help them implement their projects and goals. Adults need to listen carefully to kids in order to know how best to support them in the movement. This can be seen in Juan's statement that the "primary role of the *colaborador* is to always listen to them and to transform what we hear into something that will support them, always in a horizontal way." He suggests that *colaboradores* should listen to kids in order to synthesize kids' voices and to help provide a framework for seeing the patterns in kids' opinions. Here, listening is seen as a key task for a *colaborador* not so that they empower individual kids to speak up and help them to develop their confidence in their voices, but rather so that the *colaborador* can effectively support the movement, based on what they hear children say. This approach to listening highlights the fact that the adult listener, the *colaborador*, is supposed to both act and speak based upon what he or she hears from the NATs, whose voices are primary and highly influential in setting forth an agenda for action.

Although adolescents are usually more confident in their self-expression, younger kids' voices have a great deal of symbolic power and authority in the movement. Given the movement's discourses about childhood and the value of children's insights and children's perspectives, when young children speak up, everyone listens enthusiastically and attentively. A key part of the movement's ideology is the commitment to being "kid-led," not just "adolescent-led." Therefore, the statements of the very youngest kids are highly valued and given substantial attention. For example, in a workshop on the revisions to the national law on children and adolescents, a young boy of about eight who was quick to raise his hand was called upon more frequently than any other individual, and everyone loudly praised his contributions and his engagement during the evaluation at the end of the day. Paying particular attention to the contributions of the youngest encourages these kids' ongoing participation and gives them substantial influence in movement decisions, but it also visibly demonstrates the movement's self-professed commitment to the belief that chronological age does not define one's ability to contribute excellent ideas and valuable insights. Listening carefully to the very youngest is both an actualization of intergenerational democracy and a performance of that democracy.

While kids' voices have a great deal of power on the basis of claims to authenticity and direct experience,[9] many kids also note that they listen carefully to the opinions of the adult *colaboradores* because they "know more." As twelve-year-old Andrés said, "Their opinion is important to us—they support us and they have more experience, they are older already." This view is supported by some of the ways that adults present information, giving NATs an "orientation" to the subject at hand. Adults often have information to offer to the kids in the movement and will share this information at the very start of the relevant discussion in group meetings and assemblies. Sometimes this information is highly practical: for example, the organization has been asked whether it wants to send representatives to an upcoming event and the *colaborador* has information about both the event and the invitation. In other cases, the information being shared is far more conceptual, as when *colaboradores* talk about the goals of a particular campaign, or the various players in an upcoming legislative debate. In both of these instances, the *colaborador* knows more about a given subject than the kids and that information needs to be passed along for the group to move forward effectively in its work. The practice of *colaboradores* providing this kind of information and orienting the group is entirely understandable given that *colaboradores* often have longer histories in the movement that give them particular insights and have institutional positions that make them the recipients of pertinent information from other organizations.

However, this practice also sometimes positions adults as not just useful sources of information, but also as the primary sources of *knowledge* within the group, or as expert guides. It is this practice that leads kids who are newer to the movement to say, "*Colaboradores* orient us, respect our opinions, tell us what is good, and tell us what is bad." Or "They let us know what we are talking about, why we are talking about it, and what are the important things to focus on. They tell us what we should do." The practice of adults "orienting" kids to a subject sometimes leads kids to see adults' voices and adult knowledge as more important and more relevant than their own ideas. Movement materials are careful not to position adults as "experts," but, despite adults' desire to not be treated as expert voices, many kids continue to view adults as more knowledgeable, giving their words more authority. Their voices, even when they are less frequent, are still given significant weight due to the widespread belief that "adults know best."

One way that people in the movement try to limit the influence of adults is through the idea that adults can suggest things and can "orient" the NATs, but they do not have official decision-making power. Marco used a common phrase in the movement to articulate this distinction: "Adults only, as we say, have voice but they don't have a vote. On the other hand, we have voice and we have a vote. They are there to orient us to what options we can choose and which we can't. We are the ones who decide." Here, Marco suggests not that adults listen to kids and then work with kids' own ideas, but rather that they present options and ideas for kids to choose between. Or, as one of the adults, Juliana, described it, "We give them various orientations, various reflections, and after the decision, how it seems or doesn't, and they make their own conclusions." According to these individuals, adults suggest, provide frameworks for thinking, respond affirmatively or negatively to kids' decisions, but, in the end, the decision still belongs to the kids themselves. In order to reconcile the powerful role of adult voice in a movement that loudly states the democratic value of being kid-led, these movement participants emphasize the formal decision-making power of the kids and the absence of that formal power in the hands of adults through the idea that adults "don't vote." However, there are rarely actual votes in most movement meetings, and this framing understates the substantial informal power of adults' suggestions and orientations. By relying on the distinction between voice and vote, movement participants are able to minimize, or avoid fully confronting, the substantial influence of adult voices in what they often describe as the children's movement.

Some NATs, however, especially those who have more years of experience in the movement, try to articulate a limit on adult influence that is much more specific and stronger than the voice/vote framework. For example, Graciela gives adult voice a fairly restricted place in the movement: "The *colaboradores* have an important role in the organization as well because while we are the ones who suggest things, and we are the ones who decide, the *colaboradores*, a lot of the time, with the decisions we make, they help us make them better, more clear, more coherent, more concise." In her opinion, adult voices are not there to orient or introduce options but are primarily used as a complement, or an additional resource, to improve the already formulated position of the kids. Adults should add, but they should not be central to the making of decisions. Unfortunately, Graciela's view here is somewhat less common, and the NATs and *colaboradores* rarely talk directly about the implicit power of adult "orientation" and "guidance," or about the subtle power dynamics that emerge based on differences between how adults' and kids' voices are heard and treated in the context of the movement.

By identifying adult voices as still powerful in the movement of working children, I do not want to suggest that kids are being directed by adults or that adults are running the movement and simply using kids as window dressing. Kids' voices and opinions are absolutely vital to movement decisions, and there certainly are times when they disagree loudly and fervently with the ideas of adults, especially around how to organize particular events. For example, when planning a children's rights festival, Rosa, a *colaboradora*, and Marco had a disagreement about the inclusion of an *hora loca*, or crazy hour with costumes and music, at the end of the event. Marco was clear that this would be too chaotic and that the event should be "fun but also somewhat serious, and so we should definitely not do this." In planning this event and many others, the NATs did not simply give in to adult voices, but were comfortable resisting and disagreeing with their *colaboradores*. Thus, while adult voices may be influential, they are not determinate, and kids continue to make the movement their own.

In thinking about the question of influence, a dynamic unique to age-based power begins to emerge: the complex but intractable relationship between age and experience. On the one hand, children's ideas are treated as important and are influential in the movement because of their present-day experiences: they know what it is to be a child right now. On the other hand, adults' contributions are valued because of their many years of experience with the movement and with political action. Both of these kinds of experience are seen as producing knowledge and as generating particular types of expertise. But knowledge that is generated over time, which is knowledge more often held by adults, is more highly regarded in the larger social context. Therefore, this dominant view of expertise filters into movement interactions, with some kids still valuing adult perspectives over the knowledge and ideas of their peers.

The Power of Formal Leadership and the Age/Experience Conundrum

The tangled relationship between age, experience, and notions of expertise emerges even more strongly within another modality of power in the movement: formal leadership responsibilities. Leadership in the movement is generated via processes of annual or biannual elections, and those elected as regional, national, and international delegates take on significant authority in movement planning and organization. For example, delegates are very actively involved in setting the agendas for every meeting and event. For the Yerbateros assemblies, this meant that the base group's regional delegates would arrive an hour before the assembly to work with the *colaboradores* to plan the meeting and how they would organize each activity and discussion. For regional planning meetings, the agenda was more often discussed at the very start of the meeting, with all the NATs and *colaboradores* present adding items for consideration. Determination of the day's priorities, and therefore the movement's direction, are made in these intergenerational conversations. The NATs who participate in these decisions are the delegates, who all have at least two years of experience in the movement. As each delegate becomes more experienced in agenda setting, individual NATs take on more leadership and guide these decisions, while adults frequently try to step back.

In addition to setting the agenda for a meeting, delegates usually work with *colaboradores* to organize the political education activities of the movement. They discuss workshop goals and methodologies together, as well as the specific pedagogical strategies of educational components of assemblies and meetings. For example, when planning the workshop about the potential changes to the Código, the kids in the RedNNA discussed the need to have small groups analyzing each section of the law, in order to give everyone time to think about some of the details. The delegates play a key role during these workshops and discussions, helping to add more details and analysis to the contributions of NATs who are newer to the movement. Political education is thus not just something accomplished by *colaboradores*; kids also teach each other the movement's ideas and perspectives.

The structures and rules around electing delegates generally lead to the consolidation of this power and authority in the hands of adolescents, rather than younger kids. The requirements for election as a delegate at each level mean that it can take several years of participation before an individual reaches the national coordinating body. Each base group is encouraged to elect delegates every year who help to coordinate base group activities, working with the *colaborador* to guide the base. In MANTHOC in Lima, these delegates are also generally the ones who represent their base at the regional (Lima-wide) coordinating meetings. But in MNNATSOP, a distinction is made between delegates, who are elected by their bases, and *dirigentes*, or leaders, who are elected at regional gatherings to represent their base on the regional coordinating body. These *dirigentes* are also referred to as regional delegates (in line with the language of MANTHOC), and they must have at least one year of experience as a delegate before their election. The regional delegates of both organizations meet in regional planning meetings and have responsibility for the movement's regional actions and agenda. Regional delegates could, by regulation, be as young as nine years old, but in practice most are at least twelve. Much as the regional assembly must elect and approve each base's regional delegates, the national assembly must approve each region's proposed national delegates. National delegates must, according to movement policy, have at least two years of active participation in the movement as a whole and either be, or have been, a regional delegate. This means that they could, in certain circumstances, be as young as ten, but most are at least thirteen when they are elected. Terms are for two years, which means that any individual who goes up for election must be under the age of sixteen so that they do not age out of the movement before their term is up. Therefore, the movement's structure leads to a strong concentration of twelve- to sixteen-year-olds in the movement's regional and national leadership.

Although the movement defines these requirements predominately around years of experience rather than chronological age, the two are not entirely separable. The time it takes to become sufficiently "experienced" to take on greater leadership means that these positions are rarely held by the very youngest kids. At the MNNATSOP-Ica regional assembly during which regional delegates were being elected, I observed the complex ways that kids drew on their understandings of the interplay of age, experience, and capabilities in order to explain their decisions and votes about who was "ready" to be a regional delegate. Chronological age continued to matter in these discussions in ways that undercut the movement's argument that age does not define one's abilities.

The election of the regional delegates was preceded by a session during which the entire assembly (approximately fifty kids) evaluated each delegate. Each group's base and regional delegates were asked to come forward, one by one, to stand and receive feedback. Rodrigo, who was facilitating this portion of the assembly, explained that this was "so that we can use these comments to grow as delegates and improve in our roles." Many delegates of every age were complimented for being friendly, collaborative, responsible, and participatory. The younger delegates were praised for being enthusiastic, creative, or energetic, but were sometimes told that they were "not participating much" and that they were "shy," but that "this shyness is common when people are new and I hope that when she gets more comfortable she will participate more." Or, in another case, "He is shy, but I think all of us in our first *encuentro* were shy like this, so I want to encourage him to become more active." Such comments hoping for greater participation in a young delegate's future set up these younger delegates as still being early in their process, suggesting that they do not yet have the "experience" that leads to a more participatory and vocal subjectivity. In contrast to this type of commentary on younger kids, the adolescents who were described as "quiet" were not generally framed as "shy" or "still learning how to participate," but were instead told by their peers that they needed to "take on more responsibility" and step up more to meet what was expected of them. Older kids were either praised for being exemplary protagonist

NATs or criticized for not fulfilling their commitments and "being distracted" by other things in their lives.

These narratives about age and experience have an important impact on organizational power and who is actually elected to various positions. At the Ica event, a twelve-year-old girl and a fifteen-year-old boy were both criticized during the evaluation period for being distracted during the *encuentro* and for not always participating. The critique of the boy, however, focused more on the need to meet his obligations. He was told by several other regional delegates, "You need to fulfill more of your responsibilities. We are doing too much of the work for you, and you are not taking on your fair share." On the other hand, the critique of the younger girl emphasized that she has to grow up a bit more in the movement. The twelve-year-old was put before the assembly as a possible regional delegate, but was not voted into the position by the assembly. She was told that she needed to keep working more for her base, to develop more, that she is not yet ready for this responsibility, but that they hope she will work hard this year and take the feedback she has gotten so that she may be elected as a delegate in the future. Clearly disappointed at the lack of confidence in her abilities, she began to cry. These critiques, and their outcomes, can be quite difficult to hear. The fifteen-year-old, on the other hand, was reelected to his position as a regional delegate, despite the very similar behaviors during the assembly. When he was reelected, he promised he would "try to be better, to be more committed, to be more of a protagonist." His age, I would argue, led the kids to a different interpretation and analysis of the same behaviors, and in the process gave more movement authority to adolescents, rather than younger kids. While the twelve-year-old girl was told she needed to grow, the assembly gave the older boy the benefit of the doubt, believing he could live up to their expectations.

The critiques offered to delegates of different ages suggest that kids themselves treat age as a relevant factor in analyzing each other's potential leadership. They may frame younger delegates' actions as resulting from a lack of experience, but do not make this critique with older kids, even if those older kids may, in fact, also be new to the movement, as was sometimes the case. Older kids are expected to be more responsible, more focused, and more participatory by their peers of various ages, no matter how much (in)experience they have. In contrast, younger kids' quietness or distractedness is usually explained by their inexperience, rather than by their age, allowing movement participants to continue to argue that kids of all ages can be participatory leaders no matter their age—they just need a bit more experience. Age, then, matters in what the kids say about each other, but is also simultaneously denied as being significant for identifying leaders. The dual frameworks of experience and age thus work together and are each drawn upon for different purposes.

Adolescent NATs sometimes express concerns about the fact that older members dominate the official leadership of the movement. They would often seek to demonstrate their commitments to the ideal of intergenerational democracy through a critique of spaces that they perceived as being unjustly exclusionary on the basis of age. For example, at a national meeting of MNNATSOP delegates, the group was discussing some of the challenges in the movement's structure. Katy, a teen girl, announced to the room that she wanted to add something important to the conversation. She stood up, straightened her shoulders as if to take up more space than her tiny five-foot frame, and said, "We are all adolescents here in this room. Where are the kids? There should be kids as national delegates!" Moisés, one of the other delegates, responded, "It takes time to become a national delegate. The criteria in the movement for becoming a national delegate require some time at each of the various levels, so it is really difficult to have kids in the national committee." Katy was clearly not satisfied with this response and continued to look skeptical. One of the national *colaboradores* suggested that they could change the rules and require that all elections of delegates include 50 percent adolescents (usually understood as those over the age of twelve) and 50 percent kids. A few of the other teens nodded at the idea, but no one really took up the conversation, and the group moved on to other topics. From my perspective, one reason they didn't continue to discuss the subject is that it is incredibly difficult to reconcile the desire for younger children's full participation with the reality of the time it takes for people to develop into national leadership. There is no solution to this problem and so it is referenced regularly, but never resolved.

The invocation of the problem of a lack of children's leadership also serves important performative functions for adolescents. When Katy argued that there should be more kids in the national coordinating committee of MNNATSOP, she had also been trying to make a different point about the exclusivity of having a headquarters in Lima. It is possible that she was, in this instance, using the symbolic power of being concerned about the younger kids' participation in order to gain greater authority for herself and her faction in the main discussion about the headquarters. In this case, there was no rationale presented for the need to be more age-inclusive in organizational leadership and she did not press the issue when the group moved on and returned to the topic of the national headquarters.

In contrast to Katy's abstract expression of the value of the youngest children, NATs in a meeting assessing the strengths and weaknesses of the RedNNA explicitly articulated reasons to seek more formal leadership from younger kids. Graciela, the fifteen-year-old undisputed informal leader of the organization, presented her view that the network needs to include younger kids because their inclusion would give the group greater continuity: "If there are more *niños*, they have time in this space to develop and learn, and then they can be here for more years, helping continue the campaigns and projects for longer." She also argued that younger kids have their own distinct perspective and that they add more "creativity" and "energy" to the group. In this instance, Graciela provided a rationale for seeking more balance of age and experience in the organization. And, unlike the MNNATSOP example, the discussion of the problem was held in a space that included both kids and adolescents and was partly intended to encourage more participation from the younger members of the group. Here too, however, no substantial action was taken to ensure that this rebalancing of power would occur. In each of these examples, adolescents invoke narratives about the importance of younger children in order to reinforce claims about the arbitrariness of chronological age as a marker for insight and expertise. But, despite these narratives, older and more experienced kids tend to have significantly more formal authority and official movement responsibility than their newer (and younger) movement peers. Teenagers sometimes identify their additional power compared to younger kids as a problem for the movement, but they are also able to justify this accumulation of power and authority; they are not "in charge" because of their age, they argue, but simply because of their additional experience.

The patterns of formal authority of more experienced NATs in the movement suggest that intergenerational activism should be seen not as a dualistic space made of young people and adults, but as involving a whole array of people of different ages, with different levels of experience. Age and experience are related, but not identical, and should be considered and analyzed both in relation to one another and separately. Children and young activists are not necessarily inexperienced, but their age is still important to how they are treated by their peers and by adults, and plays a role in how their experience is understood. Further, the particular position of adolescents in the movement shows how children, when they begin participating in social movements at a young age, can become highly skilled organizers by the time they are twelve or thirteen years old. These young people draw on their years of experience as well as their social proximity to younger children as they take on leadership and make important decisions about movement activities, projects, and future directions. And, notably, adolescent leaders lay claim to their authority in the movement by emphasizing their status as NATs and as children; these leaders are also the most likely to push back vigorously against adults who they think are talking too much or taking up too much space.

However, individual NATs cannot hold this formal leadership power for very long. Movement regulations are very clear that one cannot be a delegate after one's eighteenth birthday, meaning that many national delegates serve only one term. Further, depending on one's birthday and its relationship with the two-year election cycle, NATs can age out of leadership positions at sixteen. Some of these former delegates who are not yet eighteen still stay very active in the movement, while others reduce their participation slowly. But in either case, at eighteen, an individual is no longer a NAT and must transition to becoming a *colaborador* if they wish to continue to be involved in the movement. At this time, there is a sharp break in their power and authority, as they are expected to step back from their outspoken leadership and to begin to listen more, taking on the new role of *colaborador*. On the one hand, this profound break in roles and responsibilities is somewhat arbitrary: the teen is not, after all, particularly different before and after their eighteenth birthday. On the other hand, this dividing line between kid and adult requires older teens to confront their increased power, accumulated over the years by way of both age and experience, and to figure out how to then give up that power and authority in order to keep the movement "kid-led" and pass responsibility along to the next generation of NATs.

This transition, of course, is not smooth or easy. As teens move from delegate to *colaborador*, they often struggle with the meaning of these roles and the challenge of changing their behaviors in the movement. Young adult *colaboradores* experience difficulty learning to not speak for the movement and to listen instead. As Juan described it, "In one minute you are there and everyone has to consult with you, and you are used to giving opinions. . . . Everyone used to listen to you and now you have to listen, but sometimes you might say, 'yes, but this,' and that isn't your role anymore." For some youth, making this transition to *colaborador* requires time away from the movement. Several young adults told me that they didn't feel "ready" to become a *colaborador* right away, so they took a year off from movement activity in order to more fully separate from their previous roles and responsibilities. Juliana described how "generally you have to have a break because sometimes when we finish being delegates and we are in charge of the organization, sometimes we feel like we are still the participants, even though now we are not. So, to accomplish this process, I spent a year away from the organization. I would come by the house, check on the groups, but I didn't have a direct role." Taking a break allows the youth to let go of his or her sense of control over the organization and to learn to trust others with its leadership. Juliana told me that not everyone does this, but that she thinks it is a good practice. Another young woman, Faviana, sought the same kind of distance by moving from her base group to another base. She said she felt she needed to move because the kids in her base "knew me as a national delegate. They knew me as a representative of the organization and they thought I would continue to represent the organization, and so I didn't want to work with this group, I wanted to work with a different group." She suggests here that if she had not switched groups, her original group would continue to look to her to lead and to provide direction. This suggests that the transition requires changes on the part of the newly adult former leader and on the part of the other kids. In order to change her role, Faviana had to change her context.

The challenge of learning to constrain one's participation is substantial. However, this challenge is easier for those adolescents who already, in their later years in the movement, began to focus on encouraging the participation of younger kids. Notably, the practice of encouraging the voices of younger NATs seemed to be far more common among the teenage girls than the teenage boys. For example, when I visited the Surquillo base group, the oldest participant, Lili, who was just twelve at the time, ushered all of the kids into their seats, gathering them around the table, and then invited them to introduce themselves to me. She facilitated the conversation, asking each individual to share their name and their work with me. When one of the youngest girls whispered to Lili that she wanted Lili to introduce her instead, Lili replied, "No, I'm not you—go ahead, you can talk." In my fieldwork, Lili was just one of a group of girls who were diligent in their attempts to slowly step back more within their base groups as they began to age, helping to foster the voices and leadership of younger participants. Their male peers were often very encouraging and enthusiastic about the participation of the youngest kids, but seemed less attuned to the amount of time and space that they themselves were taking up in meetings and events. Girls were often more self-aware and thoughtful about their own role in the movement and their need to transfer and share power in their base groups as they prepared to "age out" of leadership. The fact that this more inclusive mode of leadership was more common among girls highlights the gendered dimensions of leadership styles, and serves as a reminder that attempts to bring forward the voices of one marginalized group can also reproduce a different social inequality, as other less powerful individuals choose to step back to make space, while the most socially powerful group continues to dominate. Teenage girls' tendencies to reduce their own contributions and encourage the voices of younger NATs sometimes allowed teenage boys to take up far more space in movement discussions.

The teenage girls were generally more reflective about the amount of power and influence that they gained over the course of their participation in the movement, and then worked to reduce that authority. Therefore, over time, they were acting in ways that were more and more similar to *colaboradores*. For girls, age-based power seemed to be treated more as a continuum rather than simply a matter of the NAT/*colaborador* and child/adult binary. By seeing themselves as having more social power than younger kids, they also saw themselves as having a responsibility to minimize the effects of that power in the context of the movement. Their male peers, on the other hand, did not do as much work bringing forward younger children's participation, instead con-

Figure 5.1. Adolescents play a key role in the movement, often helping to bring forward the voices of younger NATs as well as taking on significant leadership and authority. A teenager and a younger child may frequently co-present information, as is happening here. Photo courtesy of Movimiento de Adolescentes y Niños Trabajadores Hijos de Obreros Cristianos—Nacional.

tinuing to develop their own individual leadership skills and capacities. They also seemed much more likely to understand themselves as *not* having age-based power in the larger society and as therefore being in the same position as younger children. This binary understanding of age-based power and their tendencies to focus on their own leadership as delegates meant that young men really confronted and reflected upon their accumulated privilege and authority only when crossing over into the category of adult.

Unlike many other kinds of inequalities, the marginalized position that comes with childhood is temporary, so individuals have to, at some point, acknowledge that they have left behind that position for the more privileged one. This is one of the distinctive elements of this particular form of alliance across difference: individuals' relationships to the categories of child, youth, and adult change over time. These transitions can provide an opportunity to reflect on the workings of age-based power. For delegates, having the experience of holding political power as a child and learning to cede some of this particular power may be a challenge, but it also gives them the chance to reflect on their own adulthood and carefully consider how they will interact with children as they age out of this category. The dynamics of how adolescents accrue and then let go of formal power and leadership in the movement of working children productively draws our attention to how age-based power cannot and should not be thought about in binary terms, with adults as the "haves" and children as the "have-nots."

Cataloguing and Disrupting Multiple Modalities of Age-Based Power

Challenging Assumptions about Childhood

The practices I've outlined here fundamentally disrupt the often taken-for-granted assumption that adults should be "in charge" of intergenerational spaces, or what I have named the power assumption. Kids and adolescents in the movement of working children are clearly powerful actors. When given an opportunity, children as young as eight will gladly and effectively take on a variety of roles and responsibilities within activist spaces. They collectively regulate the movement's social norms, reward and punish certain kinds of behaviors, plan and facilitate events, and participate actively in movement discussions. While adults may sometimes "talk too much" and kids may sometimes return to their intergenerational habitus of listening and seeking guidance, kids are always encouraged to share their ideas, disagree with adult opinions, and question adult authority. And, in many instances, they do speak up and articulate strong opinions. Younger children's voices are taken very seriously as participants strive to demonstrate their belief in equality of insight, and the pre-teen and teenage delegates in the movement play key roles in setting agendas and making movement decisions. In some ways, the movement is able to effectively prefigure the intergenerational social relations it would like to see in the wider society: adults and kids frequently listen to each other and engage in meaningful democratic collaboration and dialogue. Looking at this landscape of power dynamics, this case clearly demonstrates that children and adolescents can enact political power and authority in intergenerational social movements. Relationships between children and adults can certainly be more equal, or more horizontal, than dominant practices. Adults' power, then, should be something to examine and consider, rather than something that is assumed as inevitable.

An analysis of the power relations within the movement of working children also productively undermines the assumption of a binary difference between the categories of child and adult. Adolescents clearly mediate and complicate this binary as they access and deploy certain modalities of power in the movement based on their in-between positioning. Of course, the binary assumption has always been troubled by the very existence of the social categories of adolescent, teenager, and youth, which make clear that the adult/child distinction is not sufficient for organizing age-based power in social systems.[10] The binary logic of adult/child sits in constant tension with the linear logic of developmentalism, which uses a range of chronological ages as standards for determining specific rights, responsibilities, and access to resources: you may work at fourteen, drive at sixteen, vote at eighteen, and so forth. But rather than taking adolescents' key role in intergenerational activism as support for these kinds of age-based distinctions, we can also use this example to think more critically about *both* of these logics and the categories they produce.

The adolescents in the movement of working children, as a liminal group, clearly complicate even the movement's own binary distinction between NATs and *colaboradores*. They have greater access to some forms of power than many of their younger peers, and they also take on some of the roles of *colaboradores*, encouraging and facilitating the participation of younger children. Sometimes the teenagers identify themselves primarily as *niños trabajadores*, while in other moments, they find utility in describing themselves as *adolescentes*. This flexibility, in which they position themselves as simultaneously children and not children, enables these teenagers to play a mediating role in the movement. Instead of seeing the adolescents in the movement of working children as naturally more "mature" than their younger peers, or as having crossed various developmental milestones that allow them to accomplish particular roles and responsibilities, we can also interpret their distinctive role as the result of their location within a particular social category that is understood as a bridge between childhood and adulthood.

The Persistence of Age-Based Power

By distinguishing between multiple modalities of power, rather than treating power as a singular force, this chapter identifies which forms of power children and adolescents deploy with relative ease, and which forms of age-based power require more effort to disrupt. In this way, it helps make visible the sticky spots, or the places where challenging age-based power is more difficult. The NATs embrace their responsibility for selecting *colaboradores*, setting rules and norms of behavior, and regulating and rewarding particular modes of interaction. They also quickly take up the authority and power that come with event planning and agenda setting. However, intensive political deliberations remain more challenging for many NATs as they continue to lack confidence in their voices despite significant encouragement, and adults continue to dominate some key discussions. Good intentions, caring relationships, and rich discourses of children's *protagonismo*, equality, and horizontalism are not enough to interrupt the far more common patterns of intergenerational interaction and the deeply habituated power relations that shape these conversations. Many adults and kids revert back to the more common habitus in which adults speak and children listen, which is then justified by the movement's discourse of intergenerational dialogue and collaboration. Patterned and power-charged interactions rooted in a culture of adult dominance and children's marginalization do not simply vanish from this space, but continue to shape it in subtle and not-so-subtle ways.

Kids and adults are both habituated to their inequality and to the idea that age equals wisdom, knowledge, skills, and authority. This is what makes any kind of prefigurative politics difficult: in order to prefigure a new world, you have to unlearn the old ways. The prefigurative space of the movement is not separate or isolated from the larger contexts of people's lives. It does not entirely escape the current reality, but remains imbricated in existing social structures of power. A key point here is that age-based power is produced and defended not only by adults, but also by children and adolescents. We can see this in the ways that they question their own ideas, in how they assume adult expertise, and in how they interpret the behaviors of twelve-year-olds differently from those of fifteen-year-olds, allowing for the consolidation of leadership in the hands of teenagers. Age-based power persists not just because adults benefit from it and find it difficult to renounce or let go, but also because children and adolescents are habituated to it and therefore also perpetuate it.

The Movement as a Model for Intergenerational Politics

An analysis of age-based power in the movement of working children highlights several strategies and methodologies that can amplify and increase children's power in organizations and institutions. By electing their own adult supporters, children in the movement play a key role in determining the norms and expectations for adult behavior. They are also able to set up systems of mutual responsibility and discipline for each other, shifting disciplinary power away from adults. The formal leadership, planning, and decision-making responsibilities of the NATs also help to shift power toward younger individuals, even when "adults talk too much." These institutionalized practices offer an alternative model for children's organizations, institutions, or any space that aims to be "child-led" or even "child-centered." While there are certainly difficulties, as I've outlined above, the movement of working children is an innovative intergenerational space where young people deploy substantial power and authority.

Disrupting hierarchy requires ongoing discussion of the often subtle dynamics of power and social difference, and engaging directly with this process is one way that scholars can contribute to social movements. Ethnographers in particular can help visibilize the multiple modalities of power that are at play in a movement so that the activists involved can deepen their conversations and create organizations that better reflect their political desires. We can offer language and tools for thinking about how it can be the case that "the kids are in charge" *and*, at the same time, "the adults talk too much." By identifying and analyzing various modalities of power, adults and kids can discuss what should be done about these power relations in specific contexts and conditions. What kinds of power should adults deploy? What kinds of power should they work harder to cede to the kids? What forms of power seem to be accruing to adolescents? How, exactly, is a particular modality of power being enacted or shared in any given space at any given time? Developing a shared vocabulary around these powers can allow movements, organizations, and groups to more fully imagine and therefore pursue intergenerational horizontalism.

6

Struggles for Children's Dignity and Citizenship

Transforming Individuals and Institutions

In July 2014 the Bolivian Legislative Assembly passed a new national law on children and adolescents that removed the internationally accepted prohibition on children working below the age of fourteen, replacing it with a more nuanced approach that allows children from ages ten and up to work in certain contexts and conditions, with protection from violence and exploitation.[1] This new law was the result of significant organizing and activism on the part of the working children's movement in Bolivia, most especially UNATsBO, the Union of Working Children and Adolescents of Bolivia. When the law was originally proposed in December 2013, it had simply outlawed work for those below the age of fourteen. But working children in UNATsBO and other organizations protested this proposal, arguing that work is a vital part of their lives and that it should not be criminalized. They emphasized that they, as working children, should have a central role in the crafting of any law related to child labor. In La Paz, their protests were met with significant police violence and garnered national attention as images of children being beaten and teargassed spread rapidly through both traditional and social media. They continued to mobilize and managed to get an important meeting with President Evo Morales, at which they discussed their perspective on the issue and alternatives to a policy of complete elimination. After the meeting, Morales spoke eloquently about how making child labor illegal simply makes it clandestine and therefore worse for children and offered his support for a different approach. UNATsBO had produced its own draft proposal for a new law in 2010, and its draft law was now finally presented to the Legislative Assembly, which then went through a process of revising the original code, with the continued input and engagement of working children. The final outcome was a compromise that took working children's perspectives into account and created an unprecedented new legal approach to the issue of child labor.

Bolivia's new law very quickly became a significant international news story and reveals some of the challenges that working children's movements face as they seek to decriminalize children's work. The media coverage of this event highlighted how difficult it is for journalists to question their commonsense notions about child labor as always already a moral outrage. The image of working children as pure victims—as tragic innocents exploited by unscrupulous adults—was hard to reconcile with the widely shared pictures of these same children sitting with their president, smiling and telling him that they want to be able to keep their jobs. Working children's stories about why they like their work and why they want to work substantially call into question the frequent association of the term "child labor" only with its worst and most brutal forms. In response to this surprising image, media reports tended to either downplay the working children's voices or leave readers with a muddled picture, referencing both the UNATsBO kids who wanted to keep working in family businesses while attending school and kids who work in the dangerous conditions of Bolivia's mines, often without making any distinctions. They also did not usually discuss how the new Bolivian law would treat these two groups of working children very differently, allowing the former while still outlawing the latter. In the Global North, the media narratives consistently criticized the law as if it were utterly unthinkable for children's work, in any form, to ever be morally justified. Even supporters of the law were often presented as defending it as a "necessary evil" that makes sense only in the context of Bolivian poverty, rather than considering the possibility that some forms of work might benefit rather than cause harm to children.[2] The BBC referred to the law as "a huge step back" and a *Forbes* commentator wrote, "Of course we all agree that child labor is undesirable."[3] Further, criticisms of Bolivia's new law tended to downplay UNATsBO's involvement, or, if they mentioned the UNATsBO youth, expressed concern that these children were perhaps manipulated into their political claims, or simply moved on quickly from the children's own arguments about the validity of their work to quote adult experts who warned against work for children.[4] The UNATsBO participants were thus dismissed as not knowing what is in their own best interests.

Children's advocates from around the world had a more mixed response to the law. A handful of individuals and organizations that had long-term engagement on this issue took a supportive approach, pointing to the fact that the law would provide more protections for working children and highlighting the social scientific evidence that the abolitionist approach to child labor was both ineffective and sometimes even harmful to children. They also noted that this new law was the result of children's participation in the policy-making process, something that children's rights organizations have regularly advocated for in the decades since the passage of the UN Convention on the Rights of the Child. Those supporting the law emphasized the groundbreaking fact that the government had shown serious respect for working children's political capacities and perspectives, and sought to amplify working children's voices. Others, however, were quick to denounce the new law despite the fact that the policy changes to which they objected came from affected children themselves. It seemed that the anti–child labor position of many of these organizations and individuals outweighed their commitment to incorporating children's perspectives and listening to children. UNATsBO's successful bid to transform the Bolivian law so that it would better meet their needs pushed up against the limits of mainstream international children's organizations' interpretations of children's participatory rights, suggesting that some adult-led organizations would support children's political participation only to the extent that children agree with those organizations or have only minimal actual impact on the policy process. When working children disagreed with adults in the international and institutional children's rights domain, their participatory rights were pushed aside and replaced with claims that these adults know what is best for them.

International political institutions also responded to the Bolivian law. Members of the European Parliament raised questions about whether or not this law put the country in violation of the regulations required to maintain preferential access to European markets.[5] The International Labor Organization also made official statements decrying the Bolivian law and urging the Bolivian government to immediately replace it with a law that met the standards of the Minimum Age Convention.[6] And, when working children entered both of these institutional spaces to explain their position and express their views, they had almost no real political impact, either speaking to those who already supported them or being dismissed as nonrepresentative and insufficiently informed about the issue.[7]

Bolivia's new law was widely celebrated by other working children's movements, which sent messages of congratulations and solidarity to their peers. But, for many of the Peruvian activists, the international resistance to this legislative transformation also highlighted the profound difficulty of transforming child labor laws. When I asked NATs and *colaboradores* whether they thought this meant they might also see some policy shifts, they were quick to point out the significant differences between the Bolivian political context and the Peruvian one. Ollanta Humala, they noted, was no Evo Morales. The new policy in Bolivia was a win for the movements internationally, but no one seemed to think that it would necessarily make the fight any easier in Peru. Alejandro Cussianovich emphasized that it would be helpful to see the results of the new law, and that they might be able to use that as evidence in their case, but he remained skeptical about Bolivia's example making a major impact on the Peruvian policy, especially given the amount of international resistance that emerged.

The Peruvian movement of working children has concrete policy goals—most especially the decriminalization of children's work—but its impact and influence should not be assessed only in relation to policy outcomes. The movement also seeks to improve the daily lives of individual working children, transform widespread ideas about childhood, expand children's place in Peruvian politics and society, and create new forms of intergenerational relationship. As Enrique described MANTHOC's goals, "The objective is the development of the *protagonismo* of NATs for the exercise and defense of their rights, and for them to improve the conditions of their work, health, education, and quality of life." Beyond the individual participants, many of the movement's objectives focus on transforming how Peruvian society understands and treats working children. Joaquín, a fifteen-year-old national leader, said that the goals of the movement are "always the promotion and defense of the rights of children and adolescents in general, but particularly working children. We are always trying to get people to know that our movements exist and to value our work and to not see it as something bad." Lili, thirteen, noted at a workshop for new regional leaders, "One of our objectives is to be recognized in society as subjects of rights, and to be able to say what we think." As Luis, a *colaborador* with many years of experience, stated, the goal is "to defend the rights of children, for children to be recognized as citizens, and for the society to have a new vision of childhood." I followed up by asking him what it meant for kids to be recognized as citizens, and he replied, "People who have rights, who have responsibilities, who participate, who are not excluded, who are not marginalized from social processes." Participants speak often about wanting to change perceptions of children and wanting to replace the paradigm of children as "objects of protection" with one of children as "subjects of rights." And, as I've discussed throughout this book, they seek to prefigure more horizontal and egalitarian intergenerational relationships in hopes that their example will expand beyond the movement.

Peru's movement of working children has been an active political and organizational presence in parts of the country for forty years. This longevity is astounding, particularly if we consider it in relation to other youth formations, many of which have a tendency to be short-lived, and in relation to the Peruvian context, in which many leftist organizations struggled to survive during the period of conflict between the government and Sendero Luminoso. But the stability or longevity of an organization is not the ultimate goal of social movements. In addition to organizational continuity, what has the movement of working children accomplished in this long history? To consider this question, we have to be attuned to the movement's multiple goals. Sociologists Elizabeth Armstrong and Mary Bernstein write, "Society is composed of multiple and contradictory institutions with each institution viewed as mutually constituted by classificatory systems and practices that concretize these systems. Movements may target a diverse array of institutions (both state and nonstate), and seek both material and symbolic change."[8] This chapter therefore looks outward from the movement to explore its multiple and diffuse effects: how it has improved the lives of individual NATs who participate and how it has influenced the politics and culture of childhood in Peru. In addition to individualized transformations, the movement has played a key role in the formation of new spaces for children's political inclusion, has influenced some schools and schooling practices, and continues to try to shift the policy debates on child labor. Further, children and adults who participate in the movement certainly come to see childhood in a new light and take that perspective with them into other spaces in their lives, including family relationships. While acknowledging the difficulty of making definitive causal arguments about the impacts of social movements,[9] I trace the movement's multiple lines of influence, exploring how it has affected individuals, policy, government opportunities for child/youth participation, schools, and families.

Individual Transformations

Unfortunately, there are no systematic longitudinal data on the benefits of movement participation for the individual NATs who become involved. However, I saw significant shifts in some young people as I continued to return over multiple years, as individual NATs became increasingly confident in their ideas, skills, and potential contributions. *Colaboradores* speak often about how they have seen many NATs grow and flourish in the movement. There are countless stories told by movement activists about NATs who found important support, resources, and community in the movement. In interviews, many NATs also described how the movement had boosted their confidence, helped them face personal difficulties, and given them a sense of their dignity and value in the world. My own observations were that the children who participate in the movement are exceptionally expressive, direct, and proud of their identities as workers. They are comfortable speaking in public and more than willing to share their thoughts and ideas with adults. They are empowered by the movement experience, and are strong advocates for their rights and the rights of their peers.

Over the past forty years, hundreds of NATs have developed their political leadership skills as delegates in the movement of working children. Tania Pariona, recently elected to the Peruvian National Congress as part of the Frente Amplio, is the most obvious example of the movement's influence on these young people. An indigenous thirty-two-year-old woman from Ayacucho, Pariona began her community work as an active member and then national leader of MNNATSOP, an overarching umbrella organization for many working children's groups. She went on to get a degree as a social worker and then spent many years working for the Centro de Culturas Indígenas del Perú (Chirapaq), organizing programs for youth and promoting indigenous rights.[10] Today, in Congress, Tania Pariona continues to emphasize her pride in her indigenous heritage by being sworn in in Quechua in addition to Spanish and by wearing traditional clothing.[11] She also continues to speak out for the rights of children as workers and against an abolitionist approach to child labor.[12]

While Tania Pariona is the most visible example of the political leadership of former organized NATs, she is not the only example. *Colaboradores* with many years of experience in the movement have a variety of anecdotal tales of former national and regional delegates who have gone on to become important figures in their communities, either through participation in government, social movements, or community organizations. And, as Norma, one of the *colaboradores*, told me, even former participants who don't have these kinds of roles are confident in themselves and in their ability to speak out about issues that matter to them. She said, "They tell me, thanks to MANTHOC, I can go out and speak in public. I am not embarrassed. . . . I can say what I think." The movement has been a significant source of political learning, socialization, and empowerment for many working children.

In addition to developing their skills and confidence for organization and community participation, the movement has helped working kids to stay in school and go on to develop professional careers. Joaquín, a young man from a very poor family in a rural area outside Piura, came to Lima when he was fifteen to serve as a national delegate for MNNAT-SOP. In Lima, he attended a better school than he would have had access to in his hometown. He also improved many of his academic skills, including writing and public speaking, through his role as a leader of the movement, and then went on to attend an international school and eventually was given a scholarship to study at a small liberal arts college in the United States. Anabella, building on her experience in the movement and the opportunities it allowed her to connect with international visitors and even travel to Japan, was accepted to a good public university in Peru, where she is studying to teach English. Movement participants also have many stories of individuals who have gone on to have a great deal success as social workers, lawyers, teachers, and other professionals, and have thus experienced substantial economic upward mobility while also continuing to have a commitment to helping others via their work. The movement helps poor and working-class children enter a range of social and political locations, helping them see beyond their immediate surroundings and imagine other futures for themselves, and it gives them the support to get there. In contrast to the claims that child labor inevitably leads to low human capital and ongoing individual and national poverty,[13] these examples make clear that working children can grow up to contribute economically and politically to their communities, their nation, and the world.

The movement of working children substantially improves children's experiences in the present by giving them warm meals, relationships with caring adults, knowledge about their rights, and valuable tools for addressing problems in their lives. And there is a strong indication that participation in the movement improves working children's lives over the long term. These signs of positive individual impacts are also consistent with the social scientific research on the effects of participation in youth activism, which has found that such participation improves young people's civic skills and knowledge, psychosocial well-being, sense of efficacy, and academic achievement.[14]

The Policy Agenda

The movement of working children has not always focused its political attention on child labor law and policy. Indeed, this was not an issue for the movement in the early years, when children's work was more culturally normalized and not yet explicitly illegal. It became much more pressing in the 1990s and 2000s, as the Peruvian government ratified the UN Convention on the Rights of the Child, drafted its first national law on children and adolescents, and began to interact more with the International Labor Organization's International Program on the Elimination of Child Labor (ILO-IPEC). The UN Convention on the Rights of the Child, in article 32, states that children have a right to "be protected from economic exploitation and from performing any work that is likely to be hazardous or to interfere with the child's education, or to be harmful to the child's health or physical, mental, spiritual, moral or social development." While some have interpreted this article to mean that children should not work, others, including the movement, argue that it is not opposed to children's work per se but rather to only some kinds and conditions of work.[15] The contention between those who seek to abolish child labor and children's work, and those, like the movements of NATs, who seek to protect children from exploitative conditions and improve their work lives has defined child labor politics for decades.[16] While the ILO and other transnational political institutions sometimes soften their language and imply that they are primarily interested in the most harmful forms of work, they have tended to encourage interventions and programs that center around ending child labor, rather than regulating children's work and work conditions.[17] Throughout the 1990s and 2000s, movement participants struggled to challenge their criminalization both nationally and internationally. They worked with similar movements around the globe to try to get their voices heard at ILO conferences and gatherings, wrote proclamations and declarations, and pointed out what they saw as the deep flaws in the ILO's approach.[18] However, during this period they made little headway. Young workers spoke, but it didn't seem that the ILO or the Peruvian government was really listening.

The movement continues its ongoing contention with the international and national abolitionist legal framework, but it does this with somewhat less intensity than in the 1990s. Movement members write proclamations outlining their critiques of new ILO documents, reports, and conferences and put forward annual proclamations against the World Day against Child Labor. They also directly confront specific instances of abolitionist rhetoric in the national government. For example, in 2012 the Ministry of Labor produced and distributed stickers that said, "We don't want children working, we want children studying." These stickers appeared all over Lima, on buses and school bulletin boards, and in market stalls and restaurants. Angered by the ways that this sticker implied that working children don't also go to school, MN-NATSOP teens wrote a letter to the ministry outlining their critiques, and they were invited to have a meeting with a ministry official. At that meeting, they shared statistics on the high percentage of working children who are also in school and talked about their own experiences incorporating both activities into their lives. The ministry official said she "didn't know this" and apologized for the sticker, noting that it was not their intention to upset working children. But, when describing this meeting to me, the kids shared that they didn't think it was going to change any future publications or materials. They were glad that they raised the issue with the ministry and felt that they needed to continue to question these false claims about them, but they were not particularly confident that these actions would have long-term impact.

Kids and adults in the movement are increasingly coming to terms with the difficulty of influencing child labor policy. In a workshop for *colaboradores*, Nico, who works at IFEJANT, described what he saw as the major barriers to improving child labor law and policy in Peru. He noted that it is very difficult to withdraw from the ILO conventions because they have been ratified by Congress and because the public discourse is that children should not work and anyone who says otherwise "is described as being a bad person: this is framed in simple moral terms in the media, with the abolitionist perspective presented as common sense, and our ideas as obviously wrong." The dominant image of the working child is always thin, sad, dirty, and tragic, and when that is the image, how can anyone say they are in favor of children working? He also reminded the group that the current discourses on child labor claim that working children are "limiting national development," and that "working children are both a result of and a cause of poverty." The movement's perspective, he said, "is a marginal countercurrent" and not widely accepted. He was clear that this did not mean that he thought the movement should give up on trying to influence policy on this issue, but simply that it needed to be realistic about the difficulty of changing the laws. In a similar instance, the national leaders of MNNATSOP acknowledged the serious challenge of impacting the ILO. They were discussing their strategic plan and goals for the next ten years, and one of the teens suggested that they "want the ILO to include us in their meetings and decisions." A girl responded, "There is no way that will happen in the next ten years," and the group went on to discuss whether this was still a useful goal, or whether they should think about seeking recognition and inclusion in other spaces instead. Impacting the ILO and national child labor policy via the Peruvian Código feels like a losing battle to many in the movement, but they also don't want to give up entirely on this key part of their agenda.

The movement has not just sought to impact policies related directly to child labor; it has also been deeply engaged in a prolonged policy debate regarding revisions to the national law on children and adoles-

Figure 6.1. Two girls participating in the movement's delegation at an annual May Day march for workers' rights. Their hand-drawn signs ask for their work to be valued and respected and for their rights as children and as workers to be recognized. Photo courtesy of Instituto de Formación de Adolescentes y Niños Trabajadores.

cents (Código de los Niños y Adolescentes). For the entire time of my fieldwork, movement participants were responding to various versions of the new law. This included numerous addresses to Congress, several press releases and media campaigns, as well as a variety of public events. The movement challenged versions of the law that limited many children's rights by making them subject to the oversight and permission of parents, that did not prohibit humiliating forms of punishment, that removed the children's councils and suggested councils of adult advocates instead, and that replaced "niñas y niños" with just the "generic" masculine term. In the discussions of the Código, the movement has mostly left aside the issue of the minimum age for work, focusing instead on preventing these regressive and reactionary changes. The movement has also successfully advocated for Peru to ratify the Third Optional Protocol to the Convention on the Rights of the Child, which sets up an international complaints procedure for violations of children's rights. These

policy goals are concrete, specific, and from the perspective of the movement, more winnable, while major change on the decriminalization of
child labor seems further out of reach.

State-Based Participation

Despite the strong political differences between the working children's
movement and the Peruvian government on the topic of children's work,
movement participants are very influential in government-sponsored
spaces for children's participation, most especially the municipal Consejos Consultivos de Niños, Niñas y Adolescentes (CCONNAs) that
have developed in different cities in the past ten years. The CCONNAs
each have slightly different structures, but, in general, these consultative
councils are spaces where children who represent organized constituencies (mostly school councils and community organizations) are elected
by their peers to serve an advisory role in municipal government and
to give their opinions on issues of local concern. The government officials charged with facilitating these spaces recognize the expertise of the
movement of working children, seek out guidance and advice on how
to organize children from the adult *colaboradores*, and encourage the
leadership and active participation of the NATs because they are a constituency of children with already developed political skills. Organized
working children have become a vital part of the landscape of municipal children's politics and participation, despite the government's official
position criminalizing and criticizing their work.

In Lima, several working children's organizations are on the advisory
board for the CCONNA. *Colaboradores* attend regular meetings with
the staff member in charge of the CCONNA and with the elected youth
leaders to help them strategize and to organize educational and training
opportunities for the youth delegates. MANTHOC and IFEJANT *colaboradores* facilitate workshops for the CCONNA youth. The first national
gathering of CCONNAs was partly organized by MANTHOC, with
Ofelia taking a major lead in coordinating the event. Indeed, the press
release from that gathering had four logos at the top of it: the municipalities of Lima and Miraflores, Trabajo de Crecer (a European Council–
funded project that worked closely with MANTHOC youth for several
years), and MANTHOC, and Alejandro gave the keynote address. In

addition to working directly with the CCONNAs, IFEJANT *colabora-dores* have provided trainings for district and city officials on children's participation and *protagonismo*.

Organized NATs are also vital to the functioning of the CCONNAs and other state-based participatory opportunities. Graciela served as one of three moderators/facilitators for the national gathering, Marco was part of the four-person coordinating council for Lima's CCONNA, Rosario was asked to be a youth representative to advise her district's (adult) council, and working children in MNNATSOP-Ica played a key role in bringing youth into participatory budgeting for that city. Adults and NATs from the movement of working children are located at the very center of these participatory spaces. While the policy differences between the NATs and the government might lead us to expect working children's marginalization, instead I found that they were fully integrated, and were often the formal and informal leaders in this terrain.

Government officials in these participatory spaces engage in complicated discursive maneuvering to navigate this potentially conflict-laden situation. For example, in my interview with the national director general of children and adolescents, she was generous and congratulatory when talking about how the movement has cared for and empowered working children, noting that the "organized children have more information, they know the arguments to make for their participation, and whether good or bad, or whether we agree or disagree, at least they have this. . . . They also have a lot of wonderful fluidity and comfort expressing their ideas." However, while praising the movement for how it has encouraged children's participation and helped them to develop participatory skills, she also criticized the movement for being "dogmatic," indicating that the NATs should consider rather than dismiss abolitionism. Thus, the movement and the children in it are recognized by government actors for the quality of their participation but not for their analysis of child labor and children's work.

Government officials usually simply ignored or skirted around the contentious issue of children's work when they were present in these spaces for children's participation. But, while they did not talk about children's work, they did invoke many other ideas and concepts that are part of the movement's discursive framework, including the idea of children's *protagonismo*. At the national CCONNA gathering, both the mayor of Miraflores (a wealthy, upscale district in the larger Lima metropolitan area) and the mayor of Lima spoke to the delegates. As I listened to their comments, I was struck by the depth and sophistication of their understanding of children's participatory rights. The mayor of Miraflores, Jorge Muñoz Wells, spoke eloquently about how important the CCONNAs are not just for children's rights, but as "an ideal, a model of a space where all can be included." He emphasized his interest in "listening to your valuable messages and excellent ideas," and said that children are "not a promise for the future, but also a reality today," echoing movement claims about children as protagonists in the present, not just the future. Even more notable was the speech of Lima's mayor, Susana Villarán, who articulated her "commitment to the *protagonismo* of children and adolescents." She noted that children "should be taken into account in all the policies that affect you, and that is everything: all the policies, not just school, not just the law on children and adolescents. We need your voice in all things." This idea that children can speak to more than just "children's issues" moves beyond many understandings of youth councils and their purpose and suggests that children are not merely a specific special interest group with only limited knowledge.[19] It is not surprising that politicians at these events celebrated children's participation, but I was surprised by how nuanced and well developed their remarks were, and by the fact that they drew on language that reflected the ideas of the movement of working children. These mayors were not simply reiterating the typical stock phrases about children as the future of democracy, or the importance of them practicing for adult citizenship. They talked about children not as citizens-in-the-making, but as citizens-in-the present.[20]

The movement of working children has clearly had an impact on the Peruvian political discourses of childhood and children's rights and is well regarded by a variety of political actors for its ability to support the development of children's knowledge and skills for participation. However, this respect for *some* of the movement's ideas and activities does not necessarily generate the more radical social and political changes that NATs and *colaboradores* hope to see in Peru. Mayors and other political officials acknowledge the educational value of the movement of working children for children's individual growth and development, but consistently reject its larger claims and goals. They celebrate the idea of children's participation but do not actually listen to the content of working children's arguments and contributions. When kids talk about their participation in these government spaces, they note that they are glad to have these spaces but also frustrated with their experiences of not really being heard.

Many of these frustrations were expressed at a meeting that organized children had with Rosa María Ortiz, the special rapporteur on the rights of children for the Inter-American Commission on Human Rights in 2013. At that meeting, kids from a variety of different children's organizations who were involved in the CCONNAs noted that "the authorities don't take us into account even though there are CCONNAs," and "they should come to our events, actually consult with us more." The kids felt that the CCONNAs had potential, but that they were mostly just for show, not giving them much real power or authority in their districts or cities. Commissioner Ortiz responded thoughtfully to these critiques, saying that "the CCONNAs were the result of a lot of struggle, and now we need to improve them. I understand that you do not feel heard. There should be a commitment to improve the mechanisms of communication between the CCONNA and the authorities. I would like to know what the adults from the municipality are going to do to address this." She turned expectantly to the representatives who were there from the municipality of Lima's office for children's rights. One of them defensively replied, "We are learning; it is a new process." The other jumped in: "There are problems with the budget, problems with the schedule—the kids can't meet during the day when the authorities want to meet. We do need to do more to connect the kids directly with the authorities." Commissioner Ortiz again nodded, and said, "The municipality has to do this. Could we have a commitment from you to hold a meeting about how to improve the inclusion of the voice of children and adolescents? And I should receive a report on how this meeting went." Both municipal officials nodded, and the kids were visibly pleased at this support from the commissioner.

In addition to the specific complaints about the limitations of the CCONNAs, NATs complained about how, even when they interact with actual decision makers, they are dismissed. Dayana, for example, shared a story with me about how when the youth in Villa El Salvador asked a local official for help setting up a meeting with the mayor, he told them, "The mayor deals with adult problems, not kids' things." Dayana continued, "It is really hard because we don't vote, so they don't listen to us." Similarly, describing a meeting at the Congress in which kids from the RedNNA presented their positions on the new Código, Patricia complained that "the president of the Congress said he would support us, and he gave us some books about the constitution, but he didn't really seem to be paying attention to us, or listening to our words—he was doing lots of other things." And kids from Ica who had been involved in participatory budgeting described how when they would speak, people focused on the fact that it was kids speaking, not on what they were saying: people would come congratulate their teachers or *colaboradores* for them being so well-spoken, but only rarely did they engage with their ideas.

Each of these stories indicates some of the limits to children's political power in these state-based opportunities for participation. Kids note that they are treated differently from adult political actors—they are dismissed as irrelevant, celebrated for being involved but not taken seriously, treated as subjects to be educated on how government works, or pushed aside into their own isolated gatherings. While adult social movements are also often frustrated in their attempts to get officials to hear them, the dynamics of this are distinct in the case of young people, who find themselves ignored partly on the basis of their age. The adult officials and politicians that kids encounter in these spaces, while they articulate support for children's right to participate, do not necessarily treat children with respect and dignity as capable and knowledgeable political actors. In contrast to movement spaces, the spaces of political engagement organized by the government do not feel collaborative or horizontal, and participation can feel a lot like tokenism.

These frustrations, however, do not mean that these spaces are without their value; the NATs' engagement in these programs has accomplished several positive outcomes. In particular, the biggest and most concrete successes have come in the city of Ica, where MNNATSOP kids waged a successful struggle to be fully included in municipal participatory budgeting processes. Participatory budgeting in Ica, as in many other cities in Peru, is organized in such a way that the delegates to the democratic budget assemblies and meetings are representatives of organizations. MNNATSOP advocated for children's organizations to be included in the list of organizations that could send delegates to the budget process. Through participatory budgeting, MNNATSOP in Ica has had several project proposals selected for funding, including the creation of a physical center for working children to go for community, support, and training.

Participatory spaces also serve to make working children visible to a wide range of political actors and institutions. Because many of the spaces are representative, with children representing their larger organizational constituencies, the NATs regularly identify themselves as working children, and as part of working children's movements. In doing this, they raise awareness about the movement, share their perspective, and claim legitimacy and authority for what is often a highly stigmatized identity. The hope, then, is that when policy makers are considering the issues of "child labor," they may think about these working children whom they have encountered in the CCONNAs or participatory budgeting processes. Working children's presence becomes normalized, and working children are able to challenge the perceptions of them as tragic, victimized individuals who do not want to work. Through participation in these spaces, NATs claim public visibility and legitimacy, reminding officials that when they speak about "child labor" they are also speaking about working children—real people with real lives. Thus, even if these spaces have led to only a few concrete improvements in the lives of working children, and even if they are frustrating and tokenizing, they are also opportunities for working children to assert their value, dignity, and rights and can help change perceptions of working children.

Kids and adults in the movement are currently putting a lot of time and energy into the development of these participatory spaces, but they have lingering questions about whether or not such participation is worth the time it takes away from other forms of action and organizing. At a discussion on this topic in 2012, Gustavo, an international visitor and friend of the movement, encouraged the participants to reflect on "how we want to relate to the state and why there is now this interest from the state in children's participation, and how to manage being in these spaces of power." His perspective was that "you have to enter them, but you must reflect. Our politics are often rather vague: social justice, equality, anti-capitalism, but when you enter relationships with the state it is not just with these abstract ideas; we need concrete positions, policies." He also noted that "we also need to remember that being involved in the state is not our ultimate objective: our objective is social justice, social change, changing power relations. This participation with the state can be a tool for that, but it is not that itself." In 2012 that conversation mostly resonated with the adults—many of the kids were lost or bored. But by 2015, kids and adults in the movement were asking these questions of themselves and each other, and I heard many more debates on the value of these state-based participatory spaces. On the one hand, the creation of new spaces for citizens' participation, including children's participation, has opened up a set of political opportunities, and the movement of working children sees these spaces as potentially useful sites for increasing the influence and visibility of working children. On the other hand, many of their experiences in these spaces suggest that they are not always effective and that they can be sites of co-optation and tokenism.[21]

Schools

Schools are obviously key institutions in children's lives, and so improving the lives of working children also means improving their lives at school. A great deal of children's time is spent in school, and school experiences have a profound impact on not only children's educational outcomes, but also on their overall development and life trajectories. Further, teachers are among some of the more significant adults in children's lives. Nearly 80 percent of children in Peru attend public schools, while 20 percent are enrolled in private schools,[22] but these private schools are of widely varying cost and quality.[23] Overall, the Young Lives research project has found that poor children, rural children, and indigenous children generally have access to less effective schools and schooling opportunities and that the Peruvian school system "tends to reinforce socioeconomic inequalities rather than diminish them."[24] According to many in the movement, working children and their particular needs are not well addressed in Peruvian schools, and working children face stigmatization and harsh criticism from teachers for spending some of their time working. In addition to the challenges that poor and working children face due to structural inequalities in the educational system, teaching styles in Peru tend to be authoritarian and hierarchical, with not infrequent use of physical punishment as a form of discipline. Vanessa Rojas argues that "the application of discipline in public schools in Peru has been mainly focused on obedience and controlling the body."[25] She finds that physical and verbal violence from teachers is naturalized in many schools in Peru and that students expect an authoritarian culture in which they must follow the rules without question and be obedient and compliant subjects. Clearly, this is a mode of intergenerational interaction that sits in stark contrast to the one promoted by the movement of working children. Given the importance of schools and these profound disagreements with contemporary Peruvian educational practice, it is not surprising that the movement of working children has sought to impact Peruvian schools as part of its agenda of improving working children's lives and fighting for their dignity and *protagonismo*.

One way that the movement has sought to improve working children's educational lives is through direct and close relationships with a handful of schools. MANTHOC has itself opened and operated a few schools, including one in Lima. Located in Ciudad de Dios, one of Lima's busy, sprawling, poor neighborhoods, the school provided an education for working children who have left other, more traditional schools for various reasons.[26] According to the teacher, Pedro, the kids who attended the MANTHOC school were in much more difficult situations than many of the other children in the movement. They dealt with more family violence, alcoholism, absent parents, and intense poverty. The MANTHOC teachers sought out neighborhood kids who were not attending any school and invited them to attend this school, telling them that it was different from the traditional schools that had not worked for them.

The time I spent at the school in 2012 made some of those differences clear. In the mornings, the kids trickled in at various times because, as Pedro explained, many of them were helping their families bring things to the nearby market. He said that too many schools don't understand this and just shut and lock the door at eight, so any kid who is late can't attend school. As each child arrived, Pedro asked them how they were doing, and whether everything was all right. They each responded with some bit of information about the last day's activities or experiences. In this way, the student-teacher relationship was more personal and less hierarchical than a typical Peruvian classroom. The students used the informal *tú* form when speaking with their teacher, and they all interacted casually and with a great deal of affection. Pedro dressed in jeans and a school sweatshirt, rather than the suits and ties I often saw on other male teachers. Pedro's teaching was interactive and driven by discussion with the students, and the school highlights learning through work. Several afternoons a week they have "workshops" where they produce various items to sell: cookies, empanadas, greeting cards, and so on. In the workshop I attended on chocolate cookies, they talked a lot about where chocolate comes from and how it is made, and they practiced their math skills by multiplying and dividing the recipe into different size batches. I also went with one ten-year-old girl to the market to pick up the needed ingredients. She navigated easily through the streets to the correct stalls, gathered what the group needed, and collected and organized the receipts. After making the cookies, the kids were then each given a portion to sell. The MANTHOC school's pedagogical model explicitly enacted movement ideas about intergenerational relationships as well as the potential educational and economic value of children's work, and it provided a direct educational service for kids who had been pushed out of more traditional schools.

In the 1990s and early 2000s the school was thriving, with several teachers and classes, and a structure of student organization that connected to the movement. The kids in the school made up several base groups, and the little, brightly painted school was a vibrant center of children's activity in the neighborhood. But when I met Pedro in 2012, there was not enough money to fund the school and pay teachers. He was the only teacher still working there, and was getting paid only about 50 percent of his previous salary. The medium-sized building, with space for about six classes, was holding just his one multi-age class of about ten kids and MANTHOC's national offices. The paint was fading and the few kids and adults seemed to rattle around the too-large, once active and colorful space. When I came back to Lima in 2015, I was saddened but not surprised to learn that the school had been shuttered when Pedro moved on to other work.

In contrast to MANTHOC's direct role running its own schools, IF-EJANT works with several public and private schools, hosting meetings of school directors, training and supporting teachers, and developing and sharing a pedagogical and curricular approach to be implemented in these schools. IFEJANT's school program encourages the schools to create structures for children's self-organization and voice within the school, including student assemblies and student delegates to the governing body of the school. They also train teachers in participatory and Freirian pedagogy, encourage the integration of productive activities into the learning process, and draw teachers' attention to the particular needs and experiences of working children. One of the schools in this program, San José Obrero, is located in the distant outskirts of Lima in Nueva Esperanza, up a dusty hill cross-cut with muddy tracks and no paved roads. The school is surrounded by concrete buildings, makeshift wooden houses, and some smaller and more precarious homes made of corrugated metal and bright blue tarps. Vibrant, colorful, and noisy with the voices of hundreds of children, this school has a very different energy than that at the MANTHOC school. But, like MANTHOC's school, this school supports the *protagonismo* and education of some of Lima's poorest children. The school director has a long history of collaborating with the movement on various projects, including getting support from the movement in the process of forming and building the school.

As with MANTHOC's school, the students at San José Obrero engage in learning through production and work. Each class participates in a production workshop every week, with the primary goals being to strengthen the academic learning that they are doing in the classroom. What they produce in these workshops is then sold at the school's kiosk. A smaller group of students participates in a PROMINATs microlending and micro-enterprise program that meets one afternoon per week. The students in that program produce items to sell on their own, and they learn not just academic skills but also professional and entrepreneurial skills, like how to make a budget, set prices, and market one's products. The school also has several structures for democratic engagement and "self-organization," with a students' council, a parents' council, a teachers' council, and a school-wide governing body that includes delegates from all three of these councils. The governing body is in charge of working on institutional visions and strategic planning. Students are organized into several other committees with different tasks and projects, including a committee in charge of dealing with discipline problems and school rules, a committee that runs the kiosk, and a committee that helps organize school meals. Each committee has a teacher who accompanies and supports the students. When I visited the school, the students were quick to point out how this made them different from many other schools, and how this school is special because it treats them with respect, as subjects and as equals.

The teachers at San José Obrero are referred to by IFEJANT and by the director as *docentes colaboradores*, emphasizing that they should have a more collaborative relationship with their students. While some teachers embrace this identity and strive to encourage children's power and *protagonismo* in the classroom, others struggle with this framework and continue to teach as they had previously done. I observed several classes at the school as well as a training for teachers and noted significant range in the extent to which they incorporated the movement's perspective on childhood and intergenerational relationships. One teacher of six-year-olds told me that, from her perspective, "*protagonismo* starts here with the little kids." She used to work with the twelve-year-olds, and said that in those classes you can really see how they are in charge, how they make decisions and influence the direction of the class, but with the younger ones "it is just beginning. But we encourage them to be proactive, to be protagonists, to speak confidently in front of others, to say what they think, and to give their opinions." Schools like San José Obrero are sites where students and teachers interact differently, with less hierarchy and greater respect for students' perspectives.

But most kids in the movement are not in schools supported by IF-EJANT or MANTHOC. Attending mostly public and a few lower-cost private schools that have no relationship with the movement, most kids have to figure out on their own how much, if any, of their *protagonismo* and critical intergenerational perspective to bring into the school context. Unfortunately, I was unable to access these schools during my research, so all I know about what kids do in these spaces is based on what they told me in interviews and informal conversations, not on observations. I also spent some time at the MANTHOC Yerbateros house helping kids with their schoolwork and so learned some about how they responded to the ways their schools were structured from these experiences. Overall, the NATs were not troubled or concerned by the fact that they had such different relationships with their teachers than they did with their *colaboradores*. The movement's vision of changing intergenerational relationships did not lead them to significantly question the way that these relationships operated in school. School and the movement were separate spaces, with different kinds of adults, and while they might have wanted their teachers to have more in common with their *colaboradores*, this was not their expectation, and also not something that they felt they could do much about and so therefore not a big deal. When discussing this subject, Alejandro told me a story about a boy in the movement who had been boisterous, vocal, and quick to stand up for what he thought was right. Alejandro went with him to school one day and was astounded by the transformation: the boy was quiet and pliable, and followed all directions without a bit of complaint even when it was clear he disagreed with them. After seeing this, Alejandro asked him about this change in his personality and behavior and why he didn't speak up more or advocate for himself in school. He responded that the two were different and that he wanted to keep them separate. School was for learning particular things, accomplishing particular things, and the movement had its own purpose in his life and that they didn't need to be mixed.

In general, this seemed to be how most NATs responded to the differences in intergenerational expectations for interaction between school and the movement. The two parts of their lives were distinct, and there was no reason to try to force movement *protagonismo* and expectations into the school context. However, even without expecting a transformation of intergenerational relationships, organized NATs probably bring some of their voice, authority, and sense of their rights into the classroom and thus might, in fact, be changing classroom dynamics at their schools even without this being an explicit project or goal. Diego's mother, for example, told me that his teachers regularly comment on how he speaks up in class and defends equality and justice, and that they think he will be a politician someday. I don't know whether or not other organized NATs are also seen by their teachers as more politically engaged and expressive, but I would imagine this is not unique to Diego. However, the only example I encountered of kids directly using some of their movement experiences at school also came from Diego, who told me about organizing some of his fellow students to present evidence to their school director of a teacher who was not doing his job and was not teaching them, just showing movies in class. The students recorded several classes on their phones, brought the videos to the director, and encouraged the director to either discipline or fire the teacher. Diego took some of his movement knowledge and put it to use to improve his school and his education. Although Diego was the only student who shared a story like this, I doubt that he is the only one whose movement participation has shaped interactions with teachers, classmates, and school administrators.

The movement of working children probably has some effects on schools as kids themselves take at least a few of their ideas and experiences from the movement into these other contexts. However, it is not entirely clear how much they are doing this, and further research is needed. In addition to the actions of individual children, though, the movement impacts schools by working directly with some "friendly" schools and school directors in order to change the pedagogy and organization of these particular institutions. But changing the educational experience of working children via these schools is also difficult as some teachers resist the new models and as funding problems lead to instability and even the closure of some movement-connected schools. The movement's approach to intergenerational relationships has a great deal to offer to teachers and schools, but while the movement has been able to shape and influence a handful of schools, its substantial potential contributions to the quality of Peruvian education are not fully realized.[27]

Families

Argentine sociologist Elizabeth Jelin has argued that families in Latin America, while experiencing significant transformations due to processes of migration, growing acknowledgment of gender (in)equality and sexual and reproductive rights, and increased social acceptance of divorce, continue to be shaped by the historical legacies of hierarchy, authoritarian patriarchal control, and *patria potestad* (the rights of fathers), which were articulated and implemented in law by the Catholic Church and colonial governments.[28] Rigid gender roles, expectations of children's obedience, and strong parental authority are legacies of this history.[29] Using Peruvian census data from the year 2000, Anastasia Gage and Eva Silvestre also find that 42 percent of mothers experience physical violence at the hands of their intimate partners, 67 percent experienced physical punishment when they were children, and 60 percent use some form of physical punishment for their own children.[30] In striking contrast to this, however, Inge Bolin suggests an alternative indigenous tradition of more permissive and egalitarian parenting practices in her study of child-rearing in the Peruvian highlands.[31] For the kids in the movement of working children in Lima, family life may involve either or both of these tendencies. The movement, as a political space trying to increase children's power and authority and facilitate more horizontal intergenerational relationships, explicitly and implicitly challenges the patriarchal, hierarchical family model, while being very careful not to criticize or demonize poor and working-class parents as "bad parents." Instead, movement *colaboradores* encourage both parents and kids to understand and then challenge the contexts and conditions that have produced authoritarian and sometimes violent parenting practices. Families are seen as potential sites for implementing the "new social contract" for intergenerational relations rooted in tenderness, children's rights, and *protagonismo*.

Families and parents interact differently with the movement in the context of different base groups. For the parents of children who are in base groups situated in neighborhoods, churches, or schools, interactions with the movement are informal, infrequent, and individualized. They are sometimes visited by *colaboradores* who come to talk with them about their kids and about the movement, and they are invited to large events like the annual anniversary celebration, but their engagement with the movement is largely optional. On the other hand, parents of kids who attend the MANTHOC social service centers, like the Yerbateros house, have specific obligations to the movement in order to maintain their children's access to participation. Each family is required to send someone to help with the cooking and cleanup from lunch once per month. Usually this is a mother or grandmother, but occasionally fathers take on this role. Parents of Yerbateros NATs also participate in monthly parent assemblies, which are evening gatherings that also primarily draw mothers as well as a handful of fathers.

Movement *colaboradores* explicitly use the parent assemblies to try to influence intergenerational family relationships. They discuss children's rights with parents and seek to impact the ways that parents engage with their children on a daily basis. Mónica, from the Yerbateros house, began each of these gatherings by reminding parents that this is an important part of what MANTHOC does, that it is a movement with a particular social vision, not just a house where they can drop off their kids for childcare, food, or tutoring. One parent assembly I attended included a discussion facilitated by a psychologist, Miguel, who had been working with the parents and the kids for several months. Miguel, who aimed to look casual and relaxed rather than formal and professional by wearing jeans and a sweater, asked the twenty parents whether their kids had shared with them what they did in last week's adolescent workshop. Very few of the parents nodded, and one father answered that his daughter told him they had talked about gender and dating. Miguel described how they had discussed sexuality, taking care of their bodies, and respecting themselves. He then encouraged the parents to ask their kids about these workshops each week because this would give them an opportunity to have important discussions with their children. He noted, "Remember, what we are working on here is improving communication and dialogue with your children." In this vein, the rest of the discussion focused on identifying passive, aggressive, and assertive forms of communication. Working in small groups, parents read several scenarios to determine which form of communication was being modeled. They shared their analysis of each scenario with the larger group and had some discussion about why they thought the response was passive, aggressive, or assertive. After the activity, Miguel warned them that "parents in Peru often turn our children into passive communicators who don't express what they think, feel, or want. We reward their obedience and then they can't express themselves, and their frustrations may build up. We need to be careful not to turn our children into passive slaves to our desires and those of others." Parents clearly agreed with this assessment, and many affirmed his point with their own examples. He then defined assertive communication, emphasizing that it involves expressing oneself while respecting the rights of others to have their own opinions and to say what they think. After contrasting this with aggressive forms of communication, Miguel asked the participants how they thought parents in Peru generally communicate. There was widespread agreement that many parents use aggressive forms of communication with their children more often than they should. Miguel identified this as the result of social conditions, not parents' personal failings, telling the group that "our society is getting more and more aggressive, and we take this all in. Parents have many responsibilities, and many frustrations during their day and when they get home they may take this out on children. Parents have been made passive in their workplaces, have been treated aggressively by others, and then are tired and angry when they get home." The group discussed this, talking about how parents can work out those frustrations before they arrive home so that they can communicate better with their kids, and then Miguel left, turning the assembly back over to Mónica's leadership.

This workshop with parents on communication shows one way that the movement attempts to improve children's family life. *Colaboradores* and allies like Miguel are careful not to demonize poor parents or to place individual blame on them for hierarchical parenting practices, but they also clearly articulate their hopes for these parents and their interactions with their children. By engaging in conversations with parents about intergenerational relationships, communication, and respect for children's rights, the movement tries to provide additional support to children as they themselves attempt to make changes in their homes. Kids, the movement recognizes, may not be able to take the lessons of children's *protagonismo* and intergenerational horizontalism home with them without parents having opportunities to discuss these ideas themselves. Unfortunately, while the parent assemblies are part of the movement process for the base groups at the social service centers, they are not part of the experience of kids and families connected to other types of bases.

When spending time with kids and their parents, I found that some parents, particularly parents of kids who were not tied to the social service centers, had only minimal knowledge about the movement. My visit with Andrea and her mom provided an interesting and unusual opportunity for Andrea to explain more about the movement to her mother. Andrea's mom, Milagros, works as a nutritionist in a hospital and is out late at work most days during the week. She and Andrea have very little time together and few opportunities to talk. The day I spent with them was a rare overlapping school vacation and day off from work. As I described my research to Milagros, she began to ask questions about why MANTHOC does not provide "more benefits" for the kids. She explained that she is friendly with a doctor whose daughter is also a representative in an organization, but that they go to the theatre, are members in a pool and sports club, and get scholarships. She wanted to know why MAN-THOC doesn't provide these benefits to her daughter. Andrea defended the organization: "There are benefits!" Her mother asked her what, and she said that the benefits are "learning about our rights and how to defend them." Milagros disagreed. "Everyone has rights," she said. "It isn't a benefit." Andrea persisted, and said that not everyone knows their rights and how to act on those rights, and this is the kind of thing they learn in MANTHOC. I also chimed in that the benefits at MANTHOC are less concrete and material, more personal, educational, and social. Milagros agreed that these were valuable, but said that "Andrea spends a lot of time in this movement, goes many places, and there should be more benefits and opportunities for the kids like her." At this point, Andrea had a pretty good sense of what her mom was envisioning, and told her that the national delegates sometimes travel internationally as part of the movement. Diego just went to Italy, she told her mom. Milagros agreed that this would be wonderful, and she said, "It seems like they should put some money to things like I'm suggesting." I told her I would pass along her comments, but that MANTHOC is not very well funded compared to many children's organizations and NGOs. She suggested that they should ask for financial support from businesses and government. Andrea and I then explained that this might be difficult because of the politics: the government and many in business think that children should not work and this is not MANTHOC's position on the issue. I added that the *co-laboradores* are also mostly volunteers, they are not paid for their work, and so do not necessarily have a lot of time to pursue funding. Milagros was genuinely surprised by both pieces of information.

Andrea, feeling a bit defensive of the movement at this point, told her mother that she wanted to show her the notes she took from a recent workshop on the principles and objectives of MANTHOC. She went to get her notebook from her bedroom and brought it out to her mother, explaining what the movement is trying to accomplish. Milagros looked over Andrea's notes and said that these all were good things to work on, but that "you can't just go straight to marching and demanding, you have to also work with the government." Andrea explained that they try to do this and that last week's march was just one part of their activities. Milagros nodded, satisfied with what she had learned. At the time of this conversation, Andrea had been involved in MANTHOC for just over a year. She had been attending weekly or biweekly base group meetings and going to occasional regional Lima-wide events, but her mother knew very little about the politics of the group. She had met Andrea's *colaboradora* and knew that Andrea was involved in an organization with other kids, but did not know about MANTHOC's objectives until our conversation that day. Andrea was glad to have a chance to talk about this with her mother, and Milagros's lack of knowledge was not the result of indifference or a disinclination to talk, but simply a lack of time for these conversations amidst the hurried activity of daily household life. Parents who are not as engaged in the movement, like Milagros, may be unaware of the political dimensions of their children's activities, but this is quite understandable given the many preoccupations of Peru's urban poor and working-class families. Parents' minimal engagement with the movement should absolutely not be read as disinterest in their children's lives.

Even though parents like Milagros are not necessarily aware of the politics of the movement, kids bring the movement home with them, impacting family dynamics by drawing on what they have learned in movement spaces. Specifically, one recurring theme in movement discussions about families and parents is a direct rejection of physical forms of punishment. In addition to INFANT's annual event against all forms of violence against children, this was a central issue in the conversations about the revisions to the national law on children and adolescents. At a RedNNA workshop on the Código, the adult facilitator discussed how the kids from MNNATSOP had been trying to change the law on punishment for quite some time. She quoted one of the ex-delegates who used to say, "When a kid breaks a glass, the mother punishes, hits, or yells. But when a neighbor breaks a glass, the mother just says, 'Oh, don't worry about it.'" She then went on to tell the group that MNNATSOP had been concerned that the previous code was not strong enough in terms of preventing violence because it allowed "moderate" punishment, and that the reality is that parents, when they punish, often do so physically and we, as people who believe in children's rights, need to respond to that reality and reword the law to prohibit physical punishment. Many kids nodded at this, and the topic of the need to prohibit "moderate" punishment became a major theme in the ongoing discussions about changes to the law.

Kids have to choose whether or not to bring this perspective into their relationships with their parents. While some may leave the movement behind when they go home and allow parents to punish them as they see fit, others try to influence how their parents see punishment. For example, one Saturday morning, Patricia and her brother Julio were talking with their mother about weekend plans, while I had a conversation with their aunt nearby. We were all standing outside the local market, cleaning up the area around the family's market stalls. At one point, Patricia's mother gave her a *very* light slap on the face. Patricia and Julio both quickly glanced my way, then quickly returned their eyes to their mother, raising their eyebrows and jerking their heads in my direction, as if to remind her that a movement-related adult was nearby and that such actions were frowned upon. In this case, the two kids could have been using their mother's knowledge of the movement's position on physical punishment to remind her that she should not do this, or they could have been reminding her that she should not do this when someone from the movement can see it. In another instance, Diego used humor to remind his mother that he thought there should be limits on how she punishes him. Her phone was not working correctly and she thought Diego had done something to make it unable to answer calls. She asked him what he did to her phone, and gave him a slight whack on the side of his head. He immediately replied, "Hey! You can't hit me! I'm going to denounce you!" But he said this with a big smile to take the sting out of the words and to make clear that he was joking. Denouncing parents at the local office for children's rights is, in fact, a legal possibility for kids in Peru, but one that very rarely happens. And, while I heard a few different movement kids make this statement to their parents, it was clear in all cases that they were not *really* threatening to do this, but rather simply using this idea as a way to let their parents know that they did not like something, or that they felt they were being mistreated in some way. In both Diego's and Patricia's cases, the kids were not responding to moments of significant violence, but rather using these small opportunities to make a point about physical punishment. It was not that they actually rejected the action of the parent in that moment, or even thought they were necessarily being mistreated, but rather that these moments were times when they could express a position on the subject of physical punishment.

Diego's involvement with MANTHOC has also changed his relationship with his father. The entire family talks about how Diego and his dad now have long discussions and debates about the future of the country, the various political parties, and problems they see in Lima. Diego's mom said, "He is willing to disagree with his father—he speaks his own ideas and can talk circles around his [older] sisters!" In my visits with Diego's family, I also noticed how active he was in family conversations. He regularly shared his thoughts on any subject being discussed, from the missing family dog to the lack of a middle class in Lima. Over several meals, Diego's father liked to ask me questions about the United States, or how I saw the differences between Peruvian and US politics, and Diego would always chime in during these discussions. Diego's mom told me that all of this had come about since he began to participate in MANTHOC. She told me, "He is a lot less timid and shy than he used to be, and he has more confidence thanks to the movement." She was clearly very proud that "he has spoken in front of Congress, and he went to Italy and met with people there to tell them about his experiences." She was also happy to share that he "always defends the children—when he sees people mistreating them on the train or in the buses, he stands up for them." Through the movement, Diego has learned how to confidently express himself to adults, and he does so in his family as well as in public spaces. While Diego may sometimes use this confidence to disagree with them, his mom clearly values and appreciates it.

Kids in the movement of working children develop a strong sense of their entitlement to respect from adults, including respect from their parents. But different families may be more or less aware of the movement's agendas and goals regarding both children's work and intergenerational relationships. Kids then must negotiate their newfound expectations that they should be both seen and heard, and that they should have voice and authority within the confines of their distinctive family norms and dynamics. The movement's direct work with parents supports them in this endeavor, but kids are also doing a great deal of this social change work on their own and must decide whether, when, and how they want to bring movement ideas about adultism, children's rights, and intergenerational horizontalism into their relationships with their parents.

Expanding Children's Power

Challenging Assumptions about Childhood

The movement of working children today has a strong ideological and discursive emphasis on decriminalizing and destigmatizing children's work, and on directly challenging the ILO and Peruvian government attempts to "abolish child labor," but this goal often feels elusive and out of reach. If we understand this policy agenda as the movement's primary goal, we might be inclined to argue that it has accomplished very little. However, this policy change is only one small part of the movement's much larger social change agenda; as I've indicated throughout this book, its political vision also includes reducing age-based hierarchies, pursuing more horizontal intergenerational relationships, and substantially increasing children's political power and authority in multiple arenas and institutions. It seeks to challenge our assumptions about childhood and reimagine children's place in economic, social, and political life. These are major transformations of social and cultural norms, which are not easily accomplished or measured.[32]

But social movements should also not be held to the standard of fully achieving their most utopian visions to be considered successful. Would we say that LGBTQ activism has failed because it has not ended homophobia? Or that the US civil rights movement was a failure because there is still racism in the United States? Social movements should not be judged by their ability to fulfill their most lofty goals: ending poverty, creating sustainable communities, and dismantling global inequality are not straightforward tasks that can just be checked off an organization's to-do list. Social movement "success" is not an either/or question. And, as I've indicated in this chapter, the movement of working children *is* effectively challenging children's exclusion and increasing their social and political power in everyday life. While the movement may not have completely transformed the landscape of childhood in Peru, it has supported individual children's *protagonismo* and well-being and has expanded children's presence and authority in multiple institutions that play a key role in their lives. Children and adults, working together, have expanded opportunities for children's participation in governance, influenced policy, made improvements to schools, and engaged families in important conversations about children's rights. Their modest successes in all these areas suggest that children's lack of social and political power can be challenged and that children themselves can actively participate in this process, collectively contributing to remaking the world around them.

The Persistence of Age-Based Power

Ironically, young people's ability to influence political institutions can sometimes be amplified by their marginalized age status. Adults sometimes respond to activist children as if they are extraordinary and brilliant prodigies who are to be lauded for their insights and engagement. For example, we see this in the enthusiasm for Malala Yousafzai and her campaign for girls' education and in the widespread praise for the bravery and organizational savvy of the Parkland teens as they responded to their experience as survivors of a school shooting and took on the National Rifle Association. However, the case of the movement of working children should also serve as a bit of a warning: the public admiration gained by some young activists does not necessarily mean that our social and political institutions are actually prepared to truly engage with young people as democratic subjects. Even when governments embrace "children's participation," this participation tends toward tokenism rather than meaningful influence.[33] And, while young people, including children, sometimes do manage to shift the political and cultural landscape in powerful ways, children generally have few points of leverage to use in their struggles for recognition, dignity, and social change.

The NATs and *colaboradores* are certainly making interventions into the culture and politics of childhood in Peru, but their struggles to produce more substantial institutional and policy changes illuminate another distinctive dynamic of age-based power: children's profound lack of accumulated resources for social mobilization and political pressure. As David Oswell writes, "Children have historically been unable to accumulate capital of different forms. . . . [and] lacked the means, not of forming and belonging to networks, but of maintaining them, building them up over time, and providing the material means of their support and reproduction. In that sense, children are often thought to have the means of association, but not the means of institutionalization."[34] Children, as a social collectivity, don't have the resources that sociologists suggest enable the formation and stability of ongoing social movements (money, incentives for participation, administrative infrastructures, a dedicated cadre of organizers, widespread communications networks), nor do they have many of the requisites for the deployment of what Frances Fox Piven refers to as "disruptive power," such as "ways of enduring the suspension of the cooperative relationships on which they also depend."[35] In this sense, children's profound dependence upon adults for their ongoing well-being means that they are, even when engaged in activism for their rights and dignity, reliant upon adult allies. And, while adults in groups like the movement of working children are able to provide some infrastructure for the mobilization of some children, they are not, as a whole, an organized political entity. Children, in general, are also not a "social class" with an oppositional collective consciousness, or a collectivity that sees itself as having the power to transform its conditions. And without these characteristics, children don't possess a sufficient base of power from which they can make demands upon the institutions that shape their lives. Adults and intergenerational relationships are therefore fundamental to both the institutionalization and the impact of children's movements. Ironically, as children try to gain more power in political space, they also find themselves needing adult allies. In this sense, children continue to be dependent on adults, and age-based power persists even in movements dedicated to children's equality and collective empowerment.

The Movement as a Model for Intergenerational Politics

The movement of working children is not just a children's empowerment organization or a children's club meant to support and protect individual children. In many ways, it provides a valuable counterpoint to the countless "children's programs" in the Global South that address poverty as an individual problem and therefore promote individual solutions, such as child sponsorship, educational scholarships, health and nutrition classes, or micro-lending to children and their mothers. Other scholars have leveled important critiques of this model of global development work and child saving, highlighting ways that children's rights institutions participate in the legitimation of colonialist interventions as well as the production of neoliberal subjects.[36] Further, many children's rights and child protection institutions are able to gain leverage and funding on the basis of a supposedly neutral and universal version of humanitarian concern for children's safety and well-being, positioning themselves as being outside politics, while simultaneously supporting a particular political-economic model of development (neoliberal capitalist globalization).

In contrast to these groups, the movement of working children is an *explicitly* political, critical, and activist endeavor that deploys multiple strategies in the pursuit of a vision of social justice, rights, and dignity for poor children. The movement identifies systems of inequality that need to be challenged and suggests that they *can* be challenged by children and adults working together in horizontal collaboration. Intergenerational activism seeks to not only empower individual children, improving their lives in concrete and tangible ways, but also to influence the cultural, social, and political conditions that shape children's lives. Instead of ceding the terrain of children's programming and children's rights to neoliberalism and its promoters, radicals, anti-capitalists, and decolonial activists could learn a great deal from the example of the movement of working children and expand their work, building more intergenerational movement spaces that engage children as partners in the pursuit of social justice.

Conclusion

On March 14, 2018, hundreds of thousands of students from elementary, middle, and high schools as well as colleges and universities across the United States walked out of school as part of a growing youth-led movement against gun violence. In advance of the day's events, the *New York Times* published an article whose title asked, "How Young Is Too Young to Protest?"[1] For one school principal profiled in the article, the decision was that "third through fifth graders may walk out; second graders can observe, but not walk; kindergartners and first-grade students will remain in class for discussions on school safety in general that avoid the shooting itself." Another district decided that "it would not be appropriate for students in its elementary schools, which run through fourth grade, to participate in the walkout, but that students in grades five and up could join." Other schools, according to the article, made different age-based determinations, such as allowing elementary student participation only if parents came to the school to sign the students out for the seventeen-minute walkout, but permitting middle school and high school student participation without this parental action. In drawing these lines about which children could participate in which ways, school authorities were articulating their own beliefs about children's political capabilities at various ages. The divergent answers given to the article's question about an appropriate age to protest were not rooted in any evidence and indicate a lack of consensus on the subject. In this way, they also reveal the arbitrary quality of age-based criteria for political involvement. Social movements like the Peruvian movement of working children and moments like these student walkouts productively uncover often unspoken assumptions about childhood, exposing them as mutable cultural products rather than fundamental truths.

Children's political exclusion, as I've argued throughout this book, is not inevitable. Rather, it is the result of a set of cultural assumptions about childhood and adulthood: that children are essentially different kinds of human beings than adults; that children's particular capabilities are biological and cognitive, rather than socially and culturally dependent; that children are uncritical and passive while adults are active, agentic, autonomous, and rational; that children should be protected from engagement in the public sphere, including work and politics; and that adults' systematic power over children is justifiable and morally righteous. In striking contrast to these assumptions, the Peruvian movement of working children articulates a counter-hegemonic account of childhood. Rather than positioning working children as tragic figures or as children "without childhoods," the movement suggests that these children—and all children—are social, political, and economic actors who deserve respect, dignity, and inclusion. Drawing on a rich array of theoretical and political traditions, movement participants argue strongly for children's fundamental equality with adults. Further, their approach effectively demonstrates children's capacity for political organizing as well as young people's critical insights and knowledge about the social world. In its discourse and practice, the movement makes clear that children can, in fact, be protagonists for social change. In doing so, it demonstrates how children's exclusion from politics and social movements is arbitrary and unjust.

The desire to include children in political life is not unique to the movement of working children. Indeed, across diverse national and institutional contexts, the past few decades have seen a substantial growth in the number of programs and projects that aim to foster the civic and political engagement of both children and youth.[2] From initiatives for student voice in schools to the creation of children's councils in municipal governments, children are increasingly being invited to participate in governance.[3] While an assessment of these programs is well beyond the scope of this conclusion, the movement of working children offers a more radical alternative model for children's politics: horizontal intergenerational activism in the pursuit of social justice for people of all ages. In contrast to adult-driven institutions where children are occasionally invited to contribute their perspectives, this approach argues that children can and should be at the very center, not on the sidelines, of political advocacy efforts related to their rights and well-being. Further, compared to many programs where individual children are asked to share their personal stories and points of view, horizontal intergenerational activism emphasizes children's collective agency and the importance of pedagogical and political processes where young people can come together to develop their critical analysis of social problems. And unlike contexts that focus entirely on young people's voice, horizontal intergenerational activism aims to increase young people's real decision-making power and authority in their communities. Although elements of this approach could (and should) be taken up by many of the institutions that advocate for young people's political inclusion, horizontal intergenerational activism departs from the current dominant paradigms of children's programming, pushing into more explicitly transformative—and controversial—terrain.

Despite this context of increased interest in children's participation in governance, children continue to be primarily excluded from academic, activist, and public conversations about social movements. Sociologist Diane Rodgers has noted, "Children appear to be the most understudied of all social movement participants."[4] When activists in adult-dominated movements discuss children, it is usually either as symbolic figures who represent a promising or bleak future, as future actors who need to be educated about the movement's cause, or in the context of making sure children are welcome in movement spaces so that their parents and caregivers may fully participate.[5] And when the activism of young people does reach the public eye, it is often discussed as if each case is extraordinary. For example, the recent upsurge of youth-led activism around gun violence in the United States led to a flurry of op-eds on the importance of young people's participation in democracy and politics, with titles like "Why Demonstrating Is Good for Kids." This outpouring of support and recognition was certainly exciting, suggesting a potential embrace of young people's political subjectivity, or at least more privileged, predominately white youth protest.[6] However, in addition to the troublesome ways that race and class mattered to the articulation of support, this writing also reflected a certain kind of social amnesia about youth politics, evident in the frequent tones of astonishment and surprise about the activist skills of the Parkland teens. Interestingly, numerous articles sought to remind their readers that the #NeverAgain movement was just the latest in a long history of teenagers, and sometimes younger children, initiating substantial social change. Referencing a wide range of examples from the Greensboro lunch counter sit-ins and the 1968 East Los Angeles walkouts to the undocumented youth movement and Black Lives Matter, these articles seemed to be part of an almost desperate attempt by their writers to encourage their readers to remember that *this is not new*. But the fact that so many journalists felt the need to recover and explore this history, and even to remind the public of the existence of other present-day youth movements in the United States, suggests there is a stubborn resistance to treating young people's political activism as normal. Indeed, even though the topic of youth activism has, in the last fifteen years, garnered substantial academic and activist attention,[7] this has not necessarily normalized it or disrupted the dynamic of perpetual surprise when youth demonstrate their political capabilities.

The tendency to treat the political engagement of youth as out of the ordinary and respond to it primarily as an unusual event has serious consequences for the project of building horizontal intergenerational social movements. If youth activism always miraculously appears out of nowhere, then it is not a phenomenon that needs to be supported by organizations and institutions. In contrast, the model of horizontal intergenerational activism offered by the movement of working children suggests that children's activism can and should be intentionally cultivated by caring, engaged, critical adults who want to foster young people's political power. Rather than waiting for youth movements to magically appear on their own, this approach suggests that those of us who are concerned about social justice, human rights, and inequality should be finding ways to engage with children and youth as partners in social struggle. But in order to build more intergenerational horizontal social movements that challenge inequalities, including those related to age, we must also confront the propensity to see any adult involvement in youth movements as evidence of adults' manipulation of innocent children.

The US media coverage of the student organizing around gun violence also highlights this common trope and the ways that it discourages a more nuanced understanding of age-based power. On the one hand, opponents claimed that either the mainstream media or a vaguely imagined Left was "turning innocent children into propaganda pawns to peddle a fake news argument."[8] Or, as Ben Shapiro argued in the *National Review*, "Children and teenagers are not fully rational actors. . . . And we shouldn't be treating innocence as a political asset used to push the agenda of more sophisticated players."⁹ Young people, in his view, are just too ruled by their emotions to be capable of complex critical political thought and strategy, so they are being used by those who are more competent and skilled at politics. On the flip side, supporters tended to downplay adult involvement, emphasizing the autonomous actions of the youth and only rarely discussing the supporting role of teachers and parents. While a handful of stories about the Parkland teens mentioned encouraging teachers and parents and there were plenty of images of parents waiting in the wings to hug, cry with, and care for their children as they stepped off the stage or out of the spotlight, the political pundits and commentators sympathetic to the teens' cause tended to highlight specific individuals' extraordinary organizing skills, media savvy, and public presence. As Lyn Mikel Brown has noted, media narratives of young people's activism usually emphasize an individual youth's unique achievements, and "any mention of adult or community support kicks in another opposing narrative . . . she's a front for adult causes. This is a zero-sum game. She can't win for losing—either she does something remarkable all on her own, which ignores social reality, or she is a pawn, easily used or manipulated and worthy of dismissal."¹⁰ This all-or-nothing way of thinking fundamentally oversimplifies the relationship between society, individuals, and critical consciousness. Social change and the development of politicized perspectives on the world are always collective endeavors, and the young people (and adults) who are part of these processes are *neither* fully autonomous subjects *nor* passive dupes. But this binary thinking about age-based power is not just inaccurate; it also implicitly discourages intergenerational activism and impoverishes our ability to talk about the complexity of age-based power dynamics within social movements. When supporters of any given group of youth activists are always trying to avoid the accusation of brainwashing or using youth, they are forced to deny their contributions, claiming that it is all "just the youth" rather than engaging in more careful, critical, and thoughtful discussion of their roles and responsibilities in intergenerational social movement contexts. Rejecting this zero-sum game and the either/or model, this book argues for the value of intergenerational social movements that include children and the concomitant need for a more complex accounting of the dynamics of age-based power within these movements.

There is a rich body of scholarship on the power dynamics of race, class, and gender in social movement contexts that can and should inform our conversations about intergenerational activism. Analyzing and confronting often subtle internal power dynamics at individual and institutional levels have become important practices in many contemporary social movements that seek to organize across differences.[11] The theories and practices of intersectionality, anti-oppression organizing, and coalitional politics therefore have many conceptual and practical tools to offer, but age categories and ageism also operate with their own distinct logics. Throughout this book, I've suggested that the specificities of childhood and adulthood require a somewhat different approach to thinking about horizontal organizing across difference. Indeed, the zero-sum narrative I've just outlined is one that applies only to intergenerational activism at this point in time: it would be unimaginable to claim that the presence of some white activists in a movement of people of color indicates that activists of color are being used to further the agenda of the white individuals.

Intergenerational collaboration is also unlike many other coalitional approaches in that the roles taken on by adults in movements for children's rights are quite different from those normally associated with "allies"—those individuals who belong to a social group with more power and privilege who act in solidarity with a movement for the liberation of the social group that is oppressed or marginalized along that same axis of inequality (men in the feminist movement, white people involved in anti-racist struggles, and so on).[12] While the idea of "adults as allies" appears in several US texts about adult-youth partnerships and intergenerational social movements,[13] Hava Gordon and I have argued that the role of adults in youth movements is often far more extensive than the concept of ally-ship might suggest.[14] Ally-ship, in fact, is not necessarily a very good description for what actually happens in many intergenerational social movement spaces, where adults take on key roles as funders, logistical coordinators, repositories of historical memory and continuity, trainers and educators, or therapists and mentors.[15] Calling adults allies can thus serve to obscure the very powerful role that adults often play in youth activist spaces.

Although the idea of the ally has some presence in Peru in the context of the LGBTQ movement, it is not a term that appears at all in the movement of working children. Adults in the movement are only described as *colaboradores*, not *aliados*. The relationship of *colaboración*, or co-laboring/co-working, suggests a much more extensive role for adults than the term "ally" usually implies. *Colaboración* is a relational model that more clearly acknowledges how active adults are in the intergenerational movements. But its flip side is that it can then become a justification for habituated practices of adult dominance and control. The language of ally-ship, compared to *colaboración*, helps draw ongoing attention to questions of power and inequality and invites movement participants to continually consider the dynamics of adultism and ageism.[16] Adults, according to this framework, should be stepping back more because they are "just" the allies; the role of the *colaborador* doesn't make this dynamic as central. In short, children and youth rely upon adults in their movements in ways that are distinct from other social dynamics of inequality and difference. Ally-ship can obscure this particularity by treating age-based power as more like other forms of social power, but *colaboración* can also obscure some of the challenges of intergenerational horizontalism.

Adults clearly play a crucial role in children's movements, but adult involvement in children's political spaces can take a variety of different forms, all of which are far more complex than the polarized narrative of total autonomy versus manipulation. And while both *colaboración* and ally-ship aim to increase children's power and authority, this is not necessarily the case for all intergenerational political interactions. Adults may involve children primarily as objects of political socialization, treating them just as students or learners in political space, or they may use children as tokens, decoration, or symbols.[17] If social movements are going to try to include children as partners in struggle, as I'm arguing they should, then we are going to need to significantly expand our theoretical and conceptual vocabularies for making sense of age-based power.[18]

The movement of working children is just one of many spaces that would substantially benefit from more conversations about age-based power dynamics. Activists in the movement tend to see power only as a negative and think about it primarily in terms of coercion or prohibition. NATs and *colaboradores* also often want to proclaim that power is already equal and shared within the movement. This is understandable given the ever-present danger of being accused of brainwashing or using children, but this desire to articulate their egalitarianism can obscure how power is still functioning in less visible forms, and how it continues to be part of the fabric of the movement. Throughout this book, I've stubbornly refused to treat power in either/or terms, instead exploring the dynamic, shifting, messy terrain of age-based power relations. I've highlighted some of the particularly sticky spots in the pursuit of inter-generational horizontal relationships, noting how age-based hierarchies persist despite good intentions and a radical analysis of childhood. But rather than seeing these challenges as evidence of failure or as reasons to give up on the ideal of intergenerational horizontal social movements, I offer up the ambiguities of this work in hopes that they will stimulate a much-needed conversation about the nuances of age-based power both within and beyond this specific context. I am confident that participants in the movement of working children and in other intergenerational po-litical communities can take up these important conversations and find new and creative ways to deepen their work.

Incorporating children as partners in social movements and am-plifying their power in community life are difficult tasks, and actually achieving intergenerational horizontalism may be a utopian vision that is always on the horizon, but that does not mean we should just accept children's ongoing exclusion from politics. The Peruvian movement of working children invites us to question our taken-for-granted assump-tions about childhood and consider the (in)justice of children's margin-alization. This movement is therefore a vital theoretical and practical resource for the radical remaking of childhood. It offers a set of inno-vative discourses, practices, and methodologies that can transform the very meanings of childhood and adulthood and support the creation of social movements, institutions, and organizations that treat children with greater respect, give children significantly more decision-making power and authority, and recognize and value children's insights and contributions. Increasing children's power may be challenging, but the world's two billion children deserve a chance to be included as protago-nists and meaningful participants in the social, economic, and political lives of their communities.

ACKNOWLEDGMENTS

This book, like all books, is a collective product. The ideas shared here are not entirely my own, but were generated in community. Most importantly, I am indebted to all of the NATs and *colaboradores* who have shared their wisdom and knowledge with me. The innovative ideas about childhood and intergenerational relationships that I explore in this book are the result of their intellectual and political creativity, produced over many years of collective reflection and debate. They generously shared these ideas with me, and welcomed me into their organizations, meetings, homes, and workplaces. The staff at IFEJANT gave me a friendly base while in Lima and helped me to make connections with other individuals and groups. This project would absolutely not have been possible without their deep organizational support for research and researchers. Alejandro Cussianovich was always available to talk history, theory, and childhood studies, and continues to be an inspiring example of a teacher, advocate for justice, and public intellectual.

I am also grateful to the people who read and commented on either individual chapters or the full manuscript, most especially Deborah Levison, Anna Bolgrien, Lauren Friend, María Elena García, Lyn Mikel Brown, Patricia Zavella, Bill Myers, Aviva Sinervo, Lara Loesel, and the Childhood Studies research group at the University of California at Santa Cruz, as well as anonymous reviewers. Their insightful questions and feedback helped me think through some messy conceptual tangles and see the path forward. I have also benefitted immensely from inclusion in a vibrant international community of children's work scholars. Conversations and emails with Michael Bourdillon, Ben White, Manfred Liebel, Dena Aufseeser, Edward van Daalen, Nicholas Mabillard, and many others have been illuminating and generative. My brilliant colleagues at both Davidson College and UCSC have also pushed my thinking in new directions and created work environments where I was encouraged to explore new interdisciplinary and theoretical terrain. My partner Gabriel has been a constant and unwavering source of encouragement, listening to me talk about this project on hikes, over dinner, and in the car, and joining me on several research trips to Lima. Many of my friends, especially Ginny Browne, Christine Marshall, and Sheila Katz, have also listened to both my breakthroughs and my frustrations and offered much-needed reassurance in moments of doubt and uncertainty.

Ilene Kalish, my editor at New York University Press, has once again proven to be a great advocate for childhood and youth studies and an insightful reader. This has been a more difficult book for me to write than my previous one and I am truly appreciative of Ilene's patient support of my work. Finally, I benefitted from financial support from the American Sociological Association's Fund for the Advancement of the Discipline, the Kellogg Institute for International Studies at the University of Notre Dame, Davidson College, the University of California at Santa Cruz Chicano-Latino Research Center, and the UCSC Division of Social Sciences.

GLOSSARY OF ACRONYMS

CCONNA: Consejo Consultivo de Niños, Niñas y Adolescentes (Consultative Council of Children and Adolescents)

IFEJANT: Instituto de Formación para Educadores de Jóvenes, Adolescentes y Niños Trabajadores (Training Institute for Educators of Child, Adolescent, and Youth Workers)

ILO-IPEC: International Labor Organization—International Program on the Elimination of Child Labor

INFANT: Instituto de Formación de Adolescentes y Niños Trabajadores (Training Institute for Working Children and Adolescents)

JOC: Juventud Obrera Christiana (Christian Youth Workers)

MANTHOC: Movimiento de Adolescentes y Niños Trabajadores Hijos de Obreros Cristianos (Movement of Working Kids and Adolescents, Children of Christian Workers)

MNNATSOP: Movimiento Nacional de Niños, Niñas y Adolescentes Trabajadores Organizados del Perú (Peruvian National Movement of Organized Working Children and Adolescents)

MOLACNATS: Movimiento Latinoamericano y del Caribe de Niñas, Niños y Adolescentes Trabajadores (Latin American and Caribbean Movement of Working Children and Adolescents)

MOVICOLNATS: Movimiento de Colaboradores de los NATs (Movement of *Colaboradores* of Working Children and Adolescents)

NATS: niños y adolescentes trabajadores (working children and adolescents)

PROMINATS: Programa de Microfinanzas de los NATs (Microfinance Program for Working Children and Adolescents)

REDNNA: Red de Niños, Niñas y Adolescentes (National Network of Children and Adolescents)

UNCRC: United Nations Convention on the Rights of the Child

NOTES

INTRODUCTION

1 Alert! Alert! Alert! Look who is marching—the organized NATs of Latin America. The kids are saying it, and they are right—yes to work with dignity and no to exploitation.

2 Elizabeth Chin, "Children Out of Bounds in Globalising Times," *Postcolonial Studies* 6, no. 3 (2003): 309–25; Elizabeth A. Kuznesof, "The House, the Street, Global Society: Latin American Families and Childhood in the Twenty-First Century," *Journal of Social History* 38, no. 4 (2005): 859–72; Kristen Cheney, "Deconstructing Childhood Vulnerability: An Introduction," *Childhood in Africa* 2, no. 1 (2010): 4–7; Diane M. Hoffman, "Saving Children, Saving Haiti: Child Vulnerability and Narratives of the Nation," *Childhood* 19, no. 2 (2012): 155–68; Olga Nieuwenhuys, "Theorizing Childhood(s): Why We Need Postcolonial Perspectives," *Childhood* 20, no. 1 (2013): 3–8.

3 Johanna Wyn and Rob White, *Rethinking Youth* (Thousand Oaks, CA: Sage, 1997); Nick Lee, *Childhood and Society: Growing Up in an Age of Uncertainty* (London: McGraw-Hill Education, 2001); Nancy Lesko, *Act Your Age! A Cultural Construction of Adolescence* (New York: Routledge, 2001); Rebecca Raby, "Age: Decentering Adulthood," in *Power and Everyday Practices*, ed. Rebecca Raby, Deborah Rose Brock, and Mark Preston Thomas (San Francisco: Cengage, 2011), 133–56.

4 Philippe Ariès, *Centuries of Childhood: A Social History of Family Life*, trans. Robert Baldick (New York: Random House, 1962); Viviana A. Zelizer, *Pricing the Priceless Child: The Changing Social Value of Children* (Princeton: Princeton University Press, 1994); Allison James, Chris Jenks, and Alan Prout, *Theorizing Childhood* (Cambridge: Polity, 1998); William Corsaro, *The Sociology of Childhood*, 2nd ed. (Thousand Oaks, CA: Pine Forge, 2005).

5 Samantha Punch, "Childhoods in the Majority World: Miniature Adults or Tribal Children?," *Sociology* 37, no. 2 (2003): 277–95; Heather Montgomery, *An Introduction to Childhood: Anthropological Perspectives on Children's Lives* (Malden, MA: Wiley-Blackwell, 2009); David Oswell, *The Agency of Children: From Family to Global Human Rights* (New York: Cambridge University Press, 2012).

6 Barbara Rogoff, *The Cultural Nature of Human Development* (New York: Oxford University Press, 2003).

7 For an excellent discussion of different ways of theorizing children's agency, see Oswell, *The Agency of Children*.

8   Any quick search for news coverage about child and youth activists reveals countless blogs and opinion pieces decrying their role as pawns of unscrupulous adults.

9   Zelizer, *Pricing the Priceless Child*; Robin Bernstein, *Racial Innocence: Performing American Childhood from Slavery to Civil Rights* (New York: New York University Press, 2011).

10 As historian Robin Bernstein notes in *Racial Innocence*, not all children have access to the category of innocence, and being denied innocence can lead to significant harm and mistreatment. We only have to think, for example, of Tamir Rice, an African American twelve-year-old who was shot by police in 2014 while playing with a toy gun, to see how innocence is not equally distributed among all children.

11 Ruth Nicole Brown, *Black Girlhood Celebration: Toward a Hip Hop Feminist Pedagogy* (New York: Peter Lang, 2009).

12 Jens Qvortrup, *Childhood Matters* (Aldershot, UK: Avebury, 1994); Oswell, *The Agency of Children*.

13 Barry Checkoway, "Adults as Allies," *Partnerships/Community* 38 (1996), https://digitalcommons.unomaha.edu; Hava Gordon, "Allies Within and Without: How Adolescent Activists Conceptualize Ageism and Navigate Adult Power in Youth Social Movements," *Journal of Contemporary Ethnography* 36, no. 6 (2007): 631–68; Donovon Ceaser, "Unlearning Adultism at Green Shoots: A Reflexive Ethnographic Analysis of Age Inequality within an Environmental Education Programme," *Ethnography and Education* 9, no. 2 (2014): 167–81.

14 Manfred Liebel, "Paternalism, Participation, and Children's Protagonism," *Children, Youth and Environments* 17, no. 2 (2007): 56–73; Anne Graham and Robyn Fitzgerald, "Progressing Children's Participation: Exploring the Potential of a Dialogical Turn," *Childhood* 17, no. 3 (2010): 343–59; Nigel Thomas, "Love, Rights and Solidarity: Studying Children's Participation Using Honneth's Theory of Recognition," *Childhood* 19, no. 4 (2012): 453–66.

15 Rogoff, *The Cultural Nature of Human Development*; Montgomery, *An Introduction to Childhood*; John Wall, *Ethics in Light of Childhood* (Washington, DC: Georgetown University Press, 2010).

16 John Davis and Malcolm Hill, "Introduction," in *Children, Young People and Social Inclusion: Participation for What?*, ed. E. Kay M. Tisdall et al. (Bristol: Policy Press, 2006), 1–22; Didier Reynaert, Maria Bouverne-De Bie, and Stijn Vandevelde, "A Review of the Children's Rights Literature Since the Adoption of the United Nations Convention on the Rights of the Child," *Childhood* 16, no. 4 (2009): 518–34; Ingrid Agud Morell et al., *Participación infantil y construcción de la ciudadanía* (Barcelona: Grao, 2014).

17 Tisdall et al., *Children, Young People and Social Inclusion*; Hannah Lyford Jones, "Putting Children at the Center: A Practical Guide to Children's Participation" (London: Save the Children UK, 2010); Jaume Trilla Bernet and Ana María Novella Cámara, "Participación, democracia y formación para la ciudadanía: Los consejos de infancia," *Revista de Educación*, no. 356 (2011): 23–43.

18 Roger A. Hart, "Children's Participation: From Tokenism to Citizenship," In-
    nocenti Essays (Florence, Italy: UNICEF, 1992); Allison James, "Giving Voice
    to Children's Voices: Practices and Problems, Pitfalls and Potentials," *American
    Anthropologist* 109, no. 2 (2007): 261–72; Jason Hart, "Children's Participation and
    International Development: Attending to the Political," *International Journal of
    Children's Rights* 16, no. 3 (2008): 407–18; Rebecca Raby, "Children's Participation
    as Neo-Liberal Governance?," *Discourse: Studies in the Cultural Politics of Educa-
    tion*, no. 1 (2012): 1–13.

19 Davis and Hill, "Introduction," 9.

20 Hava Gordon, *We Fight to Win: Inequality and the Politics of Youth Activism* (New
    Brunswick, NJ: Rutgers University Press, 2010); Jessica K. Taft and Hava R. Gor-
    don, "Youth Activists, Youth Councils, and Constrained Democracy," *Education,
    Citizenship and Social Justice* 8, no. 1 (March 2013): 87–100.

21 Margaret K. Nelson, *Parenting Out of Control: Anxious Parents in Uncertain Times*
    (New York: New York University Press, 2010).

22 Annette Lareau, *Unequal Childhood: The Importance of Social Class in Family
    Life* (Berkeley: University of California Press, 2003); Marjorie Faulstich Orellana,
    Translating Childhoods: Immigrant Youth, Language, and Culture (New Bruns-
    wick, NJ: Rutgers University Press, 2009).

23 Jennifer Tilton, *Dangerous or Endangered? Race and the Politics of Youth in Urban
    America* (New York: New York University Press, 2010); Monique Morris, *Pushout:
    The Criminalization of Black Girls in Schools* (New York: New Press, 2016); Victor
    M. Rios, *Human Targets: Schools, Police, and the Criminalization of Latino Youth*
    (Chicago: University of Chicago Press, 2017).

24 A. S. Neill, *Summerhill: A Radical Approach to Child Rearing* (New York: Hart,
    1960); Ron Miller, *Free Schools, Free People: Education and Democracy after the
    1960s* (Albany: State University of New York Press, 2002); Marguerite Anne Fil-
    lion Wilson, "Radical Democratic Schooling on the Ground: Pedagogical Ideals
    and Realities in a Sudbury School," *Ethnography and Education* 10, no. 2 (May 4,
    2015): 121–36.

25 For some examples of this, see Gordon, *We Fight to Win*; Andreana Clay, *The Hip-
    Hop Generation Fights Back: Youth, Activism and Post–Civil Rights Politics* (New
    York: New York University Press, 2012); Walter Nicholls, *The DREAMers: How the
    Undocumented Youth Movement Transformed the Immigrant Rights Debate* (Palo
    Alto, CA: Stanford University Press, 2013); Soo Ah Kwon, *Uncivil Youth: Race, Ac-
    tivism, and Affirmative Governmentality* (Durham: Duke University Press, 2013);
    and Jerusha Conner and Sonia M. Rosen, eds., *Contemporary Youth Activism:
    Advancing Social Justice in the United States* (Santa Barbara, CA: Praeger, 2016).

26 Bonnie Thornton Dill, "Race, Class and Gender: Prospects for an All-Inclusive
    Sisterhood," *Feminist Studies* 9 (1983): 131–48; Bernice Johnson Reagon, "Coali-
    tion Politics: Turning the Century," in *Home Girls: A Black Feminist Anthology*, ed.
    Barbara Smith (New York: Kitchen Table Press, 1983), 356–68; Chandra Mohanty,
    Feminism without Borders: Decolonizing Theory, Practicing Solidarity, 5th ed.

(Durham: Duke University Press, 2003); Elizabeth R. Cole and Zakiya T. Luna, "Making Coalitions Work: Solidarity across Difference within US Feminism," *Feminist Studies* 36, no. 1 (2010): 71–98.

27 Francesca Polletta, *Freedom Is an Endless Meeting: Democracy in American Social Movements* (Chicago: University of Chicago Press, 2002); Marina A. Sitrin, *Everyday Revolutions: Horizontalism and Autonomy in Argentina* (London: Zed, 2012).

28 Susan A. Ostrander, "Gender and Race in a Pro-Feminist, Progressive, Mixed-Gender, Mixed-Race Organization," *Gender and Society* 13, no. 5 (1999): 628–42; Brent Stockdill, "Forging a Multi-Dimensional Oppositional Consciousness: Lessons from Community-Based AIDS Activism," in *Oppositional Consciousness: The Subjective Roots of Social Protest*, ed. Jane Mansbridge and Aldon Morris (Chicago: University of Chicago Press, 2001), 204–37; Jane Ward, "'Not All Differences Are Created Equal': Multiple Jeopardy in a Gendered Organization," *Gender and Society* 18, no. 1 (2004): 82–102; Jo Reger, Daniel J. Myers, and Rachel L. Einwohner, eds., *Identity Work in Social Movements* (Minneapolis: University of Minnesota Press, 2008); Veronica Terriquez, "Intersectional Mobilization, Social Movement Spillover, and Queer Youth Leadership in the Immigrant Rights Movement," *Social Problems* 62, no. 3 (2015): 343–62.

29 Natasha Blanchet-Cohen and Brian Rainbow, "Partnership between Children and Adults? The Experience of the International Children's Conference on the Environment," *Childhood* 13, no. 1 (2006): 113–26; Gordon, "Allies Within and Without"; Shawn A. Ginwright, *Black Youth Rising: Activism and Radical Healing in Urban America* (New York: Teachers College Press, 2010); Sekou M. Franklin, *After the Rebellion: Black Youth, Social Movement Activism, and the Post–Civil Rights Generation* (New York: New York University Press, 2014); Dana Edell, Lyn Mikel Brown, and Celeste Montano, "Bridges, Ladders, Sparks, and Glue: Celebrating and Problematizing 'Girl-Driven' Intergenerational Feminist Activism," *Feminist Media Studies* 16, no. 4 (July 2016): 693–709; Lyn Mikel Brown, *Powered by Girl: A Field Guide for Supporting Youth Activists* (Boston: Beacon, 2016).

30 Diane M. Rodgers, "Children as Social Movement Participants," *Sociological Studies of Children and Youth* 11 (2005): 239–59.

31 I am focusing on age-based power because it is distinct from other power relations and yet sheds light on the operation of power more broadly; in doing so, I hope to contribute to addressing the problem identified by Claudia Castañeda: "rarely has the question of the child translated into wider theoretical debates." Claudia Castañeda, *Figurations: Child, Bodies, Worlds* (Durham: Duke University Press, 2002), 2. In addition to Castañeda's excellent work on this topic, for more on the relevance of childhood for social theory in general, see Allison J. Pugh, "The Theoretical Costs of Ignoring Childhood: Rethinking Independence, Insecurity, and Inequality," *Theory and Society* 43, no. 1 (January 2014): 71–89.

32 Michel Foucault, *The History of Sexuality*, vol. 1, *An Introduction* (New York: Vintage, 1980).

CHAPTER 1. LEARNING WITH THE PERUVIAN MOVEMENT OF
WORKING CHILDREN

1 The other is the student organization Juventud Estudiantil Católica.

2 For more on this period in Peruvian history and the labor struggles during the
Morales Bermúdez government, see Manuel Valladares Quijano, "La experiencia
política del paro nacional del 19 de julio 1977," *Investigaciones Sociales* 11, no. 18
(2007): 243–76.

3 My understanding of this meeting comes largely from my interviews with Alejandro Cussianovich, a key figure in the movement of working children, and the
adult advisor for the JOC at this national gathering.

4 Paul Dosh, *Demanding the Land: Urban Popular Movements in Peru and Ecuador,
1990–2005* (University Park: Pennsylvania State University Press, 2010).

5 Alejandro Cussianovich, *Llamados a ser libres* (Buenos Aires, Argentina: CEP,
1974); Leonardo Boff and Clodovis Boff, *Introducing Liberation Theology* (Maryknoll, NY: Orbis, 1987); Gustavo Gutiérrez, *A Theology of Liberation: History,
Politics, and Salvation*, rev. ed. (Maryknoll, NY: Orbis, 1988).

6 Milagros Peña, "Liberation Theology in Peru: An Analysis of the Role of Intel-
lectuals in Social Movements," *Journal for the Scientific Study of Religion* 33, no. 1
(March 1994): 34–45.

7 Jo-Marie Burt, "Shining Path and the 'Decisive Battle' in Lima's Barriadas: The
Case of Villa El Salvador," in *Shining and Other Paths: War and Society in Peru,
1980–1995*, ed. Steve J. Stern (Durham: Duke University Press, 1998), 267–306;
James Ron, "Ideology in Context: Explaining Sendero Luminoso's Tactical Escalation," *Journal of Peace Research* 38, no. 5 (2001): 569–92; Katy Jenkins, "Depoliticis-
ation and the Changing Trajectories of Grassroots Women's Leadership in Peru:
From Empowerment to Service Delivery?," *Journal of Latin American Studies* 43,
no. 2 (2011): 299–326.

8 The COTADENI meetings were held during school hours, meaning that no kids
from the organization were able to attend. The kids, therefore, asked two of their
adult allies to participate in the meetings in the name of the movement, but it was
understood that these adults could not make decisions on behalf of the movement. Rather, the adults had to take the conversations in the COTADENI back
to the movement and ask the kids for their opinions, then return to the COTAD-
ENI with the kids' votes and positions. This was a confounding and unexpected
dynamic for many of the adult-led NGOs involved in COTADENI, and eventually
became too much for the network to deal with procedurally; the network was
then redefined so that it would be a network of adult staff from various NGOs,
rather than a network of representatives of each organization and movement,
leading to MANTHOC's de facto exclusion.

9 Michael Bourdillon, Ben White, and William E. Myers, "Re-Assessing Minimum-
Age Standards for Children's Work," *International Journal of Sociology and Social
Policy* 29, nos. 3–4 (2009): 106–17.

10 Anthony Swift, "El Movimiento Nacional de Niños, Niñas y Adolescentes Traba-jadores del Perú," *Revista NATs* 5–6 (2000): 122.

11 The existence of this headquarters was a major point of debate during the years of my fieldwork. It was sometimes part of the MNNATSOP structure and sometimes shuttered and replaced by a more diffuse leadership structure.

12 "Mestizo" can refer to individuals with mixed ancestry (indigenous and Euro-pean) or individuals who, "regardless of ancestry speak Spanish and claim His-panic cultural traits but are not considered blancos (whites)." María Elena García, *Making Indigenous Citizens: Identities, Education, and Multicultural Development in Peru* (Palo Alto, CA: Stanford University Press, 2005), 29. It can also be "a so-cial condition with room for both literacy and urban education and the continu-ation of regional costumbres." Marisol de la Cadena, *Indigenous Mestizos: The Politics of Race and Culture in Cuzco, Peru, 1919–1991* (Durham: Duke University Press, 2000), 30. Mestizo identity thus implies some distance from indigenous spaces, but not necessarily a full or complete distancing. See also Mariela Planas and Nestor Valdivia, "Identidad étnica en el Perú: Un estudio cualitativo sobre los discursos de auto identificación en tres zonas del país" (Lima, Peru: GRADE, 2007); and Martín Moreno and R. S. Oropesa, "Ethno-Racial Identification in Urban Peru," *Ethnic and Racial Studies* 35, no. 7 (2012): 1220–47.

13 García, *Making Indigenous Citizens*, 30.

14 James M. Jasper, *Protest: A Cultural Introduction to Social Movements* (Malden, MA: Polity, 2014), 5.

15 In addition to asking kids about their racial and ethnic self-understandings in interview contexts, I paid careful attention to the times when they would invoke particular identities in everyday interactions; I never encountered kids laying claim to a specifically indigenous or Andean identity. They might say that their families were Andean, but it was not a term they used for themselves or when describing peers.

16 For more on the Afro-Peruvian experience and dynamics of racism in Peru, see Tanya Maria Golash-Boza, *Yo Soy Negro: Blackness in Peru* (Gainesville: Uni-versity Press of Florida, 2011); Tanya Golash-Boza, "'Had They Been Polite and Civilized, None of This Would Have Happened': Discourses of Race and Racism in Multicultural Lima," *Latin American and Caribbean Ethnic Studies* 5, no. 3 (2010): 317–30; Sylvanna M. Falcón, "Mestiza Double Consciousness: The Voices of Afro-Peruvian Women on Gendered Racism," *Gender and Society* 22, no. 5 (2008): 660–80; Gonzalo Portocarrero, *Racismo y mestizaje y otros ensayos* (Lima, Peru: Fondo Editorial del Congreso del Perú, 2007).

17 Santiago Cueto et al., "Tracking Disparities: Who Gets Left Behind? Initial Find-ings from Peru Round 3 Survey" (Oxford, UK: Young Lives, 2011).

18 Ibid., 45.

19 UNICEF, "The State of the World's Children 2013" (UNICEF, 2013).

20 Ibid.

21 Cueto et al., "Tracking Disparities," 20.

22 Gabriela Guerrero et al., "Young Lives School Survey in Peru: Design and Initial Findings," Working Paper (Oxford: Young Lives, 2012).

23 Ibid.

24 Cueto et al., "Tracking Disparities," 21; Guerrero et al., "Young Lives School Survey in Peru."

25 Guerrero et al., "Young Lives School Survey in Peru," 57.

26 Rosario Aquije Valdez, "Visión del trabajo infantil y adolescente en el Perú, 2001" (Lima, Peru: Dirección Técnica de Demografía e Indicadores Sociales, 2002); UNICEF, "The State of the World's Children 2013."

27 "Magnitud y características del trabajo infantil en Perú" (Lima: Instituto Nacional de Estadística e Informática, 2016); José Rodríguez and Silvana Vargas, "El trabajo infantil en el Perú: Magnitud y perfiles vulnerables" (Lima, Peru: International Labor Organization, 2009).

28 Michael Bourdillon et al., *Rights and Wrongs of Children's Work* (New Brunswick, NJ: Rutgers University Press, 2010), 18–19; Meltem Dayıoğlu, "How Sensitive Are Estimates of Working Children and Child Labour to Definitions? A Comparative Analysis" (New York: UNICEF, 2012).

29 According to the statistics in a 2015 Peruvian survey, over 70 percent of economically active children are doing unpaid labor in the context of the family, and nearly 64 percent of all economically active children ages five to seventeen do less than sixteen hours of labor per week.

30 Rodríguez and Vargas, "El trabajo infantil en el Perú."

31 UNICEF, "The State of the World's Children 2013," 122–38.

32 Cueto et al., "Tracking Disparities," 17.

33 Armando Mendoza Nava, "Inequality in Peru: Reality and Risks," Working Paper (Lima, Peru: Oxfam in Peru, 2015); Gustavo Yamada and Juan Francisco Castro, "Poverty, Inequality, and Social Policies in Peru: As Poor as It Gets" (Peruvian Growth Puzzle, Harvard University, 2006).

34 Cueto et al., "Tracking Disparities," 17.

35 In addition to numerous peer-reviewed books and articles, there are also many unpublished master's theses and dissertations related to these movements. Further, IFEJANT has published over twenty-five issues of a semi-academic journal, *Revista NATs*, that includes both empirical research and theoretical reflections.

36 See, for example, Giangi Schibotto, *Niños trabajadores: Construyendo una identidad* (Lima, Peru: MANTHOC, 1990); Alejandro Cussianovich, "Participación y ciudadanía de los NATs," in *Niños, niñas y adolescentes trabajadores: Derechos, ciudadanía y protagonismo* (Lima, Peru: MANTHOC, 2000), 39–57; Manfred Liebel, Bernd Overwien, and Albert Recknagel, eds., *Working Children's Protagonism: Social Movements and Empowerment in Latin America, Africa, and India* (Frankfurt: IKO, 2001); Manfred Liebel, *A Will of Their Own: Cross-Cultural Perspectives on Working Children* (London: Zed, 2004); Beatrice Hungerland et al., eds., *Working to Be Someone: Child Focused Research and Practice with Working Children* (London: Kingsley, 2007); and Iven Saadi, "Children's Rights as 'Work

in Progress': The Conceptual and Practical Contributions of Working Children's Movements," in *Children's Rights from Below*, ed. Manfred Liebel et al. (London: Palgrave Macmillan, 2012), 143–61.

37 My analytic strategy places significant attention on the relationship between multiple, sometimes conflicting discourses and social practices. To accomplish this analysis, I imported all of my interview transcripts and field notes into atlas.ti, a qualitative data analysis program. I used a Foucauldian, discourse-oriented approach to coding that also draws heavily on inductive grounded theory. The coding process included "in vivo coding," which uses participants' terms as codes in order to identify narrative and discursive patterns, as well as extensive open and focused coding of practices and interactions at movement meetings and events. I looked carefully at the relationships between these two sets of codes, seeking out the connections and disjunctions between various movement discourses and movement practices. By using this strategy, I identify when and how movement ideas are deployed and made real in practice, and trace when and how these same ideas are set aside in the face of practical challenges, structured inequalities, and habituated intergenerational expectations and interactions.

38 Most of the movement's foreign visitors are from either Europe or Asia.

39 Arturo Escobar, *Territories of Difference: Place, Movements, Life, Redes* (Durham: Duke University Press, 2008), 24.

CHAPTER 2. *PROTAGONISMO* AND WORK

1 The language and terminology of citizenship is one that I use with some amount of hesitation because of the implicit connections to national legal status. The movements of undocumented youth in the United States provide an excellent reminder that active political engagement in a community is not equivalent to legal citizenship, can exist without such legal status, and may even challenge and rework definitions of national identity and belonging. When talking about children as citizens, then, I am speaking here not necessarily about their legal status or their national belonging, but instead about their recognition and experience of themselves as having "full membership in the community within which one lives." Evelyn Nakano Glenn, "Constructing Citizenship: Exclusion, Subordination, and Resistance," *American Sociological Review* 76, no. 1 (2011): 3.

2 James, Jenks, and Prout, *Theorizing Childhood*; Tobias Hecht, ed., *Minor Omissions: Children in Latin American History and Society* (Madison: University of Wisconsin Press, 2002); Castañeda, *Figurations*; Montgomery, *An Introduction to Childhood*; Anna Mae Duane, *The Children's Table: Childhood Studies and the Humanities* (Athens: University of Georgia Press, 2013); Valeria Llobet, ed., *Pensar la infancia desde América Latina* (Buenos Aires: CLACSO, 2014).

3 For this kind of discussion, see Walter Alarcón, *Ser niño: Una nueva mirada de la infancia en el Perú* (Lima, Peru: Instituto de Estudios Peruanos, 1994); Maria Emma Mannarelli, "La infancia y la configuración de los vínculos en el Perú: Un enfoque histórico" (Lima, Peru: Save the Children UK, 2002); Bianca Premo,

Children of the Father King: Youth, Authority, and Legal Minority in Colonial Lima (Chapel Hill: University of North Carolina Press, 2005).

4 Carolyn Dean, "Sketches of Childhood: Children in Colonial Andean Art and Society," in Hecht, *Minor Omissions*, 21.

5 Dean, "Sketches of Childhood," 22.

6 In the case of children in Lima, the institutions for their management and education included orphanages, religious houses, and schools. See, for example, Stefan Roggenbuck, "Historia social de la infancia callejera limeña," *Apuntes* 39 (1996): 89–112; and Bianca Premo, "Minor Offenses: Youth, Crime, and Law in Eighteenth-Century Lima," in Hecht, *Minor Omissions*, 114–38.

7 Lesko, *Act Your Age!*

8 Victoria Haskins and Margaret Jacobs, "Stolen Generations and Vanishing Indians: The Removal of Indigenous Children as a Weapon of War in the United States and Australia, 1870–1940," in *Children and War: A Historical Anthology*, ed. James Marten (New York: New York University Press, 2002), 227–41.

9 García, *Making Indigenous Citizens*, 88.

10 Quoted in Dean, "Sketches of Childhood," 46.

11 Susan E. Ramírez, "To Serve God and King: The Origins of Public Schools for Native Children in Eighteenth-Century Northern Peru," *Colonial Latin American Review* 17, no. 1 (2008): 73–99; Monique Alaperrine-Bouyer, *La educación de las elites indígenas en el Perú colonial* (Lima: Institut Français d'Études Andines, 2013).

12 Premo, "Minor Offenses," 130.

13 Ibid.

14 Jessaca B. Leinaweaver, *The Circulation of Children: Kinship, Adoption, and Morality in Andean Peru* (Durham: Duke University Press, 2008); Leigh Campoamor, "'Who Are You Calling Exploitative?': Defensive Motherhood, Child Labor, and Urban Poverty in Lima, Peru," *Journal of Latin American and Caribbean Anthropology* 21, no. 1 (2016): 151–72.

15 Mannarelli, "La infancia y la configuración de los vínculos en el Perú."

16 The racial narrative of "civilization" also continues to circulate in contemporary multicultural Lima. See Golash-Boza, "'Had They Been Polite and Civilized, None of This Would Have Happened.'"

17 Vanessa Rojas Arangoitia, "'I'd Rather Be Hit with a Stick . . . Grades Are Sacred: Students' Perceptions of Discipline and Authority in a Public High School in Peru," Working Paper (Oxford: Young Lives, 2011).

18 I address some of these dynamics in greater detail in chapter 6.

19 Robert Coles, *The Moral Life of Children* (New York: Atlantic Monthly Press, 1986); Jessica Kulynych, "No Playing in the Public Sphere: Democratic Theory and the Exclusion of Children," *Social Theory and Practice* 27, no. 2 (2001): 231–64; Wall, *Ethics in Light of Childhood*.

20 Orin Starn, "Missing the Revolution: Anthropologists and the War in Peru," *Cultural Anthropology* 6, no. 1 (1991): 63–91.

21 Inge Bolin, *Growing Up in a Culture of Respect: Child Rearing in Highland Peru* (Austin: University of Texas Press, 2006), 152.

22 Vidal Carbajal Solís, "Cosmovisión andina y procesos de desarollo del niño andino: Una mirada para trabajar el enfoque de EIB" (Lima, Peru: Ministerio de Educación, 2012), 8.

23 Fernando A. García, "Respect and Autonomy in Children's Observation and Participation in Adults' Activities," in *Children Learn by Observing and Contributing to Family and Community Endeavors: A Cultural Paradigm*, ed. Maricela Correa-Chávez, Rebeca Mejía Arauz, and Barbara Rogoff, Advances in Child Development and Behavior 49 (Waltham, MA: Elsevier, 2015), 142.

24 García, "Respect and Autonomy in Children's Observation and Participation."

25 Patricia Ames, "Niños y niñas andinos en el Perú: Crecer en un mundo de relaciones y responsabilidades," *Bulletin de l'Institut Français d'Études Andines* 42, no. 3 (2013): 389–409.

26 Albert Recknagel, "Déficits socio-culturales de la Convención de los Derechos del Niños," *Revista NATs* 9 (2002): 11–19; Jorge Dominic Ruiz, "La concepción andina de la infancia y el trabajo," *Revista NATs* 11–12 (2004): 31–39; Walter Alarcón, *Trabajo infantil en los Andes* (Lima, Peru: Instituto de Estudios Peruanos, 2010).

27 Antonella Invernizzi, "Street-Working Children and Adolescents in Lima: Work as an Agent of Socialization," *Childhood* 10, no. 3 (2003): 319–41; Robin Cavagnoud, *Entre la escuela y la supervivencia: Trabajo adolescente y dinámicas familiares en Lima* (Lima: IEP/IFEA/Fundación Telefónica, 2011).

28 Invernizzi, "Street-Working Children and Adolescents in Lima."

29 For other discussions of the figure of the child in relation to nation building, see Elena Jackson Albarrán, *Seen and Heard in Mexico: Children and Revolutionary Cultural Nationalism* (Lincoln: University of Nebraska Press, 2014); and Anita Casavantes Bradford, *The Revolution Is for the Children: The Politics of Childhood in Havana and Miami, 1959–1962* (Chapel Hill: University of North Carolina Press, 2014).

30 Joshua Tucker, "Producing the Andean Voice: Popular Music, Folkloric Performance, and the Possessive Investment in Indigeneity," *Latin American Music Review* 34, no. 1 (2013): 33.

31 These relationships are somewhat stronger in other parts of the country where the movement is active. In Lima, they are also currently being developed through the presence of Tania Pariona, the congresswoman from Ayacucho who was a national leader for MNNATSOP, remains connected to the working children's organizations, and also has a long history with Chirapaq, an indigenous association.

32 For more thorough discussions of the idea of children as becoming or as representing mutability, see, for example, Lee, *Childhood and Society*; and Castañeda, *Figurations*.

33 Ames, "Niños y niñas andinos en el Perú," discusses how twelve-year-olds are involved in community politics and political life in some rural communities in the Andes.

34 Kuznesof, "The House, the Street, Global Society," 860.

35 Chin, "Children Out of Bounds in Globalising Times," 310.

36 For a clear introductory discussion of Western visions of childhood see James, Jenks, and Prout, *Theorizing Childhood.*

37 Zelizer, *Pricing the Priceless Child*, 11.

38 Cheney, "Deconstructing Childhood Vulnerability"; Hoffman, "Saving Children, Saving Haiti"; Karen Wells, "The Melodrama of Being a Child: NGO Representations of Poverty," *Visual Communication* 12, no. 3 (2013): 277–93; Aviva Sinervo, "'No Somos Los Pobrecitos': Negotiating Stigma, Identity, and Need in Constructions of Childhood Poverty in Cusco, Peru," *Childhood* 20, no. 3 (August 2013): 398–413.

39 Kate Swanson, "'Bad Mothers' and 'Delinquent Children': Unraveling Anti-Begging Rhetoric in the Ecuadorian Andes," *Gender, Place and Culture* 14, no. 6 (December 2007): 703–20; Campoamor, "'Who Are You Calling Exploitative?'"

40 Mark Connolly and Judith Ennew, "Introduction: Children Out of Place," *Childhood* 3, no. 2 (1996): 131–45; Bourdillon et al., *Rights and Wrongs of Children's Work.*

41 Kuznesof, "The House, the Street, Global Society."

42 Invernizzi, "Street-Working Children and Adolescents in Lima," 323.

43 García, *Making Indigenous Citizens*; Leinaweaver, *The Circulation of Children*; Golash-Boza, "'Had They Been Polite and Civilized, None of This Would Have Happened.'"

44 Feminist theorists have long pointed out the problems with a public/private divide, identifying how privatizing gender relations, rather than treating them as public and political issues, serves to erase the power politics of the patriarchal family and to exclude many of the concerns of women from policy debate and public engagement.

45 Children's rights scholarship is a vast and ever-expanding literature. A useful review of different approaches to the subject can be found in Karl Hanson, "Schools of Thought in Children's Rights," in Liebel et al., *Children's Rights from Below*, 63–79.

46 Reynaert, Bouverne-De Bie, and Vandevelde, "A Review of the Children's Rights Literature," 521.

47 Gary B. Melton, "Beyond Balancing: Toward an Integrated Approach to Children's Rights," *Journal of Social Issues* 64, no. 4 (2008): 903–20.

48 Olga Nieuwenhuys, "Embedding the Global Womb: Global Child Labour and the New Policy Agenda," *Children's Geographies* 5, nos. 1–2 (2007): 149–63.

49 Berry Mayall, "The Sociology of Childhood in Relation to Children's Rights," *International Journal of Children's Rights* 8 (2000): 245.

50 Colette Daiute, "The Rights of Children, the Rights of Nations: Developmental Theory and the Politics of Children's Rights," *Journal of Social Issues* 64, no. 4 (2008): 708.

51 Ibid., 705.

52 Ibid., 718.

53 Mikaela Luttrell-Rowland, "Ambivalence, Conflation, and Invisibility: A Feminist Analysis of State Enactment of Children's Rights in Peru," *Signs* 38, no. 1 (2012): 182.

54 While they are officially supposed to be sites for children to seek out support in the defense and protection of all of their rights, according to Luttrell-Rowland ("Ambivalence, Conflation, and Invisibility"), the DEMUNAs are almost entirely used by women, not children, and are primarily used to address issues of child support, custody, and visitation rights between parents. Furthermore, at an event I attended with over fifty children and youth who are actively involved in many children's rights organizations, it was quite clear that most of these kids did not know about the DEMUNAs and/or did not know how to access them. Thus, while the DEMUNAs exist as a potential site of children's rights activity and serve as evidence for the Peruvian state's interest in children's rights, they are largely absent from kids' experiences of organizing and political or civic engagement in Lima.

55 On children's involvement in this process in Brazil, see Eliana Guerra, "Citizenship Knows No Age: Children's Participation in the Governance and Municipal Budget of Barra Mansa, Brazil," *Environment and Urbanization* 14, nos. 9–15 (2002): 71–84.

56 Roger A. Hart, *Children's Participation: The Theory and Practice of Involving Young Citizens in Community Development and Environmental Care* (New York: UNICEF, 1997); Barry Percy-Smith and Nigel Thomas, eds., *A Handbook of Children and Young People's Participation: Perspectives from Theory and Practice* (London: Routledge, 2009).

57 Daiute, "The Rights of Children, the Rights of Nations"; Matías Cordero Arce, "Towards an Emancipatory Discourse of Children's Rights," *International Journal of Children's Rights* 20, no. 3 (2012): 365–421; Emily Bent, "The Boundaries of Girls' Political Participation: A Critical Exploration of Girls' Experiences as Delegates to the United Nations Commission on the Status of Women (CSW)," *Global Studies of Childhood* 3, no. 2 (2013): 173–82.

58 William E. Myers, "The Right Rights? Child Labor in a Globalizing World," *Annals of the American Academy of Political and Social Science* 575 (2001): 38–55.

59 Alejandro Cussianovich, "What Does Protagonism Mean?," in Liebel, Overwien, and Recknagel, *Working Children's Protagonism*, 157.

60 See Jessica K. Taft, "Continually Redefining Protagonismo: The Peruvian Movement of Working Children and Political Change, 1976–2015," *Latin American Perspectives*, 2017, https://doi.org/10.1177/0094582X17736037.

61 Cussianovich, "Participación y ciudadanía de los NATs," 48.

62 Cussianovich, "What Does Protagonism Mean?," 165.

63 Alejandro Cussianovich, "Infancia como representación social," in *Niños trabajadores y protagonismo de la infancia* (Lima, Peru: IFEJANT, 1997), 24.

64 Ibid., 22.

65 Cussianovich, "Participación y ciudadanía de los NATs," 49.

66 Cussianovich, "What Does Protagonism Mean?," 169.

67 Alejandro Cussianovich, *Paradigma del protagonismo* (Lima, Peru: INFANT, 2010), 45.

68 Ibid. For other discussions of the intersection of youth activism and neoliberal governmentality, see Anita Harris, *Future Girl: Young Women in the Twenty-First Century* (New York: Routledge, 2004); Jacqueline Kennelly, *Citizen Youth: Culture, Activism, and Agency in a Neoliberal Era* (New York: Palgrave Macmillan, 2011); and Kwon, *Uncivil Youth*.

69 Cussianovich, "Infancia como representación social," 97.

70 Ibid., 163.

71 Laura Lundy, "'Voice' Is Not Enough: Conceptualising Article 12 of the United Nations Convention on the Rights of the Child," *British Educational Research Journal* 33, no. 6 (2007): 927–42.

72 Cussianovich, *Paradigma del protagonismo*, 44.

73 Ibid., 11.

74 Taft, "Continually Redefining Protagonismo."

75 Augendra Bhukuth, "Defining Child Labour: A Controversial Debate," *Development in Practice* 18, no. 3 (2008): 387.

76 "Magnitud y características del trabajo infantil en Perú."

77 Bourdillon et al., *Rights and Wrongs of Children's Work*.

78 Bourdillon, White, and Myers, "Re-Assessing Minimum-Age Standards."

79 For social scientific discussion of how the abolitionist approach to child labor has negatively impacted working children, see Bourdillon et al., *Rights and Wrongs of Children's Work*.

80 Much more could be said about the relationship between work and learning, and there are many complex debates about vocational learning, class inequality, and learning through apprenticeship. For discussions of informal learning, and learning via work, see Bourdillon et al., *Rights and Wrongs of Children's Work*, chapter 7.

81 Hungerland et al., *Working to Be Someone*; Bourdillon et al., *Rights and Wrongs of Children's Work*; Ben Kirshner and Shawn Ginwright, "Youth Organizing as a Developmental Context for African American and Latino Adolescents," *Child Development Perspectives* 6, no. 3 (2012): 288–94; Parissa J. Ballard, Lindsay T. Hoyt, and Mark C. Pachucki, "Impacts of Adolescent and Young Adult Civic Engagement on Health and Socioeconomic Status in Adulthood," *Child Development*, 2018, https://doi.org/10.1111/cdev.12998.

82 Ben Sasse, *The Vanishing American Adult: Our Coming-of-Age Crisis—and How to Rebuild a Culture of Self-Reliance* (New York: St. Martin's, 2017).

83 Elizabeth Ben-Ishai, "Paternalism," in *The Encyclopedia of Political Thought* (Boston: Wiley-Blackwell, 2015), 2663–64.

84 Corinne T. Field, *The Struggle for Equal Adulthood: Gender, Race, Age, and the Fight for Citizenship in Antebellum America* (Chapel Hill: University of North Carolina Press, 2014).

CHAPTER 3. EQUALITY AND HORIZONTALISM

1 Mayall, "The Sociology of Childhood in Relation to Children's Rights"; Oswell, *The Agency of Children.*

2 Mehmoona Moosa-Mitha, "A Difference-Centered Alternative to Theorization of Children's Citizenship Rights," *Citizenship Studies* 9, no. 4 (2005): 369–88.

3 Harry Shier, "What Does Equality Mean for Children in Relation to Adults?," paper presented for "Addressing Inequalities: The Heart of the Post-2015 Development Agenda and the Future We Want for All: Global Thematic Consultation," October 2012, www.harryshier.net.

4 Marc Jans, "Children as Citizens: Towards a Contemporary Notion of Child Participation," *Childhood* 11, no. 1 (2004): 27–44; Moosa-Mitha, "A Difference-Centered Alternative"; Tom Cockburn, "Partners in Power: A Radically Pluralistic Form of Participative Democracy for Children and Young People," *Children and Society* 21, no. 6 (2007): 446–57; John Wall and Anandini Dar, "Children's Political Representation: The Right to Make a Difference," *International Journal of Children's Rights* 19, no. 4 (December 2011): 595–612; John Wall, "Can Democracy Represent Children? Toward a Politics of Difference," *Childhood* 19, no. 1 (2012): 86–100.

5 Shier, "What Does Equality Mean?"

6 Reynaert, Bouverne-De Bie, and Vandevelde, "A Review of the Children's Rights Literature."

7 Thomas, "Love, Rights and Solidarity," 459.

8 Cussianovich, *Paradigma del protagonismo*, 14.

9 Swift, "El Movimiento Nacional de Niños, Niñas y Adolescentes Trabajadores del Perú," 106.

10 IFEJANT, "Jóvenes y niños trabajadores: Ser protagonistas" (Lima, Peru, 1997), 71.

11 Cockburn, "Partners in Power," 448.

12 Rogoff, *The Cultural Nature of Human Development*; Daiute, "The Rights of Children, the Rights of Nations."

13 Rogoff, *The Cultural Nature of Human Development.*

14 Patricia Hill Collins, *Black Feminist Thought: Knowledge, Consciousness and the Politics of Empowerment* (New York: Routledge, 1990); Mohanty, *Feminism without Borders.*

15 Donna Haraway, "Situated Knowledges: The Science Question in Feminism and the Privilege of Partial Perspective," *Feminist Studies* 14 (1988): 575–600; Joan W. Scott, "Experience," in *Feminists Theorize the Political*, ed. Judith Butler and Joan W. Scott (New York: Routledge, 1992), 22–40; James, "Giving Voice to Children's Voices."

16 Oswell, *The Agency of Children*, 235.

17 Cussianovich, "Participación y ciudadanía de los NATs," 53.

18 David Gottlieb, *Children's Liberation* (Englewood Cliffs, NJ: Prentice-Hall, 1973); John Caldwell Holt, *Escape from Childhood* (New York: Dutton, 1974).

19 Laura Martha Purdy, *In Their Best Interest? The Case against Equal Rights for Children* (Ithaca: Cornell University Press, 1992).

20 Oswell, *The Agency of Children*, 243.

21 Swift, "El Movimiento Nacional de Niños, Niñas y Adolescentes Trabajadores del Perú," 102.

22 Cussianovich, *Ensayos sobre infancia*, 165.

23 Moosa-Mitha, "A Difference-Centered Alternative," 381.

24 Other texts that offer tools for thinking along these lines include Lundy, "'Voice' Is Not Enough"; and Wall and Dar, "Children's Political Representation."

25 Lee, *Childhood and Society*; Raby, "Age."

26 Jessica K. Taft, *Rebel Girls: Youth Activism and Social Change across the Americas* (New York: New York University Press, 2011), 141.

27 Wall, "Can Democracy Represent Children?," 93–94.

28 Kulynych, "No Playing in the Public Sphere"; Berry Mayall, *Towards a Sociology for Childhood: Thinking from Children's Lives* (Buckingham: Open University Press, 2002); Caroline Lodge, "From Hearing Voices to Engaging in Dialogue: Problematising Student Participation for School Improvement," *Journal of Educational Change* 6, no. 2 (2005): 125–46; Malcolm Hill, "Children's Voices on Ways of Having a Voice," *Childhood* 13, no. 1 (2006): 69–89; Judy Cashmore, "Children's Participation in Family Law Decision-Making: Theoretical Approaches to Understanding Children's Views," *Children and Youth Services Review* 33, no. 4 (2011): 515–20.

29 Louise Chawla et al., "Don't Just Listen—Do Something! Lessons Learned about Governance from the Growing Up in Cities Project," *Children, Youth and Environments* 15, no. 2 (2005): 53–88; Greg Mannion, "Going Spatial, Going Relational: Why 'Listening to Children' and Children's Participation Needs Reframing," *Discourse: Studies in the Cultural Politics of Education* 28, no. 3 (2007): 405–20; Hava Gordon and Jessica Taft, "Rethinking Youth Political Socialization: Teenage Activists Talk Back," *Youth and Society* 43, no. 4 (2011): 1499–1527; Taft and Gordon, "Youth Activists, Youth Councils, and Constrained Democracy."

30 See, for examples, Rebecca de Schweinitz, *If We Could Change the World: Young People and America's Long Struggle for Racial Equality* (Chapel Hill: University of North Carolina Press, 2011); Angélica Rico Montoya, "Percepciones de niños y niñas zapatistas: Guerra, resistencia y autonomía," *Argumentos* 26, no. 73 (2013): 57–78; Eliud Torres Velázquez, "La participación de niños y niñas en pueblos indígenas que luchan por su autonomía," *Rayuela* 5, no. 9 (2014): 104–12; Brown, *Powered by Girl*.

CHAPTER 4. TEACHERS, MOTHERS, OR COMPAÑEROS

1 Polletta, *Freedom Is an Endless Meeting*.

2 These greetings include the ideas of Alejandro as a great teacher as well as the Quechua word for a teacher (*amauta*).

3 Paolo Freire, *Pedagogy of the Oppressed*, trans. Myra Bergman Ramos, 30th anniversary ed. (New York: Bloomsbury Academic, 2000); Alejandro Cussianovich,

Aprender la condición humana: Ensayo sobre pedagogía de la ternura, 2nd ed. (Lima, Peru: IFEJANT, 2010).

4 For a compelling discussion of this issue, see Lesley Bartlett, *The Word and the World: The Cultural Politics of Literacy in Brazil* (Cresskill, NJ: Hampton, 2009).

5 Freire, *Pedagogy of the Oppressed*, 72.

6 Social movements produce strong emotional and affective ties and generate and mobilize a range of feelings; each movement has its own distinctive emotional culture, or what Deborah Gould productively identifies as a movement's "emotional habitus." See Deborah B. Gould, *Moving Politics: Emotion and ACT UP's Fight against AIDS* (Chicago: University of Chicago Press, 2009). In the movement of working children, this emotional habitus includes visibly expressed feelings of trust, affection, playfulness, pride, and concern for others.

7 Cussianovich, *Aprender la condición humana*, 27.

8 All of this is thoroughly developed in the above text.

9 Alejandro Cussianovich, *Ensayos sobre infancia: Sujeto de derechos y protagonista* (Lima, Peru: IFEJANT, 2006), 165.

10 Martin Mills, "Male Teachers, Homophobia, Misogyny and Teacher Education," *Teaching Education* 15, no. 1 (2004): 32.

11 James, "Giving Voice to Children's Voices."

12 In contrast, a study of the parent volunteers in *salas comunitarias* in middle schools in New Mexico found that women who took on similar supportive roles were identified by the Latina students as being "like friends." Nancy López and Charlane E. Lechuga, "'They Are Like a Friend': Othermothers Creating Empowering, School-Based Community Living Rooms in Latina and Latino Middle Schools," in *Urban Girls Revisited: Building Strengths*, ed. Bonnie J. Ross Leadbeater and Niobe Way (New York: New York University Press, 2007), 97–120.

13 David L. DuBois et al., "Effectiveness of Mentoring Programs for Youth: A Meta-Analytic Review," *American Journal of Community Psychology* 30, no. 2 (2002): 157–97; Shawn Ginwright, "Hope, Healing, and Care: Pushing the Boundaries of Civic Engagement for African American Youth," *Liberal Education* 97, no. 2 (2011): 34–39.

14 Barbara Rogoff, *Apprenticeship in Thinking: Cognitive Development in Social Context* (New York: Oxford University Press, 1990); Barbara Rogoff et al., "Firsthand Learning through Intent Participation," *Annual Review of Psychology* 54, no. 1 (2003): 175–203; Ruth Paradise and Barbara Rogoff, "Side by Side: Learning by Observing and Pitching In," *Ethos* 37, no. 1 (2009): 102–38.

15 Rogoff, *Apprenticeship in Thinking*, 20.

16 Barbara Rogoff, Rebeca Mejía-Arauz, and Maricela Correa-Chávez, "A Cultural Paradigm—Learning by Observing and Pitching In," in Correa-Chávez, Mejía-Arauz, and Rogoff, *Children Learn by Observing and Contributing*, 1–22.

17 Ben Kirshner, "Guided Participation in Three Youth Activism Organizations: Facilitation, Apprenticeship, and Joint Work," *Journal of the Learning Sciences* 17, no. 1 (2008): 65.

18 Ibid.

19 Barbara Rogoff, "Developing Understanding of the Idea of Communities of Learners," *Mind, Culture, and Activity* 1, no. 4 (1994): 213.

20 Rogoff et al., "Firsthand Learning through Intent Participation," 184.

21 In my observations, I did not identify any patterns related to race, class, or ethnicity in the relationships that kids and adults build in the movement. It is possible, however, that such dynamics were present but were more submerged or subtle than I could identify, so I do not want to assert that such dynamics were necessarily absent. However, compared to gender and age, they were certainly less noticeable to me. Gender and age appeared to be more salient in this context.

22 Deborah W. Kilgore, "Understanding Learning in Social Movements: A Theory of Collective Learning," *International Journal of Lifelong Education* 18, no. 3 (1999): 191–202; Pierre Walter, "Adult Learning in New Social Movements: Environmental Protest and the Struggle for the Clayoquot Sound Rainforest," *Adult Education Quarterly* 57, no. 3 (2007): 248–63; John Grayson, "Organising, Educating, and Training: Varieties of Activist Learning in Left Social Movements in Sheffield (UK)," *Studies in the Education of Adults* 43, no. 2 (2011): 197–215.

23 Bartlett, *The Word and the World*, 36–37.

24 Gordon, *We Fight to Win*; Taft and Gordon, "Youth Activists, Youth Councils, and Constrained Democracy."

CHAPTER 5. "THE KIDS ARE IN CHARGE" BUT "ADULTS TALK TOO MUCH"

1 In my analysis here, I focus primarily on age, with some secondary attention to gender dynamics. These were the most salient differences I observed in the NATs' and adults' negotiation of their power.

2 Michel Foucault, "The Subject and Power," *Critical Inquiry* 8, no. 4 (1982): 789.

3 While formal ILO and UN reports don't directly speak this way about working children's movements, I have heard numerous accounts by children's rights advocates and practitioners about informal conversations with individuals in these institutions who see the movements of NATs in this way. This position also emerged in some of the media coverage of the Bolivian movement of NATs and their successful bid to revise the Bolivian law on children's work, which I discuss at the start of chapter 6.

4 Polletta, *Freedom Is an Endless Meeting*; Kathleen M. Blee, *Democracy in the Making: How Activist Groups Form* (New York: Oxford University Press, 2012).

5 Mannarelli, "La infancia y la configuración de los vínculos en el Perú"; Rojas Arangoitia, "I'd Rather Be Hit with a Stick."

6 For a more extensive discussion of this, see Jessica K. Taft, "'Adults Talk Too Much': Intergenerational Dialogue and Power in the Peruvian Movement of Working Children," *Childhood* 22, no. 4 (2015): 460–73.

7 Gaea Leinhardt, C. Weidman, and K. M. Hammond, "Introduction and Integration of Classroom Routines by Expert Teachers," *Curriculum Inquiry* 17, no. 2 (1987): 135–76.

8 Lodge, "From Hearing Voices to Engaging in Dialogue"; Graham and Fitzgerald, "Progressing Children's Participation"; Michael Wyness, "Children's Participation and Intergenerational Dialogue: Bringing Adults Back into the Analysis," *Childhood* 20, no. 4 (2013): 429–42.

9 James, "Giving Voice to Children's Voices."

10 Wyn and White, *Rethinking Youth*; Lesko, *Act Your Age!*

CHAPTER 6. STRUGGLES FOR CHILDREN'S DIGNITY AND CITIZENSHIP

1 For more on this law and the processes around it, see Manfred Liebel, "Protecting the Rights of Working Children Instead of Banning Child Labour: Bolivia Tries a New Legislative Approach," *International Journal of Children's Rights* 23 (2015): 529–47.

2 A good example of this narrative can be found in the BBC's story on the subject. Katy Watson, "Child Labour Laws: A Step Back for Advancing Bolivia?," *BBC News*, November 20, 2014, www.bbc.com.

3 Tim Worstall, "Bolivia Legalises Child Labour and Child Labour Might Decline in Bolivia," *Forbes*, July 21, 2014, www.forbes.com.

4 See, for example, Sara Shahriari, "How Young Is Too Young? Bolivia Debates Child Labor Law," *Christian Science Monitor*, March 26, 2014, www.csmonitor.com.

5 Edward van Daalen and Nicolas Mabillard argue that this was not necessarily directly related to the law itself, but a ploy used by the Hungarian and Croatian representatives to put pressure on Bolivia on the unrelated issue of two of their nationals who were being held in Bolivia without trial on accusations of attempted assassination. Edward van Daalen and Nicolas Mabillard, "Human Rights in Translation: Bolivia's Law 548, Working Children's Movements and the Global Child Labour Regime" (unpublished manuscript, 2018).

6 International Labor Organization, "ILO's Concerns Regarding New Law in Bolivia Dealing with Child Labour," statement, July 28, 2014, www.ilo.org.

7 Van Daalen and Mabillard, "Human Rights in Translation."

8 Elizabeth A. Armstrong and Mary Bernstein, "Culture, Power, and Institutions: A Multi-Institutional Politics Approach to Social Movements," *Sociological Theory* 26, no. 1 (2008): 87.

9 Tracing the impacts of the movement is quite challenging due to a lack of systematic data—there are no longitudinal studies, and no pre and post assessments. Further, there is also the general challenge of proving causality in any kind of individual or social transformation. However, with these important caveats in mind, I am confident that many of the outcomes that I discuss below are connected to the movement's actions.

10 "Los desafíos de Tania Pariona, congresista indígena electa," Chirapaq, May 31, 2016, www.chirapaq.org.pe.

11 "Congresista Tania Pariona juramentó en quechua y por los pueblos indígenas,"
    Diario Correo, July 22, 2016, http://diariocorreo.pe.

12 Patricia Ruiz, "La defensora de los derechos de los niños que apoya el trabajo
    infantil," eldiario.es, September 29, 2016, www.eldiario.es.

13 Alec Fyfe, "The Worldwide Movement against Child Labour: Progress and Future
    Directions" (Geneva: International Labor Organization, 2007); International La-
    bor Organization, "The Hague Global Child Labor Conference: Towards a World
    without Child Labor: Mapping the Road to 2016" (The Hague, Netherlands:
    International Labor Organization, May 2010).

14 Ginwright, *Black Youth Rising*; Cynthia Taines, "Intervening in Alienation: The
    Outcomes for Urban Youth of Participating in School Activism," *American Edu-
    cational Research Journal* 49, no. 1 (2012): 53–86; Kirshner and Ginwright, "Youth
    Organizing as a Developmental Context."

15 Bourdillon et al., *Rights and Wrongs of Children's Work.*

16 Martin Woodhead, "Combatting Child Labour: Listen to What the Children Say,"
    Childhood 6, no. 1 (1999): 27–49; Karen Moore, "Supporting Children in Their
    Working Lives: Obstacles and Opportunities within the International Policy Envi-
    ronment," *Journal of International Development* 12, no. 4 (2000): 531–48; Nieuwen-
    huys, "Embedding the Global Womb."

17 Bourdillon et al., *Rights and Wrongs of Children's Work.*

18 Jessica K. Taft, trans., "Nothing about Us, without Us: Critiques of the Interna-
    tional Labor Organization's Approach to Child Labor from the Movements of
    Working Children" (Lima, Peru: IFEJANT, 2013).

19 For a critique of youth councils and the ways that they tend to limit the scope
    of young people's political contributions, see Taft and Gordon, "Youth Activists,
    Youth Councils, and Constrained Democracy."

20 Gordon, *We Fight to Win.*

21 The question of how children and youth, particularly those with movement
    connections and activist agendas, experience state-based forms of participation
    deserves further research and analysis. Some useful reflections on these issues
    can be found in David Maunders, "Head of a Movement or Arms of the State?
    Youth Councils and Youth Policy in Australia, 1941–1991," *International Journal of
    Adolescence and Youth* 6, no. 2 (1996): 175–94; and Raby, "Children's Participation
    as Neo-Liberal Governance?"

22 Guerrero et al., "Young Lives School Survey in Peru," 3.

23 Santiago Cueto, Juan León, and Alejandra Miranda, "Características socio-
    económicas y rendimiento de los estudiantes en el Perú," *Análisis y Propuestas*,
    April 2015.

24 Ibid., 2.

25 Rojas Arangoitia, "I'd Rather Be Hit with a Stick," 5.

26 Unfortunately, due to a lack of funds, the school closed during the period of my
    field research.

27 One potential counterexample to this, however, is that Alejandro has in fact been recognized and honored by the Peruvian government and the Ministry of Education by being inducted in 2012 into the Orden de las Palmas Magisteriales, an honor reserved for those who have made substantial contributions to the nation in the fields of education, science, culture, or technology. And in 2013 he was recognized with a medal of honor for teachers from the Municipality of Lima. But these honors do not necessarily mean that his pedagogy or the movement's approach are actually being integrated into educational institutions.

28 Elizabeth Jelin, *Pan y afectos: La transformación de las familias*, 2nd ed. (Buenos Aires, Argentina: Fondo de Cultura Económica, 2010).

29 Mannarelli, "La infancia y la configuración de los vínculos en el Perú."

30 Anastasia J. Gage and Eva A. Silvestre, "Maternal Violence, Victimization, and Child Physical Punishment in Peru," *Child Abuse and Neglect* 34, no. 7 (2010): 523–33.

31 Bolin, *Growing Up in a Culture of Respect*.

32 It is fairly straightforward to determine whether or not a social movement that seeks to change a particular policy has done so, but it is much harder to assess the more diffuse impacts of movements that seek to transform culture and social interaction.

33 Michael Wyness, Lisa Harrison, and Ian Buchanan, "Childhood, Politics and Ambiguity: Towards an Agenda for Children's Political Inclusion," *Sociology* 38, no. 1 (2004): 81–99; Tisdall et al., *Children, Young People and Social Inclusion*; Taft and Gordon, "Youth Activists, Youth Councils, and Constrained Democracy."

34 Oswell, *The Agency of Children*, 82.

35 Frances Fox Piven, *Challenging Authority: How Ordinary People Change America* (Lanham, MD: Rowman and Littlefield, 2008), 30.

36 Jason Hart, "Saving Children: What Role for Anthropology?," *Anthropology Today* 22, no. 1 (2006): 5–8; Jason Hart, "Children's Participation and International Development"; Özlem Sensoy and Elizabeth Marshall, "Missionary Girl Power: Saving the 'Third World' One Girl at a Time," *Gender and Education* 22, no. 3 (May 2010): 295–311; Emily Bent, "A Different Girl Effect: Producing Political Girlhoods in the 'Invest in Girls' Climate," in *Youth Engagement: The Civic-Political Lives of Children and Youth*, ed. Sandi Kawecka Nenga and Jessica K. Taft, Sociological Studies of Children and Youth 16 (Bingley, UK: Emerald Group, 2013), 3–20.

CONCLUSION

1 Stephanie Saul and Anemona Hartocollis, "How Young Is Too Young for Protest? A National Gun-Violence Walkout Tests Schools," *New York Times*, March 14, 2018, www.nytimes.com.

2 Tisdall et al., *Children, Young People and Social Inclusion*; Barry N. Checkoway and Lorraine M. Gutiérrez, eds., *Youth Participation and Community Change* (New York: Haworth, 2006); Jason Hart, "Children's Participation and International Development."

3   Chawla et al., "Don't Just Listen—Do Something!"; Mary Elizabeth Collins, Astraea Augsberger, and Whitney Gecker, "Youth Councils in Municipal Government: Examination of Activities, Impact and Barriers," *Children and Youth Services Review* 65 (2016): 140–47; Daniela Díaz-Bórquez, Nicolás Contreras-Shats, and Natalia Bozo-Carrillo, "Participación infantil como aproximación a la democracia: Desafíos de la experiencia chilena," *Revista Latinoamericana de Ciencias Sociales, Niñez y Juventud* 16, no. 1 (2018): 101–13.

4   Rodgers, "Children as Social Movement Participants," 239.

5   See, for example, Victoria Law and China Martens, eds., *Don't Leave Your Friends Behind: Concrete Ways to Support Families in Social Justice Movements and Communities* (Oakland, CA: PM Press, 2012). An exception to this in the US context is the Regeneración Child Care Collective (www.childcarenyc.org), whose vision statement talks about including children as political agents and participants in movement culture.

6   As many scholars and activists working on race and racism noted, the praise given to the Florida teens was in striking contrast to media portrayals of the youth of color in the Black Lives Matter movement.

7   There has been a veritable explosion of writing on youth activism in the past ten years, with several books and dozens of articles published, including Gordon, *We Fight to Win*; Taft, *Rebel Girls*; Clay, *The Hip-Hop Generation Fights Back*; Kwon, *Uncivil Youth*; Nicholls, *The DREAMers*; Franklin, *After the Rebellion*; Ben Kirshner, *Youth Activism in an Era of Education Inequality* (New York: New York University Press, 2015); Conner and Rosen, *Contemporary Youth Activism*; Veronica Terriquez, "Training Young Activists: Grassroots Organizing and Youths' Civic and Political Trajectories," *Sociological Perspectives* 58, no. 2 (2015): 223–42; Genevieve Negrón-Gonzales, "Undocumented Youth Activism as Counter-Spectacle: Civil Disobedience and Testimonio in the Battle around Immigration Reform," *Aztlán: A Journal of Chicano Studies* 40, no. 1 (2015): 87–112; and Jennifer Earl, Thomas V. Maher, and Thomas Elliott, "Youth, Activism, and Social Movements," *Sociology Compass* 11, no. 4 (2017).

8   Todd Starnes, "CNN, MSNBC Using Florida Teens as Anti-Trump Propaganda Pawns," *Fox News*, February 20, 2018, www.foxnews.com.

9   Ben Shapiro, "Students' Anti-Gun Views," *National Review* (blog), February 20, 2018, www.nationalreview.com.

10 Brown, *Powered by Girl*, 22.

11 Ostrander, "Gender and Race"; Jill M. Bystydzienski and Stephen P. Schacht, eds., *Forging Radical Alliances across Difference: Coalition Politics for the New Millennium* (New York: Rowman and Littlefield, 2001); Cole and Luna, "Making Coalitions Work"; Taft, *Rebel Girls*. Of course, as others have pointed out, this kind of talk about privilege and oppression within movement spaces can also become merely performative and doesn't always effectively counter deep-seated dynamics of inequality. For a discussion of this problem, see Cindy Milstein, ed., *Taking Sides: Revolutionary Solidarity and the Poverty of Liberalism* (Oakland, CA: AK Press, 2015).

12 Mark R. Warren, *Fire in the Heart: How White Activists Embrace Racial Justice* (New York: Oxford University Press, 2010); Michael A. Messner, Max A. Greenberg, and Tal Peretz, *Some Men: Feminist Allies and the Movement to End Violence against Women* (New York: Oxford University Press, 2015). There are also a growing number of critiques of this model for coalition and solidarity, including concerns that it has become meaningless and that "ally" is invoked as a badge or identity, rather than involving a set of committed practices for creating equality and justice.

13 Checkoway, "Adults as Allies"; Gordon, "Allies Within and Without."

14 Jessica K. Taft and Hava R. Gordon, "Intergenerational Relationships in Youth Activist Networks," in *Families, Intergenerationality, and Peer Group Relations*, vol. 5, Geographies of Children and Young People (Singapore: Springer, 2016).

15 Taft and Gordon, "Intergenerational Relationships in Youth Activist Networks."

16 Checkoway, "Adults as Allies."

17 Roger A. Hart, "Children's Participation: From Tokenism to Citizenship."

18 The children's participation literature and practical advice manuals offer a variety of frameworks for identifying types of political relationships between children and adults, which can be helpful tools for organizational assessments, but do not really engage deeply with questions of power or help groups think through the complexity of age-based power relations.

INDEX

abolitionist approach to child labor, 25, 67–68, 214

active listening, 129–30

adolescents: between *colaboradores* and NATs, 180; girls, 176–78; NATS, 165–66, 173–74, 176–80, *178*; Parkland teens, 215, 221; teenage facilitators, 92–94; younger kids and, 165–66, 173. *See also* niños y adolescentes trabajadores

adultism, 7, 12, 105–6, 109–10

adults: agency of, 5–6; as allies, 224–25; assumptions about children, 5–11; children's need for, 107–8, 216; conversational domination by, 159–60, 162–63; as educators, 146–47; emotions of, 80; as experts, 166–67; young adult *colaboradores*, 176. *See also colaboradores*

affection, 124–26

Afro-Peruvian identity, 35

age: chronological, 15, 91, 113, 166, 171, 174; dynamics of, 13–14; experience and, 113, 168–69, 171–75; identity, inequality and, 14

age-based criteria, 90–91

age-based power, 79–80; challenging, 105–6; *colaboradores*, NATs and, 215–16; dynamics, 84–86; micro-relations, 152; modalities of, disrupting, 179–82; in movement, 152–53; persistence of, 112–13, 146–48, 181–82, 215–16; in student movement, against gun violence, 222–23; teenage girls on, 177–78

ageism, 7, 224

agency: of adults, 5–6; of children, 79–80

Alejandro. *See* Cussianovich, Alejandro

ally-ship, 224–25, 252n12

Amazon, 34

Ames, Patricia, 53

Andean paradigms: of childhood, 52–55, 76; of work, 75–76

apprenticeship learning, 135–36, 139

Armstrong, Elizabeth, 187

Arriaga, Pablo José, 49

assemblies: delegates at, 171; meetings and, 169–70; NATs at, 31–32, 92–95, *93*, 102, 155; parent, 207–9; Yerbateros, 39, 169

barriadas, 23–24

Bartlett, Lesley, 146

base groups: *colaboradores*, NATs in, 128–33, *130*; Yerbateros, 41–42, 71–72, 128–29

being heard, 164–69

Bernstein, Mary, 187

Bernstein, Robin, 232n10

binary difference assumption, of childhood, 4–5, 91, 97, 111, 180

Bolin, Inge, 52, 207

Bolivia, 183, 185

Brown, Lyn Mikel, 223

capacity, equality of, 89–97, 114–15

care: dynamics of, 147; networks of, 52–55

Castañeda, Claudia, 234n31

Catholic Church, 50; liberation theology, 23; on *patria potestad*, 206

CCONNA. *See* Consejos Consultivos de Niños, Niñas y Adolescentes childhood: Andean paradigms, 52–55, 76; binary difference assumption, 4–5, 91, 97, 111, 180; as category, 4; challenging assumptions about, 77–79, 111–12, 145–46, 179–80, 214–15; colonial model of, 47–52, 55; denaturalizing, 47, 81–82; exclusion assumption, 6–7, 51, 56, 61–62, 67, 78, 121, 214, 219–20; globalization, of norms, 55–58; good, 77–79; ideas of, working children on, 45–48, 111; innocence, 7, 56–57, 232n10; marginalized position of, 178; natural assumption, 5, 46–47, 63–64, 77–82; older ideas of, 45–46; passivity assumption, 5–6, 97–98, 111, 121; *protagonismo* paradigm, 62–67; rights-based approach to, 61–62; as social construction, 8–9; in US, 10–11, 77; valued, 67–76; Western model of, 35, 54, 58; work and, 56, 77

child labor, 1; abolitionist approach to, 25, 67–68, 214; Convention 182 on, 25; ILO on, 67–70, 98, 124; movement of working children on, 67–68, 71; in Peru, 36–38; politics, Cussianovich on, 127; UNATsBO on, 183–86; in US, 57; working children on, 98–99, 183–84, 199

children: agency of, 79–80; becoming and being, 55, 65; being heard, 164–69; citizenship of, 90–91; colonialism and, 49–50; of color, in US, 9, 11; dependence, on adults, 216; development of, 58–59, 62, 97; dignity of, 86–89; dismissing, 113–14; economically active, 68–70; empowered, 149–50; equal capacity of, 89–97, 114–15; equality of, 111–12; exclusion from politics, 7–8, 219–20; expanding power of, 214–17; insights of, 97–105; involvement, in politics, 9–10; knowledge of, 100–101, 105, 122–23; listening to, 53, 164–66; manipulation of, 153, 184, 222; men

working with, 126; in networks of care, 52–55; organizations of, 60; participation in government spaces, 196–98; political power and, 84, 106, 198, 214–15; *protagonismo* and, 62–67, 156–57; protecting, 56–57, 76; in public life, 15; in school, 200; silences of, 162–63; as social, political, economic subjects, 62–67, 79–80, 82; in social movements, 215–16, 226; status, in Peru, 89; well-being, 77–78, 216, 220. *See also colaboradores*, NATs and; movement of working children; niños y adolescentes trabajadores; working children

children's rights, 51; approach to childhood, 61–62; CRC on, 10–11, 25, 28, 58–60, 77, 185; defending, 186–87; *defensorías* for, 59–60; in democracy, 110; festival for, 61, 168; institutions, 216–17; international institutions, 58–62; MANTHOC on, 24–25; NGOs, 32–33; office, of Lima, 197; organizations, 60–61; *protagonismo* paradigm, 65–66; to state-based participation, 198

Chin, Elizabeth, 56

Christianity, 49

chronological age, 15, 91, 113, 166, 171, 174

citizenship, 90–91, 149, 238n1

Cockburn, Tom, 90–91

Código de los Niños y Adolescentes, 28, 45–46, 81–82

colaboración (collaboration): ally-ship versus, 225; in education, 145–46; emotional dimensions of, 123; inter-generational horizontal, 105–11, 225; modeling horizontalism, 121; practices of, 149–50; transformational intergenerational relationships, 145–50

colaboradores, 19, 26, 28–29, 41; active listening, 129–30; as *compañeros*, 133–39, 148; constraining own participation, 176–77; conversational domination, 159–60, 162; as co-participants, in

ABOUT THE AUTHOR

Jessica K. Taft is Associate Professor of Latin American and Latino Studies at the University of California, Santa Cruz. She is the author of *Rebel Girls: Youth Activism and Social Change across the Americas* and a series editor for New York University Press's Critical Perspectives on Youth series.